Out of Place:
Public Policy and the
Emergence of Truancy

Education Policy Perspectives

General Editor: **Professor Ivor Goodson,** Faculty of Education,
University of Western Ontario, London,
Canada N6G 1G7

This series aims to fill the academic gap between the study of education and the formulation of education policy, to reflect the politicalization of education, and to provide practitioners with the analysis for informed implementation of policies that they need. It will offer studies in broad areas of policy studies. There will be a particular focus in the following areas: a General Section which will seek to provide exemplary policy studies and will shop-window a range of methodologies and modalities employed in education policy analysis (Professor Ivor Goodson, *University of Western Ontario, Canada*); School organization and improvement (David Reynolds, *University College, Cardiff, UK*); Social analysis (Professor Philip Wexler, *University of Rochester, USA*); and Policy studies and evaluation (Professor Ernest House, *University of Colorado-Boulder, USA*).

Education Policy Perspectives

Out of Place: Public Policy and the Emergence of Truancy

Fiona M. S. Paterson

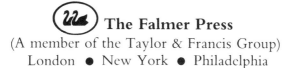

The Falmer Press

(A member of the Taylor & Francis Group)

London ● New York ● Philadelphia

UK	The Falmer Press, Falmer House, Barcombe, Lewes, Sussex, BN8 5DL
USA	The Falmer Press, Taylor & Francis Inc., 242 Cherry St., Philadelphia, PA 19106-1906

First published 1989

British Library Cataloguing in Publication Data

Paterson, Fiona M.S.
  Out of place: public policy and the
  emergence of truancy
  1. Great Britain. Truancy
  371.2'95'0941

  ISBN 1-85000-510-9
  ISBN 1-85005-511-7 Pbk

Jacket design by Caroline Archer

Typeset in 11/13 Bembo by
Mathematical Composition Setters Ltd., Salisbury, UK

Printed in Great Britain by Taylor & Francis (Printers)
Ltd, Basingstoke.

Contents

In Memoriam C.F.S.P.

Preface

This book is about a personal puzzle which became transformed into a sociological question. As someone who spent her secondary school years during a period in which children were divided into the educational successes and the educational 'also rans' by the qualifying examination (the equivalent of the English 11 +), I went to a local secondary school which was attended by children who were considered to be the academic successes of the school system. I was aware that many, though by no means all, of my peers truanted. In other ways, those who truanted were no different from those who did not — some did well in school exams, others did not; some were middle class, others were working class; most conformed, more or less, when they were in school, some did not conform. Truanting was an activity in which people engaged to varying degrees (at times skipping individual classes, at times taking half or full days off) and at different times of the year (sometimes taking illicit time off to prepare for an exam, to enjoy the sunshine on a summer day or simply to do something more interesting than go to school).

Yet much later, when I came across the Pack Report on Truancy and Indiscipline in Schools, I did not recognize the picture of children truanting described there. Turning from this to the literature on truancy, I still failed to find the image which I remembered from my school days. As a sociologist I was aware that the images of truancy about which I was reading, with their standard fare of educational failure, 'deprived' backgrounds and problem families, reflected discussions of other types of social problem. This led me to consider the gap between my 'knowledge' based on my school experience and the orthodox 'knowledge' which I could receive from books and articles about truancy and which were clearly based on a different kind of experience to my own. My puzzle about this gap, united with a broader sociological interest in the ways in which knowledge is produced, the purposes for which it is produced and how these affect each other, led me to carry out the research on which this book is based.

Like most books, there are many ways in which it can be read. Readers with a specific interest in truancy and inspectors' discussions of schooling in the nineteenth century may glean sufficient background explanation of the organization of the book from a quick reading of chapter 1, with the exception of the maps and diagrams within this. These will repay a closer reading. Chapter 1 will be of particular interest to those readers concerned with the discussion of truancy as an example of a more general argument about the way in which knowledge is produced and the importance of historical sociology in this. Within the book, male pronouns are only used as universals when they are part of direct quotations.

The process of writing this book has been enlivened by Stephanie and Edward Paterson. Although the responsibility for this book is my own, others have contributed to its production both by intellectual argument and emotional support, in particular, Ray Paterson, David Nelken, Philip Corrigan, John Holmwood, Bruce Curtis, Peter Fitzpatrick, Janet Siltanen and my parents, John and Barbara Spencer.

Thanks are due to J. D. Myers for permission to use his work, and to the National Library of Scotland for permission to reproduce the school plans in chapter 4. I am grateful to the regional council education departments who provided me with information about their responses to the Pack report. The tables from Bishop (1971) and Flinn (1977) are reproduced by kind permission of Cambridge University Press. Chapter 6 was first published as 'Schooling the family' in *Sociology*, 22, 1 (1988); a version of chapter 7 has appeared as 'Measures of schooling: Registers, standards and the construction of the subject' in *Historical Sociology*, 3 (1989).

Introduction: Truancy is Normal

It may seem surprising to begin a book about truancy with the claim that truancy is part of normality when we have a whole range of professionals working on it, writing about it and trying to develop solutions to it. After all it is not normality but problems which are usually taken as being in need of solutions. Yet in this book I shall be showing how the social arrangements which we take for granted as normal can generate problems such as truancy. This argument is not new. Durkheim, writing at the end of the nineteenth century made a similar argument about deviance (Durkheim, 1964). He held that deviance was socially generated and that it was intrinsically linked to 'normal' social conditions. Forms of deviance generally present under given social arrangements could therefore be taken as being 'normal' to those arrangements. This implies that to understand a given type of deviance we need to understand the normality to which it is linked.

It is this kind of argument which I am developing here, when I maintain that to understand the beliefs which underpin contemporary official discussions about truancy we need to look at the way in which state authorized schooling was instituted as well as at official claims at the time (during the nineteenth century) about the importance of this for the general population. I argue that state policy on schooling in nineteenth century Britain was about structuring particular patterns of living amongst the population. The impact of this upon our perceptions of education and educational problems has been profound. As I shall show, our current beliefs about truancy are intrinsically linked with prevalent views about the significance of particular patterns of schooling. Most of my discussion will be based on documents relating to Scotland between 1839 and 1872. However, my general argument that our understanding of individual pupil behaviour is dependent on our understanding of the institution of schooling and its 'normality' is of wider relevance (see, for example, the work of Curtis (1988) on Canada).

Despite the amount which has been written linking it with such problems as delinquency and poverty, *how* it is linked with these and the *significance* of this linking is rarely explored. I shall be arguing that one reason for this is that most discussions of truancy focus on the characteristics and behaviour of individuals who have been identified as truants. This has narrowed our understanding of the issues. Indeed, it is only comparatively recently that people have looked beyond descriptions of pathological individuals and problem home backgrounds and tried to assess the role which schools play in truancy. I shall be looking at why this has been the case when I argue for the importance of giving attention to the *social* parameters of understanding and beliefs.

Truancy is a sensitive topic. Expressions of concern about it are often also expressions of more generalized worries about social problems. For example, in discussions it is often linked with poverty, unemployment and delinquency. It has been variously taken as implying rejection of society now, a warning of future anti-social behaviour and a sign that the children involved are cutting themselves off from the opportunity of a better future for themselves than their parents may have had. In part, these beliefs reflect the fundamental role that schooling occupies within our society. In which other institution are almost all members of our society legally obliged to spend such a large proportion of their time during eleven of the most formative years of life? The schooling we have is produced by the type of society in which we live and it has a vital role in producing the kind of people who will live in society in the future.

Few people would argue with the view that whatever other aspects of a child's experience may reduce their chances in life, schooling should offer opportunities to all children. Indeed, it would be fair to say that underlying much that has been written about truancy is the question of how we can help children to grasp these opportunities. However, behind this anodyne assertion lie major unresolved issues. Issues involving beliefs about what schools ought to do; what they do; and what they can, under particular circumstances, be reasonably expected to do.

This book is an exploration of representations about truancy. These are located within the theories and institutionalized practices (discourse) which I shall be examining in my discussion. In the first chapter I shall indicate the sources for my discussion and explain the background to the book before going on to outline the view of schooling which underpins my argument. I shall then develop an interpretive framework of social mapping which I use within the book to help unravel the implications of past policies for our current knowledge. This will enable me to outline official knowledge and to explain the way in which this is linked with social action in my discussion of how certain representations have become orthodoxies. In chapter 2 I examine current representations and look at the ways in which they are dealt with in the specialist literature on truancy. Before developing my argument further, I shall describe the educational context of early nineteenth century Scotland.

After this my argument will proceed through three stages. Firstly, I shall deal with the issues at the level of class relations. In chapter 3 I discuss how specific programmes of power based on a way of constituting space and time which was compatible with relations of industrial capital became translated into a problem of the neutral administration of the state apparatus for eliminating problem schooling. This concludes part 1 of the book and my outline of the contours of knowledge.

In part 2 I explore the features of the maps more closely. This part begins with chapter 4 where I look at the organization of space for schooling and argue that the rules involved in implementing state regulation contained an implicit agenda for social action. This helped to structure the formal identity of teacher and, in consequence, that of pupil. In chapter 5 I shall use the example of what happened with teachers to illustrate the way in which state policy could embody contradiction. I show, not only that, once in operation, institutions spawned their own programmes, but also the way in which these could operate as constraints and resources for negotiating strategies of those involved in schooling.

In chapter 6 I further develop my discussion of the ways in which the application of state rules to existing schooling provision involved distinguishing situations and actions which were acceptable from those which were officially unacceptable. Through a discussion of dissonance between what I shall call *formal* and *in-formed* identity (that is, between officially promoted social identity and people's lived versions of it) I shall explain how this operated to marginalize particular forms of family relations by rendering them problematic for schooling. I shall then argue that as a result, there emerged the *problem family*, the key to understanding the theme of 'problematic home backgrounds'.

In the argument developed in chapter 7 I look at the way in which 'neutralized' institutional changes enabled overtly class-based concerns to be channelled into overtly individual concerns (though covertly class-based). Assessments of schooling were no longer to be based on classes of pupils, but were to become a question of counting the performance of individuals. This made possible an important shift in schooling: the dissonance between the formal identities fostered by the state regulated school and the in-formed identities of participants in the system became an *individualized* problem. An apparent harmony between formal and in-formed identity was to shift from being an indication of class members knowing their place, to becoming the basis for individuals being able to ascend the hierarchy of school assessment and, in so doing, achieve a better position.

PART 1:
The Contours of Truancy

Chapter 1

Social Mapping

Introduction

The tendency to reduce explanations of deviance to psychological terms was attacked by Durkheim (1964). He did not preclude the possibility of pathological individuals being involved in activities, such as crime, which are often considered to be socially deviant. Nevertheless, he maintained that the categorization of specific actions as deviant needs to be explained in sociological terms.

I want to stress the importance of this categorization. People's experiences are filtered through categories of knowledge both for their own understanding and for their presentation of this for the understanding of others. These categories are not 'natural' descriptions of experience but are socially constructed representations of this. Their construction should be understood as historical and in the context of the relations of knowledge and relations of power which helped to shape them. It is to these relations that I shall look in order to explain how some representations become orthodoxies and others become heresies.

Background and Sources

Discourse on truancy is characterized by three themes around which identification of this behaviour and explanations of its source are constructed:

    (i)   problematic schools;
    (ii) problematic home backgrounds;
    (iii) problematic children.

As we shall see, the predominance of particular themes changes as institutional possibilities change. The first and second were generated early in the process of state intervention into schooling. The possibilities for the third emerge, in embryonic form, with the introduction of a method of inspection which required the individual examination of pupils. At its sharpest, this individualization is expressed in the domain of twentieth century child psychiatry.

In the 1970s and 1980s in Scotland discourse on truancy traverses three different domains: the medical (consisting primarily of theories and practices of child guidance professionals; involving child psychiatrists and medical social workers); the educational (consisting of the theories and practices of schooling; involving teachers, the school inspectorate, local authority education departments, school councils and attendance officers or educational welfare officers), the social (consisting of theories and practices relating to problems of the social[1]; involving social workers, children's panels and list 'D' schools). The theories and practices within each domain define the relative importance of truancy as an issue in that sphere.

My primary focus is on the educational domain since, as I have indicated, the topic of truancy is intrinsically linked with the issue of the importance of schooling. I shall look at official views of truancy in the 1970s. These are taken from the Pack Report on Truancy and Indiscipline in Schools in Scotland (1977) and the local authority reports on truancy which appeared as a direct response to Pack. I shall also be looking at more recent literature in the area. As I shall argue, most writers have a working definition of what is meant by truancy, yet there is no consensus as to the range of behaviour to which the term refers. Some define truancy as absence of a child from school without permission of either the parents or the school. Others define it as absence without the permission of the school. In terms of the approach adopted by most researchers working in this area, to the extent to which they give any attention to this at all, such problems are held to be technical: solvable when the tools of the research, such as clearly defined categories about which there is general agreement, have been refined.

I shall argue, though, that these 'technical' difficulties relate to areas of conceptual disagreement which are indicative of broader issues. These are concerned with appropriate relations of authority; claims about normality; and claims about the role of schooling. Attendance, as a 'problem' encapsulates these issues, for to describe someone as truanting is to state that they are in the wrong physical location in respect of social customs. This judgment involves a claim about that person's temporal location: biographically, they ought to be elsewhere at that given time of the day/week/year. Truanting is being out of place and discussions of this entail questions of an individual's relation to the normality of schooling within a particular social order.

In considering this, I shall be examining the way in which schooling links particular forms of the family with the state, through relations of class, gender and age in a process of identity-formation. I shall argue that this can be understood in terms of social mapping, which will enable me to explain how one particular order of social relations has come to be defined as an educational necessity, and how, as a result, alternatives have become marginalized as problems for a system of schooling. In short, to understand truancy, it is necessary to look at the way in which the theory and practice of a state system of schooling and its problems were constructed.

The material on which my argument is based is from the Committee of Privy Council on Education and is all published in Parliamentary Papers. The Committee of Council on Education was set up in 1839 to deal with educational affairs in general, as well as to administer the state grant for education for the whole of Britain. Unlike other parts of Britain, in Scotland there was already a legally established system of education in the form of parochial schools. These were supervised by the Presbyteries and the General Assembly of the Church of Scotland's own Education Committee. In some respects the intervention of the Committee of Council can be seen as attempting to extend the scope of supervision beyond those established church schools to schools which had previously been unsupervised. The rationale underlying this was that by opening up the possibility of financial aid to them, schools would be encouraged to become more efficient. There were close links between the Committee of Council on Education and the General Assembly Education Committee, illustrated by there having been consultation between the two on the appointment of state school inspectors. In 1843 there was a protracted battle within the Church of Scotland over the nature of the relationship between church and state. This resulted in the Disruption, when the Free Church broke away from the established Church of Scotland (see Woodward, 1962, pp. 526–8 for a fuller account). By 1844 a separate inspector was appointed for the Free Church in Scotland, thereby establishing denominational inspection, which was to continue until 1872.

The Act of 1872 which introduced compulsory schooling for all children into Scotland, marks a significant change in the organization of state regulation. Up until then, though there were specific amendments to regulations sometimes made with respect to Scotland, these were *within* the overall framework of the Committee of Council on Education, which dealt with the whole of Britain. After this Act, the Scotch Education Department was created in order to oversee spending in Scotland. This legislation marks the success of state-structured schooling in claiming legitimate authority in the definition and regulation of what was to count as normal social and educational experience for the future adult population.

The Committee of Council documents consist mainly of school inspection reports and their associated regulations, although I have also looked at relevant Parliamentary committees of enquiry, such as the 1864 Select Committee on Education (Inspectors' Reports) and the 1865 Select Committee on the Constitution of the Committee of Council on Education. School inspectors' instructions covered three broad areas of interest:

> First ... inquiry in neighbourhoods from whence applications have been made for aid to erect new schools, in order to enable the Committee of Council to determine the propriety of granting funds in aid of the expenses proposed to be incurred, ...
>
> Secondly ... the inspection of the several schools aided by public grants issued under the authority of the Committee, and an examination of the method and matter of instruction, and the character of the discipline established in them, ...
>
> Thirdly, ...as incidental to and in furtherance of these duties, Inspectors may also be required by the Committee to make inquiries respecting the state of elementary education in particular districts. (XL. 1840 *Instructions for the Inspectors of Schools*)

This means that the Inspectorate played a central role in the construction of knowledge about schooling which was made available both to the government and to individual schools, many of which would otherwise have had little awareness of schooling matters beyond their own, immediate, locality. The information contained in these inspection reports should therefore not be taken as reflecting reality in any simple sense. Rather it should be understood in relation to the purpose of inspection as a means of mediating between individuals and groups interested in running schools, and state interest in giving financial aid to schooling. It should be understood as *discourse*, encompassing both theories and institutionalized practices. Reports, then, represent '... a specific order of historical reality' (Gordon, 1979, p. 34). They do not simply reflect more or less accurately the objects to which they refer. Rather they need to be understood as *practices* which *systematically form* the objects of which they speak (Foucault, 1972, pp. 48–9).

At the beginning of the period which I am discussing there was no official problem of truancy in the way in which we understand it today. This is not to deny that the word truant had been around prior to this, nor is it to suggest that children were always in school as often as we expect them to be today. However there were no special officials to deal with unauthorized absence. The official mechanisms with their associated socio-legal apparatus, which we expect to come into operation today, did not exist. Neither did the whole range of theories and practices about school attendance which are today part of our taken for granted reality. At the end of this period, with the introduction of universal compulsion we have attendance officers and school board hearings about school attendance. We have the beginnings of an official apparatus directed at dealing with school attendance. Therefore the pre-conditions for the historical emergence of truancy as an object of discourse (*ibid.*, pp. 45–8) were formed during this time.

As I have stressed, my analysis of historical material is aimed at illuminating the sociological dimensions of contemporary discussions of truancy. It follows from this that my account is not a narrative about the development of an increasingly enlightened set of agencies struggling to save wandering souls from darkness and ignorance. This is not a narrative history such as, for example, Rubinstein's (1969) work, for I am not going to try to recreate the sequence and flow of events. Rather my argument will intersect this, for I am concerned with the levels at which people engaged in producing knowledge about their world can construct 'reality'. I am not therefore dealing with the truth or falsity of knowledge claims, nor with a progressive accumulation of knowledge. What I am concerned with are the links between knowledge and its pre-conditions; between knowledge and the institutional structures to which it is integrally tied. More particularly, I am concerned with how they are linked in the case of truancy.

Historical Limits

This type of exercise has been described as involving the integration of manifest and latent history (Bailyn, 1982). That is, the uniting of events which were matters of conscious concern in their own time (in this case, constructing a form of social order by regulating the population) with those events of which contemporaries were unaware (that is, the social construction of normality/deviance) in order to show, in terms of the past, how the present has been made possible.

Given that this argument is based on official sources, there is always a danger of colluding with an official presentation of uniformity and of falsely implying that events were inevitable. Indeed the counterpart of my concentration on institutional relations of knowledge/power is that I tend to give less overt attention to relations of conflict. For example, in the nineteenth century, which was the period in which systematic state intervention into schooling began, elementary education was a controversial matter. As early as 1819 a Bill for state support of universal education for the working classes was presented to Parliament. It failed to gain support (David, 1980). In 1848, in his *Principles of Political Economy*, John Stuart Mill was arguing that state provision of education and compulsion were integral to each other. More than this, he maintained that the provision of education was a duty of the state both to children and to the community (Sutherland, 1973, pp. 117–18). Throughout the period between 1839 and 1872 there were several attempts to get Scottish Bills on this through parliament (David, 1980; Sutherland, 1973; Simon, 1970). Yet state provision and universal compulsion were not instituted in Scotland until 1872, and it was the 1880s before this happened in England and Wales.

To explain *why* this was the case would involve an examination of disputes about the nature of government intervention in relation to the role of particular religious denominations in providing schools. There were fears, for example, that state inspection would mean the regulation of the schools of non-established religions by members of the established church. This was the reason for inspection being denominational. At the level of a ruling class I would need to look at struggles between land-based fractions, who were concerned about the implications of schooling for the withdrawal of children, a cheap source of labour, from the agricultural workforce; and a rising industrial bourgeoisie concerned with the necessity of promoting a new order of social relations. The picture was further complicated by those members of the industrial bourgeoisie who were resistant to any moves which might restrict the extent to which they could benefit from the low cost of child labour. At the level of the working class I would have to consider the objections of parents who relied on their children's earnings, or who argued that universal compulsion was an insulting interference by the state because of the ways in which compulsion was associated with 'neglected' or 'delinquent' children; then there were the working class campaigns to stop child labour, those campaigns expressing the demand for publicly provided, secular schooling and, of course, Chartist and Owenite socialist demands for popular education (Simon, 1970).

There was clearly diversity in respect of education at all social levels. But this has not been my concern, for out of the diversity emerged an official uniformity. It is by focusing on *this* that I can look at the way in which a relatively small number of people in strategic locations could structure social relations in order to produce a knowledge of normality for a large number of people. This normality did not accord with the experiences of many of those people, but rather became a set of institutionalized assumptions which underpinned official judgments about the appropriateness or otherwise of different ways of living. In other words, the theories and practices of a discourse may promote the construction of *this particular* knowledge, but differing social relations could enable *other* knowledge to be constructed. In short, the models of the social world accepted within a discourse are, then, the visible result of the denial of alternatives. Now and then, glimpses of alternatives can be caught, when they appear as objects of criticism for the prevailing orthodoxy: as heresies which help to shape this orthodoxy through their negation.

Arguing for the importance of a historical sociology, Philip Abrams noted that we are in '... a world of which we are both the creators and the creatures, both makers and prisoners; a world which our actions construct and a world that powerfully constrains us' (Abrams, 1982, p. 2). As I shall show, people in strategic positions can attempt to *produce* the kinds of social relations which, in terms of their own theories of the social world, are held to be necessary for the creation/continuance of a particular social formation (Corrigan, 1977). They do this by means of programmes of power, that is, '... sets of calculated, reasoned prescriptions in terms of which institutions are meant to be reorganized, spaces arranged, behaviours regulated' (Foucault, 1981, p. 9). These programmes '... crystallize into institutions, they inform individual behaviour, they act as grids for the perception and evaluation of things' (*ibid.*, p.10). In short, programmes are both prescriptive for action and codifying of experience for knowledge. The concept of programme helps to direct our attention to such questions as *whose* programmes; *what* were they *about*; *how* were they implemented; *what* has been the *result* of this implementation? I shall be arguing that an adequate sociology of educational knowledge must be able to provide answers to each of these questions.

Discourse on truancy needs to be understood as embodying

various levels of programme. At the level of the ruling elite (or fraction of a ruling class), the programme concerns the structuring of social relations as part of the new social order of industrial capitalism, by directing schooling at the children of the working class. At the level of administration, there is the programme of the efficient implementation, at a minimum cost, of the rules set out for systematizing schooling. At the level of teachers involved in the practice of state-regulated schooling, there is the programme of professionalizing the occupation of teaching. I shall be examining the institutionalization of programmes which promoted one particular version of schooling and an associated pattern of attendance so that it came to be equated with education. In short, I shall be showing *how* state intervention into schooling effected a re-structuring of diversity in order to present it as uniformity. At the core of my argument there lies a particular view of the role of state authorised schooling and I shall now explain this.

The Social Significance of Schooling

Earlier this century when writing on education, Durkheim maintained that '... education is ... the means by which society prepares ... the essential conditions of its very existence' (1956, p. 71). The implications of this are a matter of some dispute. Michael Apple (1979a) has identified two characteristic positions on this issue. On the one hand, there are human capital theorists (for example, Denison and Poullier, 1972; and Bowman, 1972) who view schools as critical for industrial growth and social mobility, since they maximize the distribution of technical knowledge among the population. Pupils learn skills and expertise which they can 'invest', thereby becoming upwardly mobile and moving into better occupations. This, it is claimed, guarantees a supply of well-trained people which are necessary for an expanding economy. Allocation theorists, on the other hand, reject the meritocratic interpretation of the process. They argue that the teaching of technical competence is a secondary aspect of schooling since they maintain that schools allocate people within a hierarchical division of labour and inculcate into them dispositions, norms and values appropriate to their position.

As Apple (1979a, p. 117) points out, both approaches presuppose that schools are institutions of *distribution*. The first views schooling as effecting a distribution of technical knowledge which enables individuals to maximize their chances of attainment in a competitive and open jobs market. The extent to which this is an appropriate way of characterizing the jobs market is open to question (Troyna and Williams, 1986; Halsey, Heath and Ridge, 1980; Gray *et al.*, 1983). The second views schooling as a mechanism for the distribution of norms and dispositions that reinforce and reproduce economically based class positions. An example of this view has been the influential work of Althusser. Drawing on Marx's argument that '... every social formation must reproduce the conditions of its production at the same time as it produces ...' (1972, p. 242), Althusser has stressed the *reproductive* role of education within a social formation and its links with relations of economic power.

The importance of schooling as one aspect of the reproduction of social formations is accepted here. However, to restrict understanding of schooling to a reproductive role is to limit our view of the role of people in actively constructing the world in which they live and in producing knowledge about this. In viewing schooling as a mechanism for allocating people, Althusser's theory rests on a model of people as passive recipients of socialization. It is a feature of this type of model that it cannot account for deviance, it neglects ambiguity and it cannot explain how radicals emerge from, escape from, and engage with state apparatuses (Erben and Gleeson, 1978). Althusser has a narrow view of power relations, seeing them as fundamentally economic relations. As Bourdieu and Passeron (1977) have argued:

> To grant the educational system the absolute independence which it claims or, on the contrary, to see in it only the reflection of a state of the economic system or the direct expression of the value system of 'society as a whole' is to refuse to see that its *relative autonomy* enables it to serve external demands under the guise of independence and neutrality .... (pp. 177–8)

An important implication of my argument, is that schooling is about the production of individual identity and social normality. I shall argue that to understand the role of schooling we need to make explicit its links, not to some abstract notion of society, but to particular activities of people operating within the state. For the relations of legitimate authority associated with schooling are ultimately derived from its relation to the state.

On a simple level, this can be illustrated by the laws dealing with compulsion. These stipulate that it is the duty of a parent to provide a child with education and that the definition of what is to count as education is to be decided by officials whose authority is delegated to them by the state. In other words, for somewhere to count as a school and for the activities within it to be considered as education it has to be authorized. Unless this is the case then the parents of the children attending there would be liable to prosecution.

Up until the 1980s even amongst those who directly addressed the question of the significance of schooling, little attention was paid to the role of the state in this. As Dale (1982) has pointed out, although schooling in contemporary capitalist Britain is state-provided and compulsory for all children (as, indeed, it is in many other places), '... for sociologists and economists of education who effectively ignore, and for those political scientists who study, the inner workings of the "education sub-government", the State is regarded as an effectively neutral means of delivery of intended outcomes decided elsewhere ...' (p. 127).

Within the literature this reduction of political issues to administrative problems occurred partly because writers on schooling often assumed a fundamental consensus about social values and goals. This led them to focus on issues concerned with the most efficient means of achieving these. For example, looking at questions about the access of different social groups (working class/women/racial minorities) to schooling. Even amongst those, such as Young (1971), who criticized the consensual view of schooling and who recognized the importance of the political dimension to knowledge, there was a restricted view of power relations. These were viewed as relations of control and, as a result, there was a limited view of their operation.[2]

Neither consensus nor control models of social relations are adequate for an analysis of state activity in schooling. A more adequate analysis which can take into account the creation of knowledge requires that institutionalized constraints be considered as *one dimension* of knowledge/power relations. For example, at the same time as marginalizing activities which do not come within the authorized definition of what is to count as education, constraints on understanding operate as resources for the promotion of the authorized version of education and for different interpretations of this. In this way the authorized/central version of education becomes pivotal since it is in terms of this that alternatives have to be negotiated. It follows that though power relations may be about exclusion, limitation and prohibition as I have suggested, they are also about constructing '... *progammes* for the formation of a social reality' (Gordon, 1979).

During the 1980s, at a time when in Britain governmental action has brought into question previously accepted ground rules about state activity in education, the state has come increasingly into focus and there has been a growing literature on this. In particular, I shall draw on Dale's interpretation in relation to education of Klaus Offe's work on the state. It is important to distinguish the state from governments. The state consists of institutions necessary for securing the continuation of a social formation (in this case, capitalist Britain). Governments '... attempt to represent the short-term interests of the temporarily dominant coalitions within a social formation ...' (Dale, 1982, p. 139).

He explains that there are three reasons for capital being unable to secure its own reproduction. Firstly, the ground rules (i.e. legal framework of contract and property, financial guarantees) have to be specified by an apparently disinterested party which is capable of enforcing them. Secondly, since, by its very nature, capitalism generates both competitors and antagonists there is a need for protection from both internal and external attacks. Finally, particular capitals are confined within individual economic sectors. The separate conditions of optimum existence of these may be mutually conflicting. As a result of this, there are three core problem areas for the capitalist state:

  (i) support of the capital accumulation process;
 (ii) guaranteeing a context for its continued expansion;
(iii) legitimation of the capitalist mode of production and the state's own part in it (*ibid.*, p. 133).

He argues that these problems are permanently insoluble since they are mutually contradictory. Therefore they are permanently on the agenda of the state apparatus, though their prominence is variable depending on circumstances at any given time. Since these problems are also variable in content neither they, nor the means by which they will be tackled, are specifiable in advance.

Dale places two limits on this model. Firstly, on a practical level, the whole range of activities of a state apparatus cannot be seen as permanently problematic. Secondly, there is the organic limit that each state apparatus has its own history, daily practices, and individual apparatuses which, '... develop in directions, and take on a broad overall character, within the constraints of the basic demands made of them, which does not merely *not* follow the design of any one government, but can render them ineffective or inadequate vehicles for the execution of particular kinds of policy. State apparatuses are not directable at will' (*ibid.*, p. 139). Thus, though the core problems underpin the policy options available within the education system and provide an important dynamic for it, the ways in which the apparatus tackles them provides a further factor which facilitates dealing with certain questions and inhibits others.

This argument highlights the importance of the *machinery* of education, what empowers it, and how and where it is directed. Importantly, it presupposes that, 'Opposition, then, not support, must be expected and a major part of state policy is concerned with dealing with that opposition in one way or another' (*ibid.*, p. 135).

In this book I am examining the significance of the way in which the state has been linked with schooling. In pursuing this I shall argue that in order for schooling to be able to contribute to the *reproduction* of a social formation, schools must be able to facilitate the *production* of knowledge appropriate to this purpose (Apple, 1982). The importance of state involvement in the provision of schooling can be understood in terms of a more general feature of state activity. That is, the regulation of social life through the detailed definition of acceptable forms and images of social activity and individual and collective identity (Corrigan and Sayer, 1985). This is, *moral regulation* through which the fine detail of social relations characteristic of a historical and social formation come to seem natural and therefore immutable to those living within that order (*ibid.*, p. 4). In doing this, state agencies attempt to express as a unity the varying historical experiences of groups within society. I shall be drawing on this and, in particular, on Corrigan's argument concerning the need to make visible the way in which the 'public' structural features of compulsory, state provided and regulated, 'mass' schooling are differentially productive of 'private' social identities (Corrigan, 1987).

During the period in which there has been systematic state involvement in schooling the *form* of schooling has become 'naturalized' so that it is now the taken-for-granted means through which alternative educational ends may be pursued. This involved a narrowing of discussions about education to questions of access and control. This shift needs to be understood as part of a more general displacement of questions of power and problems of politics to questions of control and problems of administration. State intervention into schooling, as Corrigan maintains, is one aspect of a more general project of social formation and involves, '... an extended, protracted struggle to individualize, to place social beings in relations to institutions which appear neutral in their workings, democratic in their management and equitable in their potential outcomes' (*ibid.*, p. 5). This individualism derives from a nineteenth century belief, '... that the "children of other classes" ... needed to be "freed" from their collective moralities and cultural forms, to be made rational individuals, who could *then* take their place in the new social order' (*ibid.*).

State intervention involved an imposition of one particular model against alternative visions of the form and content of social arrangements. The resultant individualization has emerged from this contestation about social life. He argues that beyond this general project of social formation lies one of *socialization* which embodied a partially explicit psychology of the working class mind. Thus, 'Inscribed in the original structuration of schooling are images of what it means to be *rational*' (*ibid.*, p. 6). In this context he points to the *texture* of schooling, the regulation of expression within schooling, that is, performances, speech, action, which are encouraged/discouraged, approved/marginalized, and the implications which this has for the assessment and grading of people. In schools, '... forms of the presentation of a certain kind of self, a social identity, appear to in-form and structure the content of what is actually said' (*ibid*, p. 5). I shall be addressing the issue of identity formation in the next section where I shall be extending Corrigan's discussion, in order to provide an account of deviance and the production and structuring of knowledge in my argument that an important means of explaining the way in which schooling is productive of social identity is through social mapping.

In summary, an adequate account of the significance of schooling requires historical understanding and an understanding that relations of power in any social formation are multi-form and are not derived from a unitary base. Therefore their reproduction through schooling will also be multi-form. Thus, for example, an understanding of the form and the content of the family requires an understanding of power relations based on gender. These relations may be articulated to economic relations, but they are not reducible to these (Apple, 1982). Further, because relations of power are multi-form it is important to recognize that their articulation may embody contradictions which generate tensions in relations within schooling. For example, state action in structuring and regulating teaching in order to incorporate teachers as state agents helped foster the professionalization of this occupation. *At the same time* the programme of professionalism was used as a strategy by teachers for resisting incorporation. My argument will imply, then, not a passively socialized workforce, but an actively engaged population whose lived experience has been interpreted and negotiated in and through the official forms of structuring which I shall outline.

The purpose of the discussion so far has been to outline the concerns and assumptions which have underpinned my present argument. To stress, this is concerned with relations of knowledge/power and is an investigation of *how* it is that capitalist social relations are influential on the production of educational knowledge. This will be done by displaying the way in which state structured schooling is productive of knowledge; of social identities; and of deviance. In doing this I am not claiming to provide a comprehensive history of schooling, or inspection, though both these topics have contributed to my argument. I have only analyzed events in relation to their importance for the social map of truancy with which this book is concerned.

Mapping Truancy

Social mapping is an interpretive framework which focuses on relations of power/knowledge[3] and which can be used to look at the way in which the production of knowledge and the structuring of social relations are connected. In particular, it will enable me to look at the relationship between structural form, the general issue of truancy, and individual identity, the individual truant in terms of which the general issue is usually discussed.

Within this framework characterizations of power as an independent entity which people do or do not have (the zero-sum notion) are rejected. Rather, power is used here as a generic term referring to resources generated and mobilized in social relationships. Relations of power, therefore, are immanent in other forms of relation, they do not exist outside them. They are neither necessarily consensual, though consensus may be involved, nor are they necessarily based on violence. Consensus and violence reflect respectively, the strongest and weakest moments in relations of power.[4] Foucault (1982) has stated, 'The exercise of power consists in guiding the possibility of conduct and putting in order the possible outcome' (p. 221). Power relations are socially (not personally) structured and are transformed/strengthened and even reversed in an unceasing struggle (Sheridan, 1980, p. 183). This will be illustrated later in my discussion of the teaching occupation. Relations of power are therefore inescapable, though their particular forms are subject to negotiation/opposition/reversal. This definition of power moves beyond a narrow conception as exclusion/prohibition, to a definition which also incorporates the positive dimension of construction/transformation. The analysis of knowledge in terms of these concepts highlights the way in which '...

knowledge functions as a form of power and disseminates the effects of power' (Gordon, 1980, p. 69). The forms which are dealt with here are primarily those of class, gender and age; interwoven with these, at another level, are those of profession.

The issues raised in discourse on truancy can be characterized in terms of Foucault's notion of *biopolitics*. He developed this concept as part of an analysis of the new order of power relations which, he argued, emerged in Western societies from about the eighteenth century, and which led him to designate them as *disciplinary*. He maintained that the creation of techniques which enabled the development of capital accumulation was inseparable from the 'technology of subjection' which solved the problem of the 'accumulation of men' (Foucault, 1979, pp. 220 − 1).

> Historically, the process by which the bourgeoisie became ... the politically dominant class was masked by the establishment of an explicit, coded and formally egalitarian juridical framework, made possible by the organization of a parliamentary, representative regime. But the development and generalization of disciplinary mechanisms constituted the other, dark side of these processes ... tiny, everyday, physical mechanisms ... all those systems of micro-power that are essentially non-egalitarian and asymmetrical that we call the disciplines. (*ibid.*, p. 222)

Although fundamental authority within a parliamentary democracy lies in the formal representativeness of the regime, '... the disciplines provide, at the base, a guarantee of the submission of forces and bodies' (*ibid*).

Power relations characteristic of disciplinary societies can be distinguished in two basic, interlinked forms — *an anatomo-politics of the human body* and a *biopolitics of the population*. The first is '... centred on the body as a machine: its disciplining, the optimization of its capabilities, the extortion of its forces, the parallel increase of its usefulness and its docility, its integration into systems of efficient and economic controls, all this was ensured by the procedures of power that characterized the *disciplines* ...' (Foucault, 1981a, p. 139). The second form is

> ... focused on the species body, the body imbued with the mechanics of life and serving as the basis of the biological processes: propagation, births and mortality, the level of health, life expectancy and longevity, with all the conditions that can cause these to vary. Their supervision was effected through an entire series of interventions and *regulatory controls* ...'. (*ibid.*)

The deployment of biopower was therefore linked with the formation of disciplinary societies. Characteristic of biopolitical issues is that they refer to techniques of power which are strategically sited in the body, which operate through discipline and have, as their object, the regulation of the population. Essential features of biopolitics are techniques of qualifying, measuring, appraising, hierarchizing, effecting distributions around the *norm* (*ibid.*, p. 144). These techniques form the methodological core of work on truancy, which is viewed as *abnormal* activity. In biopolitical terms, truancy is out of place. It presupposes a particular organization of social space as well as the structuring of social time. As I shall show, this operated through the development of programmes of state power. Programmes aimed at regulating the place of schooling and those who were to be authorized to operate this — teachers. At the same time teachers were seeking to regulate their occupation. However, their definition of teaching profession involved autonomy and it was in trying to establish this that a strategy of struggle against state policy resulted. What was at issue was more than the regulation of spatial relations and social action which was con-sidered to be legitimate. At its core it was the structuring of perceptions of ways of living and learning. It is this action/knowledge to which I am giving attention when I refer to social mapping.

As I have implied, social mapping is an informal prerequisite for everyday social interaction. It is the reference which has to be made by people to the defining features of any category, including their social connotations, which promote a shared understanding of that category when it is used, and consequently a shared definition of the situations in which it is used. So, for example, to use the category of truancy it is necessary to understand that there is a socially appropriate location for a person during a particular period of their life and during particular times within that period. As this suggests, the ability to define a situation competently in terms of any category depends on being able to locate both the self and the situation in a general scheme of the social world. Consequently, it also embodies a specific understanding of social identity.

As a formal sociological enterprise, an account of a category involves an analysis of its constituents in relation to general concepts (i.e. concepts applicable outside this particular map) and to features specific to this map, in a way which will clarify the structural forms of the taken-for-granted aspects of the category. In so doing, this enables an explanation to be constructed of what has made it possible for the particular concepts, and that which they signify, to be taken as unproblematic ('natural'). In other words, it involves a questioning of what is often left unquestioned.

A map is a depiction of spatial arrangements which helps us to recognize our position in relation to other possible positions. It provides us with an orientation to where we are, in relation to where we are not and, importantly, an orientation to *who* we are (for example, British, French, etc.) in terms of our relation to the political structuring of territories. It is therefore also a depiction of political arrangements. Since nation states and their frontiers are not static, this depiction is historical, it intersects time. It reflects a specific set of arrangements at a given point in time, though it does not reveal the temporal processes which resulted in the possibility of any particular map. Its coordinates therefore reflect particular configurations of space/time. For example, a map of the British Empire displays the political-spatial arrangements which resulted from wars, treaties etc., but it does not display a full account of the process of any particular war, treaty etc.. Yet, by tracing the organization of domains the relations of power embedded in these are thrown into relief. In short, a map provides us with an orientation to the world in terms of strategies of power/knowledge.

These characteristics are important features of a social map, which is a scheme of the disposition of the constituents of a category of understanding. It exists in and through the construction of that category and is propagated through the institutional forms of knowledge/power relations. It operates on the level of knowledge, providing an important key to understanding social action. An integral part of any social map is an understanding of social identity. Foucault has stated '... it's my hypothesis that the individual is not a pre-given entity which is seized on by the exercise of power. The individual with his identity and characteristics, is the product of a relation of power exercised over bodies, multiplicities, movements, desires, forces' (1980, pp. 73–4).

In respect of schooling, Corrigan (1987) has pointed out that this supposedly neutral, knowledge-providing agency was structured to transform social relations and effect a particular form of socialization. This was to foster '... the presentation of a certain kind of self, a social identity ...' (*ibid.*, p. 5). This social identity in-forms and structures the content of what is said and what is done in schools and has important implications for the assessment of speech and action as acceptable/unacceptable, and for the grading of pupils.

Corrigan's argument can be extended by making a distinction between two types of identity: *formal* identity, which refers to a person's structural position and which embodies particular repertoires for social action; and *in-formed* identity, an individual's interpretation of their formal identity, which is negotiated through social interaction in any given situation. In any situation there will be a *range* of social action which participants will accept as being harmonious with the relevant formal identities. Outside of this range, social action will be defined as deviant. That is, *deviance can be understood as a dissonance between formal and in-formed identity*. The extent of the range of social action which is acceptable and the implications of any dissonance between formal and in-formed identity is, in a large part, dependent on the institutional site of the action, and would need to be specified empirically in any given case.

To put this another way, in order to be able to interact competently in any situation, people need to refer, in a taken-for-granted way, to a map, or image of a 'normal' version of that situation. This involves a range of acceptable/normal identities and repertoires which are embedded in these. The ability of people to use an acceptable repertoire of social action and therefore present an in-formed identity which is apparently harmonious with an appropriate formal identity should not however be confused with their acceptance of this. That is, '... role-performance at school need not (or, should not) be read as role-acceptance and, above all, role-internalization' (*ibid.*, p. 14).

When there is dissonance between the formal identity integral to the 'acceptable'/normal map and the informed identity of someone, then a second map comes into play. This map enables people to make sense of the content of the dissonance, by providing a version of social identities and repertoires which are held to be integral to people whose behaviour takes this particular form.

Two kinds of dissonance can be distinguished. The first results from the imposition of a particular model of normality onto existing social relations of another form. The structuring of normal family relations, which I describe in chapter 6, is an example of this. The second is dissonance which is *generated by the success* of the imposed model. Two examples here are the struggle of teachers for professional autonomy (described in chapter 5), and the contemporary problem of effecting *continuity* between schooling and wider social relations, which has emerged as a result of the success of the nineteenth century programme of structuring *discontinuity* between these (I shall discuss this in chapter 8).

To clarify this discussion the social map of the formal identity of child and its counterpart, the social map of the formal identity of truant

are illustrated. They are both derived from contemporary (late twentieth century) discourse on truancy. The first map displays the notion of
normal social relations involving children which is implicit in discussions of truancy. It involves power/knowledge claims concerning
relations of class, gender and age, and presupposes the subordination of
working class people, women and young people. These claims are
mediated through mechanisms involving relations of professional
power. When the exercise of these forms is overt and formally
supported by institutional structures then I shall refer to this as
involving legitimate authority. This map therefore expresses particular
forms of power relation in terms of the normality of legitimate
authority.

Particular social maps are institutionally propagated and embody a
particular understanding of the correct ordering of social time. This
involves a scheduling of social identities (Gurvitch, 1964). Which is to
say that someone who is truanting is out of place in terms of the social
map of normality which is propagated through state authorized schooling. This map carries within it the formal identity of pupil, which
implies child, not adult; not parent; not teacher; not worker. It implies a
particular relationship of subordination to these other identities; it
implies one whose movements ought to be authorized. It implies
someone who is physically present at authorized times in an authorized
place, i.e. school.

When a pupil's absence from school is unauthorized the social map
of normality becomes the *implicit* counterpart of the social map of
truancy. Therefore, against this first map should be set the social map of
the formal identity of truant. This displays the features of the category
'truant' in terms of knowledge/orthodoxies about truancy as a social
problem. It expresses particular forms of power relation in terms of
problems for legitimate authority: children out of control of relations of
schooling,[5] children out of parental control, priority being given to
maternal authority within family relations, parents not 'cooperating'
with (i.e. conforming to) school authority.

So far, though, I have only described a certain kind of knowledge
which state structured schooling has produced. If I am to sustain my
claim that social mapping will enable me to demonstrate *how* schooling
has produced knowledge, deviance and social identities, I shall need to
be able to explain where these maps come from. It would be a mistake
to assume that these maps of social knowledge are expressions of some
neutral central value system or some generalized consensus. These
social maps are today's result of the strategies and programmes of key

SOCIAL MAP OF FORMAL IDENTITY OF CHILD

CHILD

Acceptance of Legitimate Authority Relations
Pupil
Implies
HARMONIZE

Formal identity of teacher: the 'good teacher'			Formal identity of parents: 'good parents'
Involves:	*Implies*:	*Implies*:	*Involves*:
Class management i.e. class under control.	Attendance in designated school space during designated school hours — designation by officials in system.	In parentally organized/known space (with 'responsible' adult i.e. parent or delegated child carer of appropriate seniority i.e. over 16). May be home but key fact is that it is supervised.	Available to supervise child.
Transmission of knowledge.			Available to liaise with school about child.
Personal knowledge of children i.e. home background, friends, etc.			Supportive of relations on left of map.
Ability to identify 'needs' of child in relation to school system.			Both parents to support each other's authority, BUT priority assumed for paternal authority.
			Actions beneficial for child's welfare as defined by official agencies.

In consequence, behaves according to formal/informal authoritatively defined rules of situation. Therefore only barrier to child's achievement is individual's capability.

groups who have historically been able to negotiate successfully for the institutionalization of *their* programme over those of other groups.

At the level of knowledge, I have referred to a social map. I shall use an institutional diagram at the level of action. This diagram provides an explanation of the action which has made possible the social maps and, as such, can also be seen as a key to the organization of the book. The programmes and strategies outlined in the diagram need to be understood as operating at several levels:

(i) at the level of a ruling elite or fraction of a ruling class;
(ii) at the level of administration;
(iii) at the level of professionalization.

The institutions through which they operated acted as pressure points

SOCIAL MAP OF FORMAL IDENTITY OF TRUANT

Absence

Authorized

Unauthorized

School phobic

TRUANT

Involves:
Not in designated school space during designated school time. Not acquiescent to legitimate authority relations. Endangered as not in responsibly supervised space (out of vision/socially isolated).

Potential risks:
Delinquency, out of place — outside the law.
Poor schoolwork — can't achieve, insufficient reception of knowledge. Inability to cope with being a member of the workforce — shorthand for responsible, contributing member of the social order.

ROOTED IN

Problem families

Dissonance between formal and in-formed identity of parents. Authority relations not harmonizing with those of the school.

Implies:
Inability to reconcile 'needs' of parents with 'needs' of child.

Over-caring relations involving dominant mothers and recessive fathers.

Problem schooling

Structure and content inappropriate for approved identity formation.

Implies:
Locality — 'deprived' areas, council estates — carries implication of structural location, i.e. working class.

Structural deviation from formal family, for example, single parent family.

Faulty authority relations within family — uncooperative child, out of control, inadequate parent.

Parents unavailable to liaise with school or supervise children, their leisure pursuits and their friendships i.e. 'uncaring'.

for the application and modification of the programmes and strategies. As Dale has pointed out, in considering this it is important to consider the implications which particular institutional mechanisms may have.

It is also important to consider the contradictions which may be embodied in particular programmes and strategies. For example, to raise the status of teachers as purveyors of authorized social relations within their local communities, there was the programme of structuring the social identity of teacher and of professionalizing the occupation. This involved the propagation of a professional identity among teachers. One result of this was that legitimate authority over schooling was the subject of contest between the state and teachers. Thus, there were the unsuccessful struggles of the Educational Institute for Scotland to assert professional power/knowledge, claiming it to be the basis for

**DIAGRAM OF LEVELS OF INSTITUTIONAL ACTION
WHICH MADE POSSIBLE THE SOCIAL MAPS OF CHILD AND TRUANT**

	Ruling Elite/Fraction of Ruling Class[1] Administration[2]
	Technology of inspection[3] involved: The structuring of space and the structuring of identities within schools[4]
Professionalization of teaching[5]	The structuring of time through the problem, in terms of the social division of labour, of a clash between in-formed identity and formal identity in school. Formulation of the content of the curriculum to be relevant to appropriate identity formation[6]
Attempt to make administration cost-efficient: Revised code	The structuring of individuals through tighter implementation of regulation and supervision beyond inspection visit. Used mechanisms of the register and individual written examination to construct a hierarchy of achievement[7]

Notes:
1 Aimed to propagate social relations congruent with industrial capitalist order. Central problem of schooling the working classes set the parameters for institutional action.
2 Education office structured and implemented rules for allocating grants.
3 The key officials (i.e. inspectors) mediated between the education office and the sector of the social world which it was to structure. Their reports constituted 'knowledge' of that world in terms of the parameters of the administrative rules. They show *how* these regulations relate to that world, by stating problems and advantages of implementation. That is, they are the point of the visible application and modification of the programmes.
4 This was to provide a model for extra-school relations.
5 Involved the contradiction of teachers' strategies based on this power form in conflict with the institutionalized programme.
6 This made possible the construction of a particular knowledge of the problem of schooling working class children: that of *knowing their place*.
7 This made possible the shift to the problem of schooling as being concerned with *the ability of individual subjects to achieve a position*.

legitimate authority over what happened in education. This was against the institutionally supreme class power which successfully claimed legitimate authority on the basis of ruling class responsibility.

The institutional action embodied in the diagram involved a specialization of spatial arrangements, which were aimed at moulding thought and action. This presupposed a generalization of individuals — a moulding of individuality in relation to a formal identity. It also involved a structuring of temporal relations through the social division of labour which regulated rhythms of population life (a compartmentalization of living). Further, there was the structuring of what was to count as good teaching practice and its transformation into what was to count as teaching. What it was to be a good pupil and to provide efficient schooling coalesced to produce one particular pattern of school attendance as *regular* attendance. A shift from the structure of schooling to the content marks another level of institutional action. It is the *content* of this structure of normality/abnormality which constitutes the core substance of the map of the social problem. This content is based on one particular form of family relations: male-dominated, with the woman's primary task being to service the needs of her husband and children.

A final shift in terms of institutional action signalled the emergence of the possibility of an ontological and epistemological shift. Schooling, aimed at structuring social relations and producing knowledge of/for a class, had involved the generalization of individuals. Changes in the mechanisms for regulating schooling in the 1860s involved the individualization of general school assessment. This facilitated a shift to schooling being aimed at fostering individual achievement. This shift from an overtly class-focused concern to an overtly individualistic concern was a prerequisite for the emergence of the individual problematic child — the truant.

Having set out what is involved in social mapping, the questions it has enabled me to ask and the kinds of answers which it will help me to display, I shall be able to begin considering the four questions which, I have argued, will need to be answered. These concern: with whose programmes I shall be dealing; what they were about; how they were implemented; and with what result. I shall be providing answers to each of these during the course of my argument. However, before embarking on this I shall take a closer look at twentieth century representations about truancy.

Notes

1 'The social refers to a *particular sector* in which quite diverse problems and special cases can be grouped together, a sector comprising specific institutions and an entire body of qualified personnel ('social' assistants, 'social' workers).... The social sector does not merge with the judicial sector, even if it does extend the field of judicial action ... (it) does not merge with the economic sector either, since ... it invents an entire social economy and lays new foundations for marking the distinction between the rich and the poor. Nor does it merge with the public sector or the private sector since ... it leads to a new hybrid form of the public and the private' (Deleuze, Foreword to Donzelot, 1980, pp. IX–X).

2 For example Young (1971) in his argument for the self-styled 'new sociology of education', stressed that those wishing to understand education needed to give greater attention to the political character of knowledge.

Young argued that definitions of what is to count as knowledge depend on the meaning systems through which we understand the world. He maintained that these reflect political interests. Since for him society was a product of competing definitions of knowledge and claims to its legitimacy, some meaning systems take precedence over others. In other words, knowledge and schooling are political in nature and this, he maintained, is expressed in its control. However, his restrictive definition of power as relations of control, meant that his exploration of power/knowledge was only in terms of the institutional constraints on these relations. As a result, his work remained internal to the education system. He neglected the relations of power which underpin schooling and, because of this, he was forced to presuppose power differentials, but was unable to provide an explanation of them. (For a fuller discussion and criticisms see, for example, Whitty, 1977; Demaine, 1981; Apple, 1979a).

3 Others have used spatial concepts in discussions of knowledge, in particular, Berger and Luckmann (1971). The argument I develop here owes much to the work of Foucault. See in particular in Gordon, 1980, pp. 63–78.

4 Foucault's discussion of the relationship between power and violence is unclear. He argued that violence, though not a defining characteristic, can be an instrument/result of power (1982, p. 220). Yet, *at the same time*, he argues that: (a) the defining characteristic of a relationship of power is that it is a mode of action which acts upon actions (either present or future) rather than directly on others. It involves the recognition of the 'other', over whom power is exercised, as one who acts, and opens up a field of possible responses/results etc.; and, by contrast, (b) a relationship of violence acts upon a body, or upon things, closing off all other possibilities. This definition of violence precludes it from being an instrument of power, since that which *closes off* possibilities cannot be an instrument/result of that which *opens up* possibilities. By the same token, that which is distinguished by action on objects, rather than action upon action, cannot be an instrument of action upon action.

5 Note the linking of *truancy and indiscipline* in the Pack Report.

Chapter 2

Social Problems and Educational Knowledge

Introduction

Ann spends most days helping her mother look after her two younger sisters. None of the children attends school regularly. ('I don't mind what I do — shopping, cooking, washing up, or cleaning, so long as I stay at home.')

Ann's two favourite occupations are taking her younger sisters to the local park and visiting her grandmother. She can see no point in attending school as she believes that her mother needs her help and enjoys her company. Jim, her father, a long-distance lorry driver, cares little that his eldest daughter misses school. He believes that 'mitching' never did him any harm!'. (Reid, 1985, p. 5)

The 'irregular pupil' has generally a weakly mother who requires a great deal of help. She has a number of delicate brothers and sisters who require a wonderful amount of nursing. She is very liable to catch cold, and is a martyr to 'sore heads'. 'Washing day' occurs twice in a week, and half the family is kept to assist. The irregular pupil is blessed with many relations, near and far off: and if a father's second cousin happens to visit them, the whole family is kept at home in consequence. John is absent today, because he had to go with his father's dinner, and Mary will be absent tomorrow if she has to go to the 'shop' — for two red herrings, perhaps. (Lecture given to the National Association for the Promotion of Social Science by George Leith, a member of Greenock School Board, 1877. Quoted in Withrington, 1975)

Truancy, it seems, is an intractable problem. Over 100 years separates the first depiction of an absentee child from the second characterization of truanting children. Yet their features are identifiably the same: irresponsible parents, children doing adult tasks when they should be in school. In this chapter I am going to look at research on truancy and examine the way in which it has dealt with the topic. I shall argue that writers have generally failed to identify the social meaning of truancy. Linked with this are the difficulties which people have had in developing an agreed definition of the concept of truancy, or in getting particular definitions to be used systematically. Researchers generally consider that these problems hinder our understanding of truancy. However, I shall show how, by looking at these problems differently, they can be used to further our understanding of this subject.

There are three central themes within the literature, these are concerned with: the school phobic; the endangered truant; and the disaffected truant. By exploring these, I shall identify both the strengths and the limitations of existing work in helping us to understand the social dimensions of the problem. For truancy is fundamentally a *social* problem which is embedded within the institutional network of schooling. Yet, as we shall see, within the many papers, articles and books which have been written about it, writers have rarely treated it as such. Instead they generally deal with it in *individual* terms. That is to say, they focus on the individual characteristics and behaviour of children who have been identified as truants. To a certain extent this is understandable, after all, it is individual children with whom the concerned professionals are dealing. Yet, as some recent writers are beginning to recognize (Sayer, 1987) this has narrowed our understanding of the issues. These issues concern the standardized pattern of school attendance which forms part of what is generally taken as being the normality of one particular pattern of living and learning. It is this fundamental pattern of normality which throws alternative patterns into relief and, in so doing, informs our views about deviance.

The Individual Problem of Truancy

Even a cursory glance at the literature on school attendance reveals that most work is focused on deviance rather than normality. In this, as in the individualization of the problem, the work shares the characteristics of 'correctionalist' research (Rubington and Weinberg, 1971) in the area of social problems. Correctionalist research is aimed at finding out how to reduce or eliminate deviance. The sorts of questions which are concentrated on within this type of work are:

'Who is deviant?
How did he/she become a deviant?
Why does he/she continue in deviance, despite controls brought to bear on him/her?
What socio-cultural conditions are most likely to produce deviants?
How may deviants be best controlled? (Hargreaves, *et al.*, 1975).

The individualization of issues within this type of work is at its most pronounced within psychiatric literature on deviance. In accounts of school attendance problems this takes the form of a concern with *fearful truants*, often referred to as school phobics. Worries about this group of children differ from concerns expressed more generally about truanting children. As one writer has put it, 'A psychiatrist often feels responsible for a patient's life if he is aware that the patient is suicidal. The child who refuses to go to school is being self-destructive. Contacts outside the family are avoided, the career is jeopardized, and the future is cut off, in a way that could be described as social suicide' (Kahn and Nursten, 1962, p. 710).

There is some confusion within the specialist literature about what school phobia is. It is variously held to be a *symptom* (Model and Shepheard, 1958), an *illness* (Hersov, 1979, p. 466), a *maladaptive avoidance response maintained by fear reduction (ibid.)*. It is an *indication* of a more deep-seated problem of separation anxiety, or it is *caused by* separation anxiety. This is attributed to faulty family dynamics, typically, indulgent and over-bearing mothers, submissive and disinterested fathers, double-bind families. This is contrasted, though usually implicitly, with a favourable school situation. The nature of school phobia, then, seems to vary according to the theoretical pre-disposition of the writer.

The key to understanding why there should be such confusion, lies in the background to the emergence of school phobia as a distinctive phenomenon. Those writing about the fearful truant are generally members of staff of child guidance clinics. These clinics emerged in the first half of the twentieth century as one strand of more general moves to establish child medicine as a professionally distinctive field.[1] Those who advocated a specialist child medicine were concerned with investigating the physiological bases of childhood problems and with developing theories about the causes of these. Among those interested in child guidance, this aim of controlling disease was transformed into the control of relations underpinning social disease. Characteristically, they focused on the impact of the social environment on child and family relations, and tried to rationalize the kinds of interventions which were made by the many external agencies which dealt with families.

Child guidance operates through the 'case conference', which consists of a discussion with all agencies involved in a particular case. The purpose of this is to encourage people's adjustment to outside agencies by exorcising their internal problems. This method illustrates the interplay of psychiatric and psychoanalytic theories and practices which permeate these clinics. As I have said, it is at this point that individualistic explanations of difficulties are at their most extreme, for it is here that medical theories and educational theories coalesce in the *problematic child*. The literature often emerges in the form of case histories and seeks to generalize theories from particular family relations which have been defined as being a problem. This offers some explanation for the conceptual confusion which I have already mentioned, for this method of working means that writers' theoretical assumptions remain taken for granted. Assumptions, as Jencks argues, 'embody the values and interest of the theorist, which in turn generate normative models of the social world' (1982, p. 10). As a result of this neglect of assumptions, the object of knowledge, school phobia, comes to be treated as existing independently of theories about schooling, children and social relations. It provides reinforcement for the notion of the *normality* of an uninterrupted experience of schooling for children, and distracts attention from this as being something which is based on a historically specific understanding of appropriate patterns of living and learning.

The *fearful truant* first emerged in 1932 with Broadwin's description of two cases seen at a clinic; by the 1940s and 1950s a body of knowledge about this phenomenon had been built up. This was based on the possible treatment and detection of 'cases' discovered in child guidance clinics, and was disseminated through professional journals. By 1959 researchers (Waldfogel *et al.*, 1959) were instructing teachers in signs of 'incipient school phobia' and scouring classrooms for 'undetected cases'. However, despite these difficulties, and the fact that the distinctiveness of school phobics as a group is a matter of some debate (Turner, 1974), there are certain features about which most writers are in agreement.

ENDANGERED TRUANT	FEARFUL TRUANT
1 Voluntary absence	Involuntary absence
2 Wanders streets	Remains at home
3 Doesn't like school	May want to go to school but is unable to do so
4 Lacks caring parents	Over-caring parents
5 Comes from a poorly kept home	Comes from a well kept home
6 Schoolwork inadequate	Schoolwork fine

The fearful truant, then, contrasts with a more central theme within the literature, that concerning the *endangered truant*. Within this theme worries focus on links between truancy, delinquency, poverty and failure to achieve. Children believed to be involved in truancy are often viewed as endangered for truancy has been described as the 'kindergarten of crime' (Healy, 1915, quoted in Tyerman, 1968, p. 49). According to West (1982, p. 153) truants and delinquents have shared characteristics. Therefore to be concerned about delinquents implies concern about truants since truanting children, it seems, drift into delinquency. They often wander away from school because they cannot cope satisfactorily with their difficulties, for 'The typical persistent truant is unhappy at home, unpopular at school, and unsuccessful in his classwork' (Tyerman, 1974, p. 10).

Writers tell us that truanting children will tend to come from decaying inner city areas or council estates, live in overcrowded conditions, be poorly dressed, have broken homes or parents with unhappy marriages. They are likely to come from large families (that is, families with four or more children), to have at least one sibling who is a truant and who may be a delinquent as well. The parents will set a poor example to their children, having low standards, neglecting their off-spring and being ineffective in their supervision. On the whole, the children tend to be intellectually and academically inferior to their peers and, though they may be sociable, are unreliable, showing little perseverance at school. Poor attendance increases the difficulties of keeping up with the work of other children. Thus a vicious circle of failure and truancy is established.

This endangered truant theme resonates throughout the literature, despite difficulties with some of the work. For example, Tyerman indicated that, 'Of 137 pupils whose parents were prosecuted for their children's truancy during the ... period which I studied, sixty-four had police records by the end of the following year' (Tyerman, 1968, p. 49). However, he told us nothing of the seventy-three cases in his group who did not subsequently have police records. As Galloway (1985) points out, 'Part of the folklore of many magistrates and many teachers is that truancy and delinquency are indissolubly linked' (p. 48). Yet the significance of this link remains unclear. Even if it were accepted that juvenile delinquents often are truant from school, this would not justify a further conclusion, sometimes drawn, that children playing truant are heading towards delinquency. Such a view is implicit, for example, in West (1982) who argued that truanting often starts before officially recorded delinquency and so could be used to identify individuals 'at risk'. This view is one for which investigations have produced only equivocal support. For example, Farrington (1980) found that at age 15 less than 20 per cent of his sample of 411 males said that they had never played truant. Finding that there was little difference in the extent of truancy between those who did and those who did not become delinquent, he argued that truancy and delinquency have the same underlying causes but that they do not cause each other (*ibid.*, p. 60).

Work by Galloway (1985), confuses the picture further. In Sheffield in 1976 Galloway looked at all 11–16-year-olds who were part of a survey on persistent absenteeism. He found that only 17 per cent of the absentees were known by the police to have been convicted in juvenile court or to have been given a formal police caution by 1 September 1977. Although the percentage of offenders increased with age, in no age group were more than 27 per cent of boys and 15 per cent of girls known to the police (pp. 49–50). Out of this confusing picture there emerges a sense from the literature that there are a number of features of social life with which truancy is associated, yet the significance and extent of this association remains a mystery.

The significance of links between truancy and delinquency remain unclear primarily because work is not directed towards investigating this. The methods generally adopted are therefore not appropriate for finding out about meanings within social life. To illustrate this I shall look at some work which has been cited as providing authoritative support for statements about the close links between truancy and delinquency. This is Belson's (1975) investigation into the causal factors of juvenile theft (cited, for example, by West, 1982). The study consisted of interviews with a sample of 1425 boys aged between 13 and 16 years, and chosen at random from several London polling districts. Among the hypotheses which Belson was setting out to test was that, 'Boys who play truant from school are thereby made more likely to be involved in stealing' (Belson, 1975, p. 384). He concluded that truancy is 'a potent factor in the development of stealing' (p. xvi). Nevertheless, a closer inspection of the work reveals that the nature of the link between truancy and delinquency was found to be unclear. All boys in the sample admitted to some stealing (p. xii) and the stealing was 'widely spread through the different occupational strata, with the sons of the professionally occupied sector being quite substantially involved' (*ibid.*). When asked about playing truant, 44 per cent said that they did so and 56 per cent of the sample said they never did so. Belson found that frequency of truanting was linked to amount of stealing.

When boys were asked to say what they did when playing truant, however, only 2 per cent said that stealing was an activity during truancy. (Most said that they were involved in 'informal/unstructured' activities, such as walking around or going to friends' houses, many simply went home.) When asked directly about whether they stole while truanting, although the boys' answers indicated that 'an appreciable amount of stealing goes on during truancy' and that 'this occurs more often amongst those who play truant more frequently', Belson did not find strong support for this within the evidence. For example, of those who claimed to be truant once a week, 62 per cent claimed never to steal while truanting and only 9 per cent claimed to do this 'fairly often'. In comparison, of those who claimed 'hardly ever' to truant, the percentages were 81 per cent and 1 per cent (*ibid.*). Belson suggests that the explanation for the discrepant results may be that although those involved in truancy had greater involvement in stealing, the stealing would not necessarily occur while they were truanting. This, he maintains, implies that 'truanting does not operate directly and spontaneously as a causal factor in thieving' (*ibid.*) and concludes that there is a need to investigate the *way* in which truancy is linked to stealing (*ibid.*, p. 390).

In short, at the end of the study, as with other work of this type, we are left with a puzzle about the *meaning and nature* of the relationship between truancy and delinquency (see Galloway, 1985, for discussion). It's not surprising though that we are left with this. For the model of research with which Belson is operating is one which involves the testing of hypotheses about dependent and independent variables. This model is often used within the natural sciences. However, when applied within the social sciences it has been found to be restrictive because of its lack of sensitivity to that which is specific to these sciences, namely, the importance of meaning in social life. Indeed, it is significant that Belson does not define the concept of truancy. He assumes that its meaning can be taken for granted. Yet, as I shall show, this is far from being a tenable assumption. As with other work which employs a natural scientific method, to the extent to which human interpretation is given any recognition at all, it is treated as a problem which needs to be minimized by the introduction of certain controls.

For example, this was the case with Robins and Ratcliffe (1980), who, like Belson, found that the greater people's involvement in delinquency the greater also was their likely involvement in truancy. They used information from school attendance records in their investigation of whether days absent during someone's school career was a predictor of that person having long-term behavioural problems. Although Robins and Ratcliffe indicated that they were aware that attendance records are an imperfect index of truancy, they maintained that such records had the advantage of being independent of the judgments of teachers (*ibid.*, p. 67). In making this kind of assertion they were implicitly assuming that, by using the criteria of absences being massed (that is, 20 per cent or more days' absence within a given quarter of the school year) and there being no recorded explanation for these absences, the judgments of researchers would be technically objective and therefore more valid. The kind of knowledge about individual absentees which teachers would be likely to bring to bear in deciding whether or not an absence should be defined as truancy, was thus considered to introduce a technical problem into the study.

The issue of what is to count as valid knowledge is rooted in two fundamental and associated problems which plague writings about truancy and which, if looked at closely, undermine the certainty of much that is argued there. These are: the problem of reaching an agreed definition of what is to count as truancy; and the problem of classifying absences appropriately. Although these are recognized by others (Farrington, 1980; Galloway, 1985; Reid, 1985), they are generally treated as technical problems. That is, solvable when the tools of research, such as clearly defined categories about which there is general agreement, have been refined sufficiently to enable absenteeism to be properly analyzed and truants to be identified (Reid, 1985). However, I shall argue that if we look beyond this view and start to recognize these as being conceptual problems then we can exploit them in such a way as to help us begin to move towards an understanding of truancy as a social issue.

Identifying Truancy

The significance of the technical problem presented by there being no generally agreed definition is illustrated by the difficulties which people run into when attempting to discover the incidence of truancy. For some writers (Turner, 1974; Institute for the Study and Treatment of Delinquency, 1974) truancy is an increasing problem whereas for others (Tyerman, 1974; Galloway, 1985; Reid, 1985, Raffe, 1986) it is not. The Pack Report on Truancy and Indiscipline in Schools in Scotland argued that it was on the increase though they undermined this assertion when they noted in the same report that when the Committee was set up in 1974, '... comprehensive information about the incidence in Scotland was not available. The SED no longer gathered information on attendance rates and figures provided by those submitting evidence had been prepared under a variety of circumstances and for a variety of purposes, making meaningful comparisons difficult' (Pack, 1977, p. 14). They therefore commissioned their own survey.

There have been other attempts to discover the extent of the 'problem'. For example, the D.E.S. 'snapshot' on 17 January 1974 which quantified 'unjustified absences' — those for whose absence the school knew of no legitimate reason by 23 January 1974. However, as with similar attempts by the ILEA in 1971 and on 13 May 1981 (St. John-Brooks, 1982), results were difficult to interpret as, 'Unfortunately the nature of many of the school returns makes it impossible to separate the unacceptable and the unknown' (Williams, 1974, p. 25). As Coombes (1974, p. 94) points out, such 'snapshot' methods tend to produce artificial figures since schools make a special effort to reduce the number of absentees on the particular day by, for example, warning pupils that registration procedures will be more strictly enforced on the date in question.

Absence rates themselves, though, provide little information on the nature of these absences. Coombes notes, 'A teacher with thirty children in a class will produce an acceptable percentage attendance of 90 per cent throughout the month. This may well mean that three pupils were absent throughout this period, or six pupils had two weeks off, or every child in the class had every Friday afternoon off' (*ibid.*, p. 93). School registers are the only source of figures which are kept as a matter of routine, but their inadequacies are notorious amongst researchers, some of whom believe that these are sufficiently serious as to outweigh their possible usefulness for research purposes. Registers don't reveal the number of children who leave school after registration, nor those who arrive too late to get marked present, nor can they give information about the number of children who are on the school premises but not in classes. As one writer puts it, 'Taken at face value, attendance registers tend to mislead and obscure true attendance patterns' (Reid, 1985, p. 13).

The difficulties in compiling the figures are compounded by the doubt concerning what would constitute accurate figures. Though most writers clearly have a working definition of what is meant by truancy, there is no common agreement as to the range of behaviour to which the term refers. For Tyerman (1974), truancy is 'unjustified absence on a child's own initiative without permission of parents or school' (p. l0). Whereas Pack (1977) includes what is sometimes referred to as parent-ally condoned absence, 'Truancy is unauthorized absence from school, for any period, as a result of pre-meditated or spontaneous action on the part of pupil, parent or both' (p. 18). Because of such discrepancies surveys are rarely comparable, as they rarely share the same definition of their object of study. Further, surveys often start out with (in their own terms) clearly established absence rates, but end up with *estimates* of truancy rates (Pack, 1977; St. John-Brooks, 1982; Reid, 1985).

But the problem goes beyond that of being able to assess the incidence of truancy. For it is not the inability to do this which limits our understanding. Rather it is the failure to address the significance of teacher knowledge in terms other than as being either less valid (Robins and Ratcliffe, 1980) or as having privileged validity (Tyerman, 1974). Writers who have drawn attention to issues of meaning have noted that most research relies on teachers' definitions and perceptions of truants when samples are being selected for study. This issue was raised by Fogelman and Richardson in their work for the National Child Development Study (1974). To define a truant they used 'teachers' knowledge of the attendance behaviour of each study child' (*ibid.*), supplemented with their information on personal characteristics and circumstances of the children. Their findings remained largely consistent with those of most other work but they stressed that their data could not be taken as conclusive. This was partially because of the position of the children in some of the categories they used (for example, ratings of above/below average ability; impressions of parental interest; and general comments on the child) relied on judgments of teachers and could therefore be influenced by a 'negative halo effect', perhaps in terms of teacher expectations of working class children, or their expectations of truants.

Rather than considering factors about any pupil independently, teachers are likely to rate a pupil either positively or negatively on a given factor according to their general (positive or negative) impression of that pupil. It is the operation of this halo effect within teacher judgments which makes researchers wary of their validity. Farrington (1980) has attempted to assess whether and how such an effect might operate. His work was part of the Cambridge Study in Delinquent Development, a longitudinal survey of 411 males from six primary schools in a working class area of London. Information about the boys' truancy was derived from questionnaires which the children's teachers had filled in about them at ages 8, 10, 12 and 14. As well as this, when the boys were 14, and again when they were 16, they were given a self-report delinquency questionnaire which included a question on truancy. By combining results of teacher questionnaires at ages 12 and 14 a group of seventy-three boys were identified as secondary school truants, either because they had 90 per cent or less attendance and this was attributed to truancy or because they were rated as frequent truants. This group were then compared with a second group, which were those who, at the age of 14, admitted frequent truancy on the self-report. There were seventy-two in this group, that is, 17.8 per cent of the sample of 405 who were contacted at this stage.

Farrington found that the self-reports were less closely linked with attendance records than were secondary school teachers' ratings of truancy. He also found that in almost all cases secondary school truants were rated more negatively than were the self-report truants. Both groups, as well as the primary school truants in the study, were said to be 'lazy, uncaring, rebellious and aggressive' (*ibid.*, p. 54) in class. Teacher-rated truants at both primary and secondary school were said to have a low position in class and to be poor readers. Although the self-reported truants also had low positions in class this was less marked, further, 'they were not significantly likely to be identified as poor readers' (*ibid.*). They were also less likely than teacher-rated truants to have neurotic symptoms ascribed to them. All groups of truants had poor school results, but only the teacher-rated children had low IQs. Low achieving boys were therefore more likely to be identified as truants by their teachers.

Farrington has highlighted features of teachers' knowledge which seem to affect their identification of truanting children. A narrow interpretation of these findings, together with a more general finding that more children admit to truanting than are identified by teachers (Galloway, 1985), would take this as simply reflecting on the problem of the accuracy of teachers' knowledge. However, instead I want to take a broader view for the operation of a halo effect underlines the general importance of the meanings which are attributed to social action by those involved. It raises questions about the processes by which individuals become defined as being involved in truancy.

A labelling approach has been used to investigate questions such as these in relation to other types of social action which is held to be deviant. This approach to deviance takes it to be a relative phenomenon which is a question of social definition: 'deviance may be conceived as a process by which the members of a group, community, or society (1) interpret behaviour as deviant; (2) define persons who so behave as a certain kind of deviant; and (3) accord them the treatment considered appropriate to such deviants' (Kitsuse, 1962). Rather than asking 'who is deviant?', those doing this type of work want to know, 'What are the circumstances under which a person gets set apart, henceforth to be considered a deviant?'. Instead of 'How did he become a deviant?' the concern is to find out 'How is the person cast in that social role?'. In other words, labelling directs attention to the ways in which individuals get categorized as being certain types of people, or become associated with a particular 'halo'. It looks at the implications which this has for our understanding of those individuals' behaviour.

David Hargreaves' influential work on deviance in schools (Hargreaves *et al.*, 1975) illustrates the use of a labelling approach. Through a detailed analysis of classroom conduct he and his colleagues attempted to 'explicate the common-sense knowledge by which teachers are able to link acts to rules and thereby define the act as deviant' (p. 105). They argued that deviance involved breaking formal or informal rules in a given context. For example, in some classes pupils speaking to each other might be defined by the teacher as rule-breaking, whereas in others a teacher might only consider this to be the case if talk was not related to the lesson in hand. They found that, where there might be doubt about whether or not an action had been deviant, the identity of particular pupils influenced teacher decisions on this since teachers assumed that a pupil would usually act according to the type of person which they were considered to be. Thus, for instance, sometimes a teacher would ask a pupil to account for their late arrival. But if, because of the kind of person they believed a pupil to be, they thought that the reason for latecoming was likely to be legitimate, then they might not ask that pupil for an explanation.

Researchers found that teachers typed pupils according to a range of constructs, such as their appearance, conformity to discipline, likeability, and their peer group relations. Using these, teachers would type children on the basis of their colleagues' knowledge (for example, through 'comparing notes' in staff room talk), through their knowledge of children's older siblings, as well as through their direct experience of the children. Though the researchers found that teachers would revise their hypothetical typings of particular children if the children's behaviour did not confirm these, teachers were more sensitive to the repetition of acts on which their original typings were based. Once typings became stabilized any transformation of type was unusual, partly because teachers didn't expect this to occur and partly because deviant pupils saw teachers as being unwilling to give up the stabilized deviant typing. They therefore saw little point in trying to transform.

By directing our attention to alternative meanings and definitions in situations this work implies a view of the social world as consisting of groups which are in conflict over legitimate definitions and control of social situations. A recognition of this has been a feature of some recent work on truancy. This work is characterized by a concern with the *disaffected truant*. In contrast with work investigating the endangered truant that involved methods which treated people as the objects of enquiry, research dealing with the disaffected truant treats people as thinking, feeling subjects who engage in meaningful social interaction. This leads researchers to investigate the meaning of particular organizational forms for pupils. Thus while they share some of the concerns of those writing about the endangered truant, in that issues of family and social environment are recognized, these are understood as being background to the focal site of the problem which is located within schools (see Reynolds, 1987, for a discussion of this shift).

There is a growing body of work which supports the contention that the particular organization of individual schools does make a difference to pupil attendance. Further that, depending on their internal organization, some schools can protect children while others seem to offer them no defence against drifting into delinquency (Power, 1967 and 1972; Rutter, 1979; Gray *et al.*, 1983; Reynolds, 1987). (However, Farrington's work (1980) does not support this argument.) Aspects of labelling have been incorporated into recent discussions (Reid, 1985; Galloway, 1985) as a warning that teachers should take care about the kinds of labels which they use. Its implications about the influence of social interaction in the development of particular behaviour are that changes in teacher attitudes and action can do much to temper the kinds of images which pupils develop of themselves and therefore could improve the ways in which they behave.

It is clear that it does make a difference to pupils whether they feel stigmatized because of their own past behaviour or that of their siblings. However, as Grimshaw and Pratt (1987) have cogently argued, the formal procedures for dealing with children considered to be truanting restrict discussion to a narrow range of issues. These are defined as relevant in terms of the institutional arrangements for dealing with truancy. In this respect they are making a similar argument to Galloway (1985) who used educational welfare officer judgments about absences despite an earlier finding (Galloway, 1980) that educational welfare officers were not reliable in categorizing pupils (i.e. they did not seem to use the same criteria — either between different schools or in individual schools over a three-year period — for categorizing children's absences). Galloway set up seven categories of absences within his study. These were based on discussions with senior members of the educational welfare service and were: (1) mainly illness; (2) some illness but other factors also present; (3) absent with parents' knowledge, consent and approval; (4) parents unable or unwilling to insist on return; (5) truancy — defined as: absence without parents' knowledge or consent; (6) socio-medical reasons (for example, infestation, scabies etc.); (7) school phobia or psychosomatic illness. An eighth category was provided for absences which did not fit in to the other seven or which could not be rated. His reasons for using these were that they represented an 'informal classification system' (*ibid.*, p. 35) which these officials expected that their colleagues would use when investigating non-attendance. 'It would be extremely difficult in practice for educational welfare officers *not* to use these categories, or similar ones, when justifying a decision to take legal action against the parents or the child' (*ibid.*).

These categories signal an official agenda about what is to count as relevant knowledge in decision-making on absences. As he points out, other categories could be drawn up which might focus on school factors rather than family factors and suggests examples such as, bullied at school; personality clash with particular teachers; crippling sense of educational failure. However these categories are not on the official agenda. This means that knowledge about these is marginal to administrative decisions where weight is given to the official agenda. It is in relation to this official agenda that he considers his categories to be valid [he refers to this as 'administrative validity' (*ibid.*, p. 36)]. Educational welfare officer judgments are assumed to be valid *for all practical purposes* when official decisions are made about whether or not to take formal action in any given case. This validity therefore relates to official administrative requirements but should not necessarily be assumed to reflect what we generally understand to be accuracy of judgments.

The issue to which I want to draw attention in this is not that of the relation of particular official judgments to the activities of the children and their families. Rather I am arguing for the need to give more detailed consideration to the official agenda of relevance which under-pins these judgments in order to understand the social nature of the problem of truancy. This takes us beyond the question of the validity of the knowledge of educational welfare officers or teachers and the relative merits of this over researcher or pupil knowledge, to a consideration of the institutional pre-conditions for the definition of some knowledge as relevant and the resultant definition of other knowledge as irrelevant/unreliable/invalid.

It takes us to a recognition that those occupying the (structural) position of teacher (or educational welfare officer) are *authorized* to have their definitions accepted as legitimate. This legitimacy derives from their structural relationship to the institution of schooling, which derives its authority from its position within the social order. At worst, within the literature the social meaning of action is ignored. At best, work on truancy incorporates some recognition of the importance of being sensitized to the 'recipe knowledge' (Schutz, 1976) which people use when attempting to deal with the contingencies which arise during interaction. The official categories in terms of which concern about behaviour needs to be expressed in order to trigger institutional action, remain embedded within the official agenda of relevance. It is this agenda which needs to be understood in order to explain the problem of truancy.

The Social Map of Truancy

Clarke (1975) has argued that an adequate account of how a social problem arose requires a theory of how a particular social order is organized and operated. A research paradigm which only makes it possible to analyze social order in terms of symbolic interaction between individuals is inadequate for this task. This is because it directs attention to the way in which behaviour is fitted into a particular category. It does not further the development of an understanding of the category itself — where it comes from, why this particular category is available to be drawn on and what implications the category carries with its use.

Those influenced by labelling theorists recognize the use of cognitive maps or filters through which we understand the world, but their concentration on the processes of negotiation in specific contexts have led them to neglect these maps and the institutional sites through which they are operationalized. To categorize absence from school as truancy is to make use of such a map. It involves the designation of absence as unauthorized and, consequently, as problematic. If it is accepted that the perception of a child and the perception of that child's behaviour are integrally linked (as the notion of the halo effect implies), and that ways of behaving are only intelligible by way of categorizations and their component parts, then it becomes important to explore the social construction of the classification truancy. Therefore, to enquire into truancy is to ask about one particular map which provides available sets of meanings in this area.

The features of the *endangered truant* theme are characteristic of discussions of social problems. It is typical of these discussions that they implicitly refer to people of low status. Often they are concerned with threats to the social order, which is held to be a 'natural' order, and are based on the direct linking of cultural practices with people's structural position (for example, neglectful parenting with being poor and working class) (*ibid.*). It presupposes a particular and strictly limited notion of the extent to which it is appropriate for children to act autonomously. This conception and its legitimacy is historical, though it is often taken, by those involved in the practices, to be 'natural'.

Explanations for behaviour are linked to forms of upbringing, in particular, family background. The family is held to occupy the principal site in which cultural practices are linked with structural position. It is therefore an object of interest for those developing theories about social behaviour. It is also a practical target (Burchell, 1979). For it is the focus for a series of interventions aimed at securing an upbringing for the future adult population which will reinforce the existing social order. These interventions are almost always aimed at the child and at the relationship of the child to adults, especially to the mother and father (Hodges and Hussain, 1979). Class position is usually signified by locality, with some localities being seen as particularly problematic (for example, 'decaying inner city areas' and 'council estates'). The cultural practices which are assumed to be connected with these are seen as predisposing parents to being neglectful, having low standards and being inadequate at supervising their children. Thus communities within such localities are seen as being characterized by problem behaviour and therefore as requiring more intense intervention by outside agencies.

Yet, as Galloway (1985) has pointed out '... although absentees are more likely to come from disadvantaged backgrounds, only a minority of children from such backgrounds become absentees.' (p. 12). The assumed link between people's structural position and their cultural practices often leads writers to neglect to consider those people who occupy the same structural position but who are not involved in problem practices (i.e. children from these areas who attend school and who are not delinquent).

A closer examination reveals that the 'technical' difficulties of defining truancy and categorizing absences are related to areas of conceptual disagreement which are indicative of broader issues. Definitions generally share the notion that legitimate responsibility for a child's behaviour rests ultimately with someone other than the child. Some view both parents and school as having authority over the child, others recognize as legitimate, only the authority of the school. Neither understands that the existence and nature of legitimate authority over children is historically variable and therefore requires investigation rather than assertion. However, in common with most work on children, within these definitions, 'the child emerges ... as a formal category and as a social status accompanied by programmes of care and schemes of education' (Jencks, 1982, p. 11).

The question of truancy refers to the contention that social actors who are children should be physically present in particular places at specific times. 'Problem children' are acting in a way which challenges this definition of appropriateness as, at times, are their parents (either by wilfully ignoring the necessity of school attendance for their child, or by lacking insight into the implications of their behaviour within the family). Indeed, Jencks has argued that 'any view of the child reflects a preferred, but unexplored, model of the social order' (*ibid.*, p. 13).

It is a consensual functionalist model of the social world which constitutes the core of unexplicated assumptions on which most discussions of truancy rest and which has, therefore, limited the extent to which the topic has been explored. Thus, Kahn and Nursten (1962), for example, maintain that rejecting school is equivalent to rejecting society, and Tyerman (1974) claims, 'Most persistent truants are not precocious youths, but maladjusted children who would become unsatisfactory employees instead of being unsatisfactory pupils' (p. 14). For these writers, the condition of the possibility of a happy, well-adjusted citizen is the passing of a certain period of life within the education system. As Clarke (1975) has pointed out, this view disguises '... the fact that the social order may be changed to suit the interests of certain groups rather than others and still remain an order and not necessarily disintegrate into total disorder' (p. 409).

The institutional site which is of focal concern in respect of truancy is the state school. I maintain here that these issues are linked with the standardized pattern of school attendance which forms part of the normality of one pattern of living and learning. It is this fundamental pattern of normality which throws alternatives into relief and in so doing informs our views about deviance. Truancy is viewed here as the deviant counterpart of normal school attendance. Its social map is therefore integrally linked to the theory and practice of a system of schooling. In other words, to explain the social significance of truancy I shall need to explain the significance of the pattern of living and learning which we have come to associate with schooling. This pattern has emerged as a result of social action in the past. It therefore needs to be understood historically, in order to explain the thematic core of the way in which truancy is officially discussed in the present.

Historical Overview

As I indicated in chapter 1, the theory and practice of schooling involves issues of biopolitics. In looking at the preconditions for popular education being discussed as a necessity in nineteenth century England, Jones and Williamson (1979) have already explored the usefulness of concepts of biopolitics and disciplinary relations. They found that in nineteenth century writings on education concerns were expressed about: the expense and difficulties of poor relief administration; the threat posed to governmental authority by the extent of immorality; and the increase in crime, particularly juvenile crime registered in police and judicial statistics. These three areas were treated as *moral* problems, that is, problems of the principles and habits (mores) of the population.

The need for popular education in relation to the state of the poor was discussed in terms of the expense of poor relief (which was viewed, nonetheless, as economically and politically important for national prosperity and strength). If poor relief was necessary, it was argued, then it should encourage independence not dependence. Therefore it was important to teach destitute and orphaned children a trade so that they could support themselves by their own labour. The concern with the state of public morals took as its object a range of behaviour from licentiousness to free thought and irreligion. This behaviour was viewed as a deterioration in the state of popular habits and was held to be subversive of governmental, legal and religious authority. Popular education was defined here as a need for the diffusion of true and religious principles of conduct among the whole population. The increase in crime was seen as being connected with a proliferation of criminal habits among a population basically devoid of moral principle. Popular instruction here was a tactic to develop true principles of conduct as the basis for the formation of useful habits.

They argue that after 1830 discussions of the need for popular education were characterized by a number of themes which were related to a set of problems. These were: the rate of crime and especially of juvenile delinquency; the extent and growth of pauperism; and the problem of habits of cleanliness for public health. But 'it was formulated in relation to these problems ONLY in so far as they were represented as being determined by the existence of conditions (moral topographies) which trained up children continually to crime, to pauperism and to unhealthy habits' (*ibid.*, p. 86). In this period there was a predominance of two types of intersecting statement. *Topographical statements dealt with spatial* themes, identifying types of conduct (for example, criminality) with features of a particular area; variations in these features were seen as predisposing the people of that area to a corresponding change in their mores. *Historical* statements dealt with *temporal* themes. Sectors of the population, distinguished by habits of life (for example, criminals, paupers), were held to have passed through a series of stages on the way to their particular habits; in turn, this was used as an explanation for the habits of the population concerned.

Classes were defined in terms of these two dimensions: knowledge of classes being constituted in relation to concerns about moral topographies and the upbringing assumed to be implicit in these. For example, the growth in criminality implied a moral contagion between the criminal and other classes. Indeed, the expression 'dangerous classes' was generally a way of formulating political and social problems (*ibid.*, p. 83). All this opened up the possibility of *topography management*. Directed at eliminating topographies of the 'dangerous classes', this took two forms: one operated on general characteristics of topographies (for example, routing new roads through the centre of criminal districts); the other created separate spaces of moral training to take the place of that which people would otherwise receive as a result of the moral topography of their class (*ibid.*, p. 85). Similarly, time was treated as a dimension of the process of moral transformation, raising the issue of the necessary duration of a child's attendance at school in order to ensure optimal moral education.

In short, Jones and Williamson show that early nineteenth century schooling was not simply a means of socialization or social control. It was a means of securing public morality and preventing crime, a means for forming a population with useful habits through the instrument of good principles in order to secure a moral foundation for governmental and religious authority. 'Similarly, in a later period schooling begins to exist specifically as a means for regulating the relations between the classes of the population by forming an instrument which is able to modify a class's moral topography, that is the very conditions that were perceived to define a class in its essential traits. Schools then became a set of techniques specifically adapted to class characteristics forming together with the other conditions of a class's existence a new regime for the correct upbringing of that class's juvenile members.' (*ibid.*, p. 60).

In the conclusion to their argument, Jones and Williamson note a shift which underlay a redefinition of the function of schooling and consequently a reversal of opposition to compulsion. This shift involved the belief that the competitiveness of British manufacturers was not so much hindered by the removal of a cheap source of labour, as helped by a workforce which could introduce and quickly adapt to innovations in productive techniques. This presupposed a numerate and literate, that is, a schooled workforce. Further it involved a change in the representation of schooling as a condition of individual liberty. They maintain that within political discourse this was basically seen as the ability of a person to organize their own affairs rationally and to participate in a friendly society or cooperative. It therefore presupposed the ability to read, write and count.

The statement of the necessity for compulsory schooling was, then, founded on a discursive field which had a discourse on institutions at its centre. This was intersected by a political discourse on the conditions of freedom within a liberal state, and a political–economic discourse on the conditions of competition within world markets (*ibid.*, p. 101). In the later part of the book I shall be looking in some detail at the way in which state inspection changed in the 1860s and shall be arguing that this administrative change had fundamental epistemological and ontological implications for education. This made possible the emergence of an argument for the necessity of universal compulsory schooling in the form already outlined.

The way in which issues of biopolitics are embedded in theory and practice can be further illustrated by contrasting the pattern of attendance which is today considered as normal with that of early nineteenth century Scotland. Today, for people between the ages of 5 and 16, full time attendance at a purpose-built location where specially trained adults offer instruction, authorized by the state, is considered to be normal and appropriate. However, the situation in nineteenth century Scotland, prior to the intervention of the state, was very different. A school, at this time, was simply any place where instruction (usually in reading, though sometimes in writing and arithmetic) was offered, and a teacher was anyone who offered the instruction. A dame school, for example, usually referred to child care offered by a single woman in her kitchen. In isolated areas, such as in the Highlands and Islands, where instruction was available only intermittently, an itinerant teacher, who might be a pupil from a neighbouring school, would give instruction in a local house (XL 1840 *Remarks from the Educ. Statistics*).

An elite of schools had secure funding; teachers who were trained or had some experience of university; and offered the possibility of studying a range of subjects at a level sufficiently advanced to enable successful pupils to enter university. Generally speaking, these would be the more affluent endowed schools, most burgh schools, some parochial schools[2], and, even more rarely, affluent schools run on a teacher's own adventure. It is on the basis of these schools, and, in particular, on the formal possibility of a pupil moving from parish school to university, that Scotland's reputation of educational egalitarianism generally rests (see chapter 3).

Most schools, though, were not of this sort, and the sparse evidence indicates that they were often makeshift affairs, being held in lofts, sheds, or similar premises, taught by those, such as failed businessmen and people unable to continue their normal occupations because of injury, who were unable to sell their skills in other labour markets; or, alternatively, who mixed teaching with other occupations. The schools often continued for as long as the teacher was able to eke out a living from them, and ceased to exist when a sufficient income could no longer be made and the teacher moved on. Even where this was not the case, facilities were likely to be limited, '... the typical turn-of-the-century schoolhouse was a small drystone or stone and mortar building, with a thatched or divoted roof, measuring about 30′

in length, 12–18′ in width, and 6′ or 7′ in height. The interior, lighted by three or four small windows, was partitioned, with only the master's living section floored. The common practice of the master taking boarders added to the already cramped conditions' (Simpson quoted in Myers, 1970, p. 1).

A pattern of schooling as part of a hierarchy of instruction, and therefore as antecedent to other activities, similar to that which is today considered as normal, was at this time merely one of a number of patterns which co-existed. For the young people who might potentially attend school, it was one aspect of a way of life which was circumscribed by seasonal rhythms and opportunities to participate in the local labour market. For example, reports of state school inspectors note districts where agricultural labourers attended school three months every year in winter, but extended their attendance over so many years that in some of the inspected schools some of the pupils might be older than their teacher. The interspersing of schooling with periods of wage-earning was a common pattern.[3] In rural districts or fishing villages schools might cease to exist at periods such as harvest-time, when the teacher, as well as the pupils could be engaged in other tasks related to the harvest. Often, though, rather than ceasing to exist altogether, a school might run with fewer pupils, for example, if weather conditions prevented pupils from reaching the school. Or, alternatively, it might run with a teacher-substitute if the demands of a teacher's other occupation meant that they needed to be elsewhere, for example, if the teacher was a trainee ('stickit') minister who would have to attend university for a few terms.

In short, schooling at this period was a diverse phenomenon. Schools did not tend to be purpose-built, or characterized by particular architectural forms in the way that they are today. The space given to schools was, like the time allocated to them, largely dependent on the local way of life. People attended school as and when they felt it appropriate, there being little uniformity either to the rhythm or the overall duration of their attendance. The shift from multiple patterns of schooling and fluid social identities such that pupil/teacher/worker were not mutually exclusive categories to that of today, where any pattern other than that of full time school attendance, involving participation in a hierarchy of instruction prior to other activities is considered as deviant, and where the social identities of teacher and pupil are clearly demarcated, involved both a change in common practices as well as a closing off of alternative possibilities in favour of one particular pattern of social action which was to become the norm.

By contrasting these two situations it can be seen that the creation of the 'normal' also involved a change in the social constitution of time and space.

I shall be looking at how it was possible to move from this first situation to the second. For it was in and through this institutional shift that the contours of the problem of truancy were outlined: for the shift involved the creation of an authorized time and place for schooling and truancy is, first and foremost, about being in an unauthorized place at an unauthorized time. At another level, therefore, my argument is concerned with the construction of a particular theory and practice of normal spatial/temporal relations. Durkheim (1976) maintained that, 'At the roots of all our judgments there are a certain number of essential ideas which dominate all our intellectual life; they are what philosophers since Aristotle have called the categories of the understanding: ideas of time, space ... They are like the solid frame which encloses all thought ...' (p. 9).

This discourse, the structuring of events both at the level of knowledge and action, was being constructed in a world in which the social relations of industrial capitalism were eclipsing pre-existing social relations. The categorization of space and the counting of time were therefore important for the construction of a new social order. Spatial arrangements will be shown to be important because, more than simply the physical context of action, they were predicated on a theory of moral action — bad habits being identified with problematic spatial organisation. Similarly, temporal relations were important not simply because they specified a time of day, week, year when schooling was to be experienced; but because schooling was about the correct upbringing of the population, therefore it was to precede full participation in the social order. It pre-supposed the social identity of pupil as involving children and precluding the social identity of worker.

The regulation of schools was, then, about the regulation of areas of life, in the sense of physical locations, forms of social interaction and individual biography. It was about the structuring of what was viewed as a social necessity and its transformation into an educational necessity. The mechanisms through which this was operated will be examined in the next chapter.

Notes

1 The first Child Guidance Clinic was established in 1927 in London's East End. It was specifically concerned with the problems of cultural clash of East European Jewish immigrant children which were leading to problems of adjustment for these children in the home and in the school.
2 An Act of Scottish Parliament established the parochial system in 1696. This was supported by fees and assessment of local landowners. It made provision for a school in every parish, supervised by the church, though by the nineteenth century local supervision was a formality (Myers, 1970).
3 This was also true for England. For discussion, see Madoc-Jones in McCann, 1977, pp. 41–66.

Chapter 3:

The Regulation of Nineteenth Century Schools: Whose Programmes?

Introduction

A social map is today's result of yesterday's programmes of power and it is this which is the key to understanding the map of truancy. In this chapter I am going to examine state involvement in schooling in order to explain the framework in terms of which 'knowledge' about schooling and attendance were produced. By doing this I shall look at a topic which has virtually been ignored within histories of schooling: that is, the way in which the kind of knowledge which could be produced in inspection reports was structured.

My discussion needs to be set against two different kinds of account of the material with which I am dealing here. These are administrative histories (for example, Ball, 1963) and histories of Scottish education (for example, Scotland, 1969). Both kinds narrate tales of events, in terms of the interplay of organizations and individuals. These tales are punctuated by pieces of legislation and are characterized by the tendency to assume, often implicitly, that in talking about changes in education they are referring to a, more or less smooth, process of evolution towards an enlightened and *enlightening* expansion of schooling provision for the mass of the population. Such histories see state intervention in the form of inspection as a logical step in this rational progression, and equate inspection reports with KNOWLEDGE about the reality of schooling.

However, these accounts are limited for they leave a number of anomalies unexplained. [1] For example, they cannot explain why official attempts were made to limit the interchange of views amongst inspectors [that is, other than in terms of the personal intransigence of individual politicians or state officials]. From about 1846 school inspectors met annually in London to discuss their mutual problems.

Gradually, this conference became a forum for expressing opinions on official education policy and by the mid-fifties controversial matters were being put to the vote. It was at this point that the process of suppressing these meetings began. Initially, the Lord President (Earl Granville) and the Vice-President (C B Adderley) disputed the right of inspectors to criticize official policy, on the grounds that they were civil servants, and the practice was stopped. Finally in 1859 the conferences themselves were stopped by the new Vice-President, Robert Lowe (Bishop, 1971, p. 82).

To appreciate the significance of this restriction we need to understand the structural and institutional position of inspectors. We also need to recognize that official insistence on social action being authorized at all levels of the institutional hierarchy had profound implications for producing and sustaining a social order. This quickly reveals the impossibility of sustaining accounts of these events in terms of an evolutionary progression. Ultimately, such accounts must be rejected as inadequate. For even though some may provide us with descriptions of the fine detail of events, they all miss the integral linking of these to wider social relations. At best, this aspect is construed as the *context* or background against which organizations and individuals are sited: an asserted linking of occurrences in a narration containing no examination of the means or the significance of their linking. At worst, it is absent altogether from an inward-looking description of events (for example, Morgan,1927. For a fuller discussion of the failings of the history of Scottish education see Humes and Paterson, 1983).

In contrast, I am maintaining that state intervention into the structuring of schooling involved the transformation of general pro-grammes of class power, in the form of issues of the social organization of space and time, into the neutral administration of economic and efficient education. I show this by directly examining the links between relations of state power, the legitimizing authority of the education office and the inspectorate. In developing my argument I shall first outline, briefly, the way in which existing social relations were con-sidered to be a problem. I shall then explain with whose strategies I am dealing and why the state was a target for the adoption of these as programmes of power, before going on to indicate the reason for these programmes being supported in Scotland beyond the relatively small group of people who were involved in their initial promotion. After this I turn my attention directly to describing, in relation to a discussion of schooling, what was involved in the nineteenth century state in Britain. This description will then enable me to examine more closely, the mechanisms through which the programmes to which I have referred were institutionalized. I shall do this by examining the Committee of Privy Council on Education, the education office and the relationship between these.

A description of mechanisms and the initial purposes for which they were set up provides only a partial account of institutionalization. A full account needs also to explain how the implementation of these programmes was sustained. I shall argue that this was partly achieved by ensuring that personnel were recruited through patronage. It was further sustained by the strict interpretation of Committee of Council minutes, the censorship of inspection reports and the restriction of inspectors' interaction. It was this form of institutionalization which underlay the production of a *particular class-based knowledge* of schooling and its problems. *A knowledge* which, because of the particular way in which it was produced, was to become 'neutralised' later being equated with KNOWLEDGE OF EDUCATION and its PROBLEMS.

Problems and Programmes

In what way was the old order of relations of social space and time a problem for industrial capitalism? My description of pre-regulation schooling is a reflection of a wider social situation prior to the large-scale organization of industrial production. At this period rhythms of living were governed by natural seasons and irregular task-work. In consequence, mixed occupations were not unusual and the home was often also the place of productive work. The division of labour in this generally reflected family authority relations. These relations of space and time were not an obstacle for early forms of industrialization, involving for example, the putting out system, which used the home-based family as a unit of production. It became a problem, as Thompson (1974) has pointed out, with the use of technical innovations involving the development of large-scale organization and machine power. These required the synchronization of ordered activities and clock-time was an important feature of this. It fostered a compartmentalization of living. This is illustrated by the setting up of special locations for work which could no longer be home-based. Moving away from the home-based family unit of production also meant moving away from the discipline of family authority relations in the workplace. This opened up the political problem of the control and regulation of the workforce.

Smelser (1974), in his analysis of the textile industry, has argued that initially this problem was avoided by employing family groups in the workplace — following the traditional pattern of father as skilled worker and mother and children as auxiliary workers. However, the demise of this pattern, in the 1820s and 1830s, accompanied an increase in the scale of factories and technical developments which reduced the need for skilled workers and increased the need for the unskilled (for a fuller discussion see also Anderson, 1978, Hartmann, 1979). This shifting of the authority relations of the family back to the home, no longer considered as a place of work, opened up the need for the development of a different form of work discipline. The authority relations of the family had acted as a bridge between an older social order and a new one which was to be '... marked by time-thrift and by a clear demarcation between "work" and "life"' (Thompson, 1974, p. 66). The problem of the old order of space and time was that of the organisation of industrial capitalism. It was a problem of the construction of a new social order involving authority relations and popular mores which would facilitate the organization and discipline of a workforce. At this level, it was an issue of class control.

But for whom, in particular, was this an issue of schooling and what were the factors which made it possible for it to be understood in this particular way? Johnson (1977) has identified certain 'experts' as being important agitators for a state educational system. 'Expertise is best described through a kind of composite biography, focusing on central or symptomatic individuals, but "placing" them socially' (*ibid.*, p. 81). In the early nineteenth century, after Malthus' *Second Essay on Population*, economists were endorsing education. Further, the political ideas of the utilitarian philosopher James Mill (1773–1836) were based on a psychology which required a general 'rational' education. By the 1830s philosophic radicalism, especially utilitarianism, had become important amongst intellectuals and radical politicians. As Finer has argued:

> Any Benthamite was automatically an educationist, since his philosophy depended on the perfectability of society through the free play of its members' ENLIGHTENED self-interest ... Education was desirable because it prevented juvenile delinquency and mendicancy, because it increased a labourer's skill, productivity, and earning power; because it prevented the growth of criminal classes; and because it led the workman to realize his true interests lay not in 'communism' or Chartism,

but in harmony with his employers (quoted in Parris, 1969, p. 279).

Although the direct influence of Benthamism was waning by the late 1830s, Johnson has suggested that by this time it had already become a fundamental component of middle class common sense. This London intellectual milieu were influential on the Society for the Diffusion of Useful Knowledge, mechanics' institutes and the middle class end of the attack on the Taxes on Knowledge (Johnson, 1977, p. 83). However, despite its importance, he has stressed that it would be a mistake to identify 'expertise' with Benthamism or a particular intellectual milieu. 'The precipitating moment of "expertise" was the contradictory juxtaposition of liberal theories and the observation, out of a bourgeois culture, of working-class behaviour ... Only provincial men could gauge the gulf between political improvement and the actual state of the class' (*ibid*.).

Some of Johnson's educational 'experts' held positions in government by 1835 (for example, Edwin Chadwick of the Poor Law Commission; Leonard Horner of the factory inspectorate; G R Porter, the Head of the Statistical Department of the Board of Trade; Nassau Senior, an economist and personal adviser to Whig ministers from 1831). James Kay's career was typical of the younger 'expert' pattern. Coming from commercial origins, his family being in cotton, calico printing and banking, he had views which were largely compatible with the industrial bourgeoisie. He trained in Edinburgh and also became involved in statistical enquiry. He had contacts with Chadwick and Senior and was appointed as a Poor Law Commissioner. There were:

> ... certain nodal points where experts met and discussed their enthusiasms: London salons, the London and provincial statistical societies, the annual meetings of the Statistical Section of the British Association for the Advancement of Science, the provincial networks of organizations like the Society for the Diffusion of Knowledge, caucuses around particular government enquiries or departments, especially the Poor Law Commission, and the friendships and contacts tying Edinburgh to London' (*ibid*., pp. 86–7).

Two aspects of this which are of particular importance for my discussion here are the Edinburgh–London connection and the interest in statistics. Most important government figures at this time had received part of their education in Edinburgh.[2] During the period in which these men were attending university major figures of the Scottish Enlightenment were teaching there. For example, Dugald Stewart succeeded Adam Ferguson to the Chair of Moral Philosophy in Edinburgh and held it between 1785 and 1809. He taught James Mill and introduced both Horners and possibly Kay to the ideas of Adam Smith and Ferguson. Indeed, he was a major disseminator of Adam Smith's views (Chitnis, 1968), his influence extending to Henry Brougham, Sidney Smith and Francis Jeffrey who in 1802 formed the Edinburgh Review, an important Whig journal which provided a medium for a wider broadcast of these ideas (Hurt, 1971).

Links between these 'experts' extended beyond their university experience. For example, Corrigan indicates that from 1808 James Mill with, later David Ricardo, Francis Place and, acting as Bentham's secretary for a while, J. S. Mill, discussed the ideas of the Scottish Moralists and those of political economy, although there were some differences in their views. Further, that by 1832 James Kay was also influenced by Nassau Senior and Benthamite circles (Corrigan, 1977, p. 18). Experts

> ... did not form a 'group' in the classic sociological sense, nor even, united by a single organization, a 'movement'. But personal links WERE quite dense, and expertise DID have a definite social character and a real ideological coherence. At its heart was a coalition of liberal intellectuals with strong personal or ideological links with industrial capital. The apparent excep-tions to this — men from landed or clerical backgrounds — none the less adopted the viewpoint of capital as a perspective and city or industrial populations as an object of concern. (Johnson, 1977, p. 87. See also Markus, 1982, for discussion.)

If these were the kind of people who were advocating strategies involving education as a solution to the problems of the new order, what were the reasons for education being seen in this way, and why was the state being seen as a means to this end? As I have suggested, these 'experts' viewed industrialization as basically progressive. How-ever, they were also concerned with its accompanying problems. Some difficulties were seen as unsolvable because they were 'providential'. For example, periodic crises of capital accumulation were naturalized by being discussed as 'storms' or 'seasons'; the inequalities of class were also dealt with in this way (*ibid.*). The danger of these was that ignorance might lead some people to see them as causes for discontent.

Problems which were not viewed as 'natural' were not held to be connected with large-scale industrial capitalism. Rather, they were discussed in terms of metaphors of 'invasion' and 'disease' (*ibid.*, p. 88) and were viewed as problems of the principles and habits of the population (Jones and Williamson, 1979).

Johnson (1977) pointed out that two possible kinds of politics are embedded in these views, '... a populist, anti-aristocratic radicalism or an alliance with "reforming" politicians to "change the people"' (p. 88). Both kinds shared a deflection of responsibility for these problems from industrial capitalism and in the writings of the 'experts' the two responses were not mutually exclusive since the moral engineering necessary for changing people required the persuasion of aristocratic politicians to act. Thus, though policies differed in relation to the specific problems with which their advocates were concerned, they all stressed the importance of transforming working class belief and behaviour (*ibid.*, p. 89). Schooling, therefore, was seen as an important means for achieving this end. It should be emphasized that this transformation was to be structured from the perspective of these 'experts' with their shared aims and interests, and not, for example, from the perspectives of Chartism, Owenism or trades unionism all of which were advocating national provision of schooling at this time. The strategies of the 'experts' in advocating state intervention into schooling were not simply concerned with the provision of something which was lacking. As I have indicated, there were schools already in existence. State intervention was to be aimed at correcting that which was already present.

Although 'experts' were advocating a national system of education, because they did not constitute a united 'movement', there was no unity as to what was meant by this. Further, as Johnson has stressed, they were working within the limits of a politics of education dominated by disputes between religious factions. As a consequence they canvassed maximum and minimum versions of their proposed programmes. These ranged from proposals involving a complete state system (i.e. Ministry of Public Instruction, control over curriculum, books, the training and certification of teachers, compulsory attendance, separation of religious and secular instruction, the statutory levying of school rates and the creation of a structure of local administration), to municipal solutions requiring enabling legislation.

But the commonest form of programme envisaged, as the key priority, the founding of a government department ... with a few limited but strategic functions. The model of government action was 'incremental', persuasive, directive — a matter of educating the educators ... Government should thus supply ... 'the great element of all state organizations — a central, controlling and directing power'. (*ibid.*, p. 92)

Political economists at this time were in favour of state action since they maintained that as education was unlike other commodities, laissez-faire was an inappropriate principle on which to base schooling. The reason for this was that it was believed that an endogenous demand could not be assumed since a taste for schooling required cultivation. To fail to do this was to open the way to 'neglect' or to Socialist or Chartist agitators. In addition to this, existing philanthropic educational practices were being criticized both because of organizational failings and because they could not extend to cover a sufficient number of people. In making this second type of criticism 'experts' used statistical information.

A defining feature of 'expertise' was the political use of educational statistics to reveal the inadequacies of philanthropic provision of schooling (*ibid.*, p. 93). But these 'facts' were not only understood as demonstrating that there were an insufficient number of day-schools. They were also used to display the qualitative poverty of private schools and the intrinsic organizational deficiencies of philanthropy. By definition, philanthropy was reliant on the fluctuating interest of benefactors. Therefore resources were often inadequate for the maintenance of existing schools and any improvement or expansion was out of the question. Lacking in adequate supervision, the existing schools were held to be often wasteful and inefficient. 'Only the state could bring direction to its "zig-zag course", coherence to its "education in sections", and regular supervision and guaranteed support to its intrinsic impermanence' (*ibid.*, p. 94).

The class fraction to which I have been referring in this discussion constituted a relatively small number of people. Yet, in Scotland the impact of these ideas carried beyond this narrow grouping of 'experts' and into the large areas of the country which were not directly affected by the changes in urban industrialization. In order to account for this I want further to consider the development of statistics. The interest which the 'experts' showed in statistical enquiry can be related to what Hacking (1981) has referred to as 'statistical utilitarianism'. This contributed to the nineteenth century 'avalanche of numbers' and was an intrinsic part of the moral classification of things and people at this time. An early major statistical work was Sir John Sinclair's 21-volume *Statistical Survey of Scotland (1791 −1799)*[3] which was compiled from responses of Church of Scotland ministers to questions about the state of their parishes. The word 'statistical' in this work was used to denote '... an inquiry directed at the conditions of life of a country, in order to establish the quantum of happiness of the inhabitants' (quoted in Hacking, 1981, p. 25).

By the middle of the century the 'avalanche' was well and truly under way, fostering a method of solving practical problems by the collection of data, '... classifications multiplied because this was the form of this new kind of discourse. Even though any new single classification usually had a straightforward motivation that can be reported by the external historian; the very fact of the classifications and of the counting was internal to a new practice' (*ibid.*, p. 24). Although Sinclair and the Calvinist ministers of the Church of Scotland were not Benthamites, they shared a Benthamite interest in a 'calculus of felicity' (*ibid.*, p. 25). This affinity makes it possible to understand the broader impact of these ideas in Scotland, and brings into consideration the significance of the Scottish dimension. A notable feature of Scottish culture has been the impact of presbyterianism. Indeed Johnson (1977) has argued that one aspect of the importance of an Edinburgh education among the 'experts' was that it contributed to the cultivation of a distance from English religious entanglements and therefore an avoidance of the tendency to polarize for either Church or Dissent.

Max Weber, in discussing the compatibility of protestantism and capitalism, has argued that the Reformation meant the instigation of a total regulation of conduct which permeated all aspects of public and private life.[4] In particular Calvinism, the doctrinal core of Scotland's established religion, maintained that a Christian's social activity in the world (including that which served the mundane life of the community) was for the greater glory of God. 'Brotherly love ... is expressed in the first place in the fulfilment of the daily tasks given by the lex naturae; ... that of service in the interest of the rational organization of our social environment. For the wonderfully purposeful organization and arrangement of this cosmos is ... designed by God to serve the utility of the human race' (Weber, 1971, pp. 108−9). Weber held that this was the source of the utilitarian character of Calvinist ethics. 'The God of Calvinism demanded of his believers not single good works, but a life of good works combined into a unified system' (*ibid.*, p. 117). The methodically rationalized ethical conduct demanded by Calvinism was compatible with other forms of utilitarianism. It reinforced the movement towards the disciplinary society which was involved in the form of industrial capitalism being developed in nineteenth century Britain. Because of the status of Calvinism in Scotland, there were institutionalized moves towards a disciplinary society being made by ministers throughout the country, even in non-industrial areas.

However, compatibility does not necessarily mean an identity of interests; for the order with which the Calvinists were concerned was that of God, not that of industrial capitalism. Thus, class was not a feature of primary importance in their view, as it was in the view of members of the Committee of Council on Education. This was because the Calvinists held that there was no way of knowing who were among God's elect. *Everyone*, therefore, had to live *as if* they were. This was the reason for life-style and habits being so important to adherents to the religion. This *overlap*, as opposed to *direct coincidence*, of concerns indicates the reason for Scottish inspection reports being less overtly class focused than the English. It also illuminates the outrage expressed in Scottish petitions to the Committee of Council concerning moves which were obviously class-based, such as the requirement of the Revised Code of 1862 that a child's parents should be identified in terms of their social class in school documentation. The fourth article of the code stipulated that enquiries should be made about the occupation and incomes of parents in order to ensure that state aid would only be given to those children whose parents 'support themselves by manual labour'. This was in direct conflict with a Scottish education tradition which stressed the importance of schooling for *all* (see Bone, 1968, pp. 55–7; for a fuller discussion of the code see chapter 7).

This discussion of the significance of Calvinism should not, though, be construed as implying that Scotland was a haven of egalitarianism. This type of belief has been analyzed by McCrone *et al.* (1981) who argue that, 'No myth is more prevalent and persistent than that asserting Scotland is a "more equal" society than England (or Britain) and that Scots are somehow "more egalitarian" than others in these islands (p. 1). They stress that like most myths, it exemplifies a set of social beliefs and values from which are derived accounts of the world and social identities for the believers. As such, it draws selectively on the past and should not, therefore, be taken to be an accurate description of the distribution of resources and opportunities in the social structure.[5] 'The ideological hero is undoubtedly the "lad o' pairts" born into poverty but succeeding in the world despite formidable obstacles. ... Success came because the institutional means to mobility were there and every encouragement was given to the young man who sought a university education.' (MacLaren, 1976, p. 2).

In particular, it is often referred to in the context of discussions of Scottish education. This can be related to the early attempt in Scotland to make widespread, systematic provision of schooling and was the result of presbyterian effort to adhere to Knox's argument, in the First Book of Discipline (1560) concerning the importance of providing a school in every parish. However, assertions of egalitarianism are not so much made on the basis of what is intrinsic to the Scottish situation as *relative* to what is held to be lacking in England (*ibid.*): it is a way of establishing distance from English hierarchy and aristocratic status structures (McCrone *et al.* 1970, p. 28). Thus many parishes, especially the poorer ones, didn't achieve Knox's ideal (MacLaren, 1976, p. 2). The organization of the Church of Scotland was more democratic than that of the episcopalians in that ultimate control lay in the kirk sessions, which had powerful voices in presbyteries and the General Assembly. However, elections of members were managed, and although their composition in rural and Highland parishes tended to be different, in cities and smaller towns this meant middle class control (*ibid.*, pp. 3–4).

Further, the upper classes of society tended to send their children to school in England. Thus Grant (1876) noted that children attending burgh schools (the schools which are often referred to in discussions of educational mobility) tended to belong to social classes which could loosely be described as upper working or lower middle. As Myers (1970) has pointed out, 'two groups of Scots may be said not to have attended the parish schools, the aristocracy and wealthy classes and the lower echelons of rural and urban proletariat' (p. 141). It would therefore be more appropriate to take the kind of mixing of social groupings often implied in respect of Scottish education as referring to a *formal possibility* rather than an actual description of the social mixture.

In fact, the term 'egalitarianism' is quite misleading for in education it referred to the *formal possibility* for an able male pupil to proceed from parish school to university (McCrone *et al.*, 1981, p. 12). In other words, it was used to indicate *equality of (male) opportunity* — a notion which would today be characterized as *elitist*. The myth is premised on the existence of a hierarchical social order rather than a classless society (*ibid.*, p. 15) and signified a commitment to the social hierarchy of the parish (*ibid.*, p. 16); '... it refers to the individualism of the petty property owner, it is the equality and democracy of the 'elect' — it is the equality of the Kirkyard and the kailyard' (*ibid.*, p. 32).

A major task for the state in the nineteenth century was the generation of authority relations and popular mores which would be appropriate for the population of an emergent industrial economy. Many significant figures whose strategies pre-figured the programmes which became embedded in the power structure of the state were involved in government at this time. They had shared social and intellectual concerns, partially rooted in common educational experiences. This gave them an agreed basis from which to define problems and debate solutions. This was important for the form which relations of government took. For example, the concern with the collection and classification of information, especially in statistical form, contributed to the emergence of a new kind of state servant who would be able to carry this out: that is, the inspector. But how did these programmes of power, deriving their coherence from the coalescence of particular strategies, became institutionalized within the apparatus of the state?

Mechanisms of the State

I have been stressing that state formation, especially in respect of the agencies established in the 1830s and 1840s had, as a major facet, the moral regulation of the population: that is, the production and reproduction of particular moral norms, attitudes and expectations within the population generally (Corrigan, 1977, p. 82). It follows from this that the agencies of the state need to be understood in terms of the structuring of social relations. They were, '... at once promoting, (but, of course also restraining) the reproduction of a political classification; *and* suppressing alternative ways of being; or of conceptualising social life' (*ibid.*, p. 59). Underlying this political classification was a view of society as consisting of a series of ranks, each in its place, the preservation of society being equated with the preservation of those ranks (Morris, 1970, p. 15).

As we could expect from this the institutional form of these agencies was hierarchical. Their organization should be understood in terms of the nature of the changes in the mode of governing Britain in the nineteenth century. The roots of this have been located as early as the 1780s. At this time changes of personnel gradually shifted from being changes of individuals within government, this being the government of the sovereign and therefore continuous from their accession until their death (Parris, 1969), to the replacement of governing teams by alternative teams. This was the precursor of the nineteenth century party system. Possible problems of continuity raised by this development were met by a gradually emerging permanent civil service.

These alterations have been well documented (*ibid.*; see also Corrigan, 1977, for a summary of the literature), especially in relation to the way in which, from about the 1830s onwards, governing was increasingly delegated to officials outside of Parliament and this administrative machinery began to take shape. As Parris (1969) has argued, 'At the beginning of the nineteenth century, parliament was in a very real sense a legislature ... It was parliament, not a minister of the interior, which authorized the construction of roads and the paving of towns' (p. 184). In contrast, by the end of the century, '... to say that the administration legislated through Parliament is not to say that Parliament legislated. Only in form was Parliament a law-making body: in substance the law was made elsewhere' (*ibid.*). The particular 'elsewhere' which is of concern in relation to state intervention into schooling is the office of education which was under the formal control of the Committee of Privy Council on Education. The minutes of this Committee, the codes into which they were collected and their supplementary rules, illustrate the significance of this form of governing through administration.

The Committee of Council on Education was established in 1839, not through Parliament, but by an Order in Council from the Privy Council office. The by-passing of Parliament was a politically expedient move for Lord Melbourne's government. It was believed that sectarian arguments about the role of the established church in England in relation to schooling would prevent a Bill being passed in the House of Lords, and the government was on the point of collapse at this time (for a fuller account see Bishop, 1971; Campbell, 1972). The work of the Privy Council office mainly consisted of the management and preparation of such Orders which, unlike statutes, do not require the sanction of Parliament since they are '... issued by the sovereign by virtue of the royal prerogative ... (though) in practice they are only issued on the advice of the ministers of the crown ...' (*Encyclopaedia Britannica*, 13th. edn, p. 187). Thus the Committee of Council was created as an arm of *executive* government and, as such, was constrained by government policies and exchequer controls rather than by Parliament. Although minutes and inspector reports were laid before Parliament, apart from on rare occasions, this was a formality.

Initially, its membership consisted of the Lord President, the Lord Privy Seal, the Chancellor of the Exchequer and the Home Secretary. Its composition, though, was not fixed. Members could be chosen on the Lord President's authority though a few, such as the Chancellor and the Home Secretary, were self-selected; there was no necessity for any other office to be represented (Bishop, 1971). Disquiet over its lack of responsibility to Parliament led to an Act being passed in 1856 which sanctioned the appointment of a Vice-President. This was to be a Minister of State who must also be a member of the Privy Council. He was to assist the Lord President, acting for him in his absence, as well as representing the Committee of Council in that House of Parliament where the Lord President might not happen to sit. In reality, as the Lord President was generally from the House of Lords, the Vice-President sat in the House of Commons.

LORD PRESIDENTS OF THE COUNCIL

Marquess of Landsdowne	18 April 1835
Lord Wharncliffe	3 September 1841
Duke of Buccleuch and Queensberry	21 January 1846
Marquess of Landsdowne	6 July 1846
Earl of Lonsdale	27 February 1852
Earl Granville	28 December 1852
Lord John Russell	12 June 1854
Earl Granville	8 February 1855
Marquess of Salisbury	26 February 1858
Earl Granville	18 June 1859
Duke of Buckingham and Chandos	6 July 1866
Duke of Marlborough	8 March 1867
Earl de Gray and Rippon	9 December 1868

VICE-PRESIDENTS OF THE COMMITTEE OF COUNCIL ON EDUCATION

William F. Cowper	2 February 1857
C. B. Adderley	6 April 1858
Robert Lowe	6 July 1859
Henry A. Bruce	26 April 1864
Thomas L. Corry	26 July 1866
Lord Robert Montagu	19 March 1867
William E. Forster	9 December 1868

SECRETARIES OF THE EDUCATION DEPARTMENT

James Phillips Kay (Kay-Shuttleworth)	26 August 1839
Ralph Robert Wheeler Lingen	8 January 1850
Francis Richard Sandford	1 February 1870

Source: Bishop, A. S. (1971) *The Rise of A Central Authority for English Education*, Cambridge, Cambridge University Press, pp. 218–2.

However relations between the Committee of Council, the education office and the legislature had not been properly clarified and their respective spheres of responsibility were not clear either. The Act of 1856 served to reinforce rather than remove the confusion. This can be illustrated by the circumstances surrounding the resignation in 1864 of Robert Lowe, the Vice-President. Accusations had been made in Parliament that the education office was censoring school inspector reports which were critical of the Revised Code (see chapter 7 for a discussion of this). Lowe argued that if the Vice-President was responsible for reports then he should have the right of censorship. If not, then inspectors, who were permanent members of the civil service, were responsible and there was a risk of the office being seen to express views which were contradictory to its own policies. (For a fuller discussion of this and the resulting Committee of Inquiry, which exonerated Lowe from blame, see later in this chapter.) This resignation was the earliest arising out of a minister's responsibility for those under him, and the case was the last in which MPs seriously asserted that civil servants were directly responsible to Parliament (Parris, 1969).

The precise role which the Committee of Council played is difficult to determine, either on a formal or an informal level. This difficulty is exacerbated because no record of its proceedings were kept (1865 VI *1865 Committee Lingen's evidence*: questions 223–226) so that only those minutes which were passed are available for examination. Further, there are problems in assessing the frequency of meetings after February 1841 and any attempt has to rely primarily on guesswork. The reason for this is that though a record of attendance was started in the Office Minute Book on 11 April 1839, and the first volume of manuscript minutes was completed by February 1841, later manuscript records have been destroyed. In his discussion of various sources of information on this Campbell (1972) suggests that by the 1850s meetings were sporadic and that, aside from a burst of activity during the drafting of the Revised Code, they continued to decline and most ministerial responsibility was devolved to the education department (*ibid.*, p. 198).

The evidence given to the 1865 Select Committee to enquire into the constitution of the Committee of Council provides support for the view taken here, that the Committee of Council was a formal device for ratifying the decisions of the education office. This claim is not simply based on the hostile opinions of witnesses such as Adderley, (Vice-Pesident, 1858–1859) who described it as a 'farce' and a 'useless encumbrance' (1865 VI *1865 Committee Adderley's evidence*: questions 63–64) to the education office; or the Marquess of Salisbury (Lord President, 1858–1859) who, noting that members were not always interested in educational affairs, stated that when he summoned the Committee, 'It was generally ill-received when he proposed it, and, in the event, none of the members attended, so he acted on his own responsibility' (Bishop, 1971, p. 60). Rather, it is based on the remarkable uncertainty of witnesses who had been involved with it as to what its role had been and even as to when it had met. Thus, no one had any clear idea of when the last meeting had taken place, and when asked how often he had summoned the Committee, Salisbury 'thought he did so' on three or four occasions.

Reviewing the evidence given to the 1865 Committee, Bishop notes, 'Upon the major issues of functions and powers, the views of no two witnesses coincided; frequently they contradicted each other and even themselves' (*ibid.*). For example, Lingen (Secretary, 1850–1870) said that it *advised* the Lord President and Vice-President but had little control over them (1865 VI *1865 Committee*: question 118), later he said that it simply *ratified decisions previously made* by the Lord President and Vice-President (*ibid.*, questions 129–133). Whereas Granville (Lord President, 1852–1854 and 1855–1858) maintained that the Lord President was not bound by the majority if he differed on a matter of principle, Russell (Lord President, 1854–1855) held a contrary view, that the majority could overrule the Lord President. Had the Committee of Council been more than a formal device, it is likely that there would have been more consistency and less vagueness as to its work.

The creation of a Privy Council Committee was not, in itself, a new phenomenon. There were plenty of precedents in the conduct of government affairs for the establishment of temporary boards, and at the outset, the Committee of Council was not intended to be permanent. Indeed, this uncertainty was a factor which contributed to the failure to define the precise role of the Committee of Council in educational affairs. Initially clerical staff were from the Privy Council office and the senior post, that of secretary, was temporary and part-time. The first secretary, Kay-Shuttleworth, was encouraged to retain his superintendence of the pauper school at Norwood and consequently his formal connection with the Poor Law Commission, on the grounds that the continued existence of the Committee of Council was uncertain. The architect for the Committee of Council was also the architect to the Poor Law Commission. The apparently casual manner in which the business of the Committee of Council seems to have been conducted was in accordance with other temporary boards and, as we shall see, contrasted sharply with the precision which was demanded of those lower down the institutional hierarchy in schools.

What marked the Committee of Council as characteristic of the new mode of government was its creation of an administrative machinery to enforce the regulation of the statutory provision of finance for schooling. The key mechanisms of this were the inspectorate, which dealt with visits to schools to assess their suitability for financial aid, and the education office which related requests for aid to the minutes governing its provision, and who processed inspection reports. The main work of the Lord President, in relation to his heading of the education office, was concerned with questions of policy and patronage, this last being the way in which members of the education department were recruited.

In the last section I argued that those involved in this changing mode of government had shared aims and interests. But the explanation of the creation of a phenomenon does not necessarily explain how that phenomenon is sustained. Patronage was the normal method of recruitment at this time and was one means of helping to ensure an overall continuity in departmental action as well as conformity within its parameters. One analysis of the family backgrounds of 140 inspectors throughout this period found them to have shared social and educational backgrounds, most coming from 'the upper ranks of the middle class' and none coming from the working class (cited in Myers, 1983, p. 124). Though Scottish inspectors tended to be from lower social class backgrounds than their English counterparts, their outlook, despite being significantly coloured by what I have termed the 'Scottish dimension', was not radically different.

This was the period of the emergence of the proto-typical civil servant, 'Upper-middle-class in origin, Oxbridge education, proficiency in literary studies: such were the marks by which they were known' (Parris, 1969, p. 159). After the Northcote-Trevelyan (1853) investigations into the civil service and the introduction of examinations for assessing recruits, the education office was one of the slowest parts of the civil service to comply. Patronage continued in this department long after other departments had formally introduced competitive examination (Bishop, 1971, p. 73), Lingen (Secretary to the Education Office, 1850–1870) arguing vigorously that, '... since rank and wealth held the keys to advancement socially, politically and commercially he saw no reason for the abolition of patronage' (*ibid*., p. 41). The class-specific nature of this view is underlined by the fact that this was the period in which the education office was advocating the use of examinations for assessing children in schools. However, apart from noting this distinct class division in methods of assessing people, I don't want to overstress the significance of the failure to introduce examinations for, as Parris has noted, 'The Administrative Class type was not created by Open Competition. Open Competition served to perpetuate a type which had already come to the top.' (1969, p. 159; see also Corrigan and Sayer, 1985).

Most of the day-to-day running of the office was in the hands of the Secretary who, unlike the Lord President, did not sit in one of the Houses of Parliament. Initially the nominal Secretary was the Clerk of the Council who was ex-officio Secretary to all Privy Council Committees. At this stage most of the work was done by the Assistant Secretary, Kay-Shuttleworth, who later became Secretary. After the appointment of a Vice-President problems of building grants were usually dealt with by him. One witness to the 1865 Committee argued that the Vice-President did about nine-tenths of business and the Lord President about one-tenth, there being little contact between the Secretary and the Lord President (l865 VI *1865 Committee*: Lingen's evidence). After the introduction of annual grants in 1846 two examiners, Fred Temple [a future Archbishop of Canterbury] and Ralph Lingen [a future Permanent Secretary to the Treasury], were appointed to read inspection reports.

The rules issued by the office were generalizations of decisions which arose in daily practice of interpreting minutes in the education office (Parris, 1969, p. 194). New minutes had to be placed before Parliament unless they were defined by the office as *declaratory*. That is, unless they were simply clarifying existing policy (as in the minutes forbidding inspectors to criticize department policy). Officially, the Lord President would instruct the Secretary to draft a new minute, it would then be circulated confidentially to Committee of Council members who would send remarks on it; a Committee meeting would be called to pass the minute, which would then be sent to the House of Commons. In practice, though, the instruction might come from the Vice-President and the meeting was sometimes dispensed with. The placing before Parliament was generally seen as a formality and, for example, a major change in minutes such as the Revised Code, was laid before Parliament on the day of pro-rogation [6 August 1861] (*ibid.*, p. 195). The Secretary was a key figure in the office, acting as a 'gatekeeper' in relation to what was or was not to be referred to the Vice-President or Lord President. The importance of this role has been stressed by Bishop (1971, p. 69) who argues that *effective* control of education lay, within broad limits, with the Secretary.

Therefore it is the work of the higher officials in the education office, as well as that of the inspectorate, which is important for an understanding of how it was possible for the problem of schooling working class children to shape the definition of what constitutes problems for the education system. For though officials may have had shared educational and social backgrounds these do not *of themselves* necessarily indicate an alliance of outlook on all matters. Recruitment and patronage therefore offer only *part* of the explanation as to how the general underlying aims of these state mechanisms were sustained.

Foucault has argued that the institutional form of knowledge/power relations within a disciplinary regime is hierarchical and acts invisibly through the definition of modes of operation as 'practical' within a given context. It is to the techniques involved in this that we must give our attention in order to identify the ways in which the fundamental aims of regulating the population became enmeshed within knowledge about education. The work of state servants should not, therefore, be interpreted as dealing with neutral administrative concerns. Such a view would pre-suppose, without explaining, the institutional constraints within which state servants operate. Though inspection reports, the education department's primary source of information on schools, were aimed at 'fact-gathering', what counted as a relevant 'fact' was always *in relation* to this concern with schooling working class people. Knowledge of schooling and its problems was produced within the constraints of an organization with class-specific terms of reference.

The Production of Knowledge

I am arguing then, that an important aspect of power relations is the ability to get a particular view accepted as taken-for-granted knowledge. More than this, that the translation of the parameters of class-directed policies into 'neutral' ground-rules for their administration and implementation was what secured the continuity of the initial purposes for which the machinery for regulating schooling was constructed. This is the 'secret of power' with which I am dealing, 'Power is tolerable only on condition that it mask a substantial part of itself...secrecy...is indispensible to its operation' (Foucault, 1981a, p. 86). If the mask slips, as it does in the evidence given to the *Select Committee on Education (Inspectors' Reports)* (1864 IX *1864 Committee*), its construction can be examined and its implications made visible.

Unlike the Poor Law inspectorate, or the factory inspectorate which provided the model for the Committee of Council's inspection arrangements, the role of the school inspector was permeated with ambiguity. This was because the primary function was not the enforcement of a law. As an agent of the Committee of Council he gathered information about schools in terms of an official list of headings (see appendix) which defined information to be considered as relevant for the appropriate administration of government money. Though the minutes of the Committee of Council altered some aspects, for example, the extension of instructions to Scotland (*ibid*, letter from J P Kay to John Gordon, 4 January 1840) the basis of these instructions remained fundamentally the same during this period. In summary,

> The reports of the inspectors are intended to convey such further information respecting the state of elementary education in Great Britain as to enable Parliament to determine in what mode the sum voted for the education of the poorer classes can be most usefully applied. With this view reports on the state of particular districts may be required...' (*ibid*, quoted in report: iii).

The aim was to encourage local efforts 'for the improvement and expansion of elementary education', as well as the development of expertise through experience and observation to create and disseminate a body of knowledge about 'good' schooling. It was maintained that inspection was not intended as a means of controlling schooling but was aimed at assisting schools (1840 XL: letter of appointment to inspectors, 4 January 1840). This wording, according to Hurt (1971, p. 32–8), was necessary because of conflict between the English established church and the Committee of Council over control of the provision of schooling. The wording has sometimes been taken at face value by historians working in this area (for example, Ball, 1963). However, the question of the extent to which controlling and assisting were mutually exclusive categories rather than differing dimensions of this form of state intervention is raised by evidence submitted to the

1864 Committee during a discussion of an extension to the system of grants which was introduced in the mid-1840s.

> As soon as annual grants began to be made in 1846, a very considerable change in the duties of the inspectors took place. Previously they had merely to visit the schools, which were opened to their inspection, and to report upon them, very much at their own discretion. But as soon as annual grants began to be made to schools and to depend upon certain conditions, which were embodied in the minutes of the Committee of Council, the duties of the inspectors in the examination of particular schools from that time had to conform more strictly and uniformly to the minutes in question. They had to verify the conditions upon which those grants were dependent ...' (1864 IX *1864 Committee*: answer 9 Lingen's evidence)

Further, during this period it was ruled that no annually renewable grants would be made, '... unless the right of inspection be retained, in order to secure a conformity to the regulations and discipline established in the several schools, with such improvements which may from time to time be suggested by the Committee' (Ball, 1963, p. 27). The objects of aid and knowledge, schools, were also to be the objects of regulation. This gave the role of the collectors of knowledge its ambiguity, for they were both to gather, classify and disseminate information about schooling in terms of its greater or lesser efficiency; and to maximize the effectiveness of the parliamentary grant by ensuring that it was concentrated on areas which lacked the means but supplied the evidence of the possibility of developing efficient education. Some information might appear to suggest that inspection reports only had a limited impact on schooling, and that this impact would in part be limited by the Committee of Council's own rules. For example, the instruction to inspectors not to interfere with teaching and complaints by inspectors that reports went unread and advice unheeded; especially after the change from issuing the Blue Books (books of inspection reports) free to all districts, to restrictions on their issue which were brought about by financial constraints.[6]

However, after this, (i.e. starting in 1858) school managers were sent the full report of their school. Though this practice was later altered, a summary was still sent to the managers (1864 IX *1864 Committee Report*: iii). Thus the results of an inspection visit were still communicated to school managers as the relationship between inspection and the awarding of the grant would imply. Further, Myers (1970,

p. 125) has pointed out that inspection reports were reviewed and commented on by the periodical and public press. It was the possibility of finance which would enhance the reception of reports and which sets the context in which the above limitations must be assessed, for grants were paid after the annual inspection with the education office indicating areas required for improvement and withholding payments if necessary (1864 IX *1864 Committee*: answer 133 Lingen's evidence).

I have argued that the minutes of the Committee of Council provided the formal parameters within which inspectors could express their experience of visiting schools. The 'secret of power' referred to earlier is revealed by extending this argument to show that informal constraints amounting, in some instances, to actual censorship of reports by staff in the education office were being operated. In April 1864 accusations were made in the House of Commons that the Committee of Council was destroying the value of inspection reports by exercising indiscriminate censorship. There followed a Select Committee investigation (1864 IX *1864 Committee*) which concluded that,

> ... the supervision exercised in objecting to the insertion of irrelevant matter, of mere dissertation, and of controversial argument, is consistent with the powers of the Committee of Council, and has ... been exercised fairly. ... No objection is made to statements of facts observed by the Inspectors within the circle of their official experience, whatever may be their bearing on the policy of the Committee Council' (*ibid., Report*, p. v).

At the same time, though, it was also agreed that, '... the heads of the office have exercised a censorship over the Inspectors' reports as to the insertion of argumentative or irrelevant matter ...' (*ibid.*, p. vi); holding such power to be essential to the department's work. However, the evidence presented to the Committee indicates that more complex procedures were involved than this conclusion, at first sight, suggests.

I am not arguing that censorship operated in such a way as to eliminate *all* disagreement, as the House of Commons accusations seem to suggest. Nor am I suggesting that at *all* times the minutes were uniformly applied to *all* reports. What I am maintaining is that the minutes provided a framework in terms of which inspectors' reports were assessed and that this framework made it possible to set up a distinction between 'acceptable' and 'unacceptable' disagreement. The implications of this can be explored by examining the evidence presented to the 1864 Committee, as well as extracts from censored reports where these are available. When an inspector's report was received in the education office it would be read by an examiner who would bring doubtful passages to the attention of the secretary. If the secretary felt they were important the report would be sent to the Vice-President. This form of censorship had been present from the inception of the education office, 'From the earliest times of my connexion with the office ... the secretary has discharged ... a sort of editor's duty; previously to 1858 this came to very little, a private note or personal communication might pass, most frequently with a view to condensation' (*ibid.*, answer 17 Lingen's evidence). The strictness with which the minutes were applied varied though, for in 1860 a controversial report was published.[7]

However, following this there was a review of the instructions to inspectors relating to the regulation of reports. The result of this was that a *declaratory* minute was issued on 31 January 1861 to the effect that,

> ... Inspectors must confine themselves to the state of the schools under their inspection and to practical suggestions for their improvement; if any report ... does not conform to this standard, it is to be returned to the Inspector for revision; and if on its being again received from him it appears to be open to the same objection, it is to be put aside as a document not proper to be printed at the public expense' (*ibid.*, quoted in Report, p. iv).

A clarification of this minute was issued in a letter of instruction to inspectors dated August 1863, stating, '... by the term "state of schools under your inspection", you will understand facts observed within the circle of your official experience; and by the term "practical suggestions for their improvement", you will understand suggestions consistent with the principles of Minutes sanctioned by Parliament' (*ibid.*, *Report Appendix F*: 53). This formal constraint was confirmed by Lingen in his evidence (*ibid.*, Lingen's evidence question 320 and following) that practical suggestions which were not consistent with the principle of existing minutes were forbidden. This interpretation of '*practical*' as '*consistent with minutes*' represents a visible aspect of a phenomenon which also operated at the less visible level of inspectors recognizing what would be acceptable and what would not be acceptable in reports. For example,

Question 384:   You state that you took a great deal of care in drawing that report up?

Answer: I did.

Question 385:   That is, you took a great deal of care to keep from it all opinions adverse to the policy of the Committee of Council?

Answer: I did.

....

Question 387:   The result was that if you entertained any opinions unfavourable to their policy you did not express them?

Answer: I did not.

When asked if the report was an 'imperfect transcript' the witness responded,

Answer 389:   It was not a full account of all that I had seen and all that I had heard, but it was a faithful one.

Question 390:   It was faithful, so far as it went; but you were obliged to omit opinions, and also things that you had heard and seen, because you felt that your report would be suppressed unless you did so?

Answer: Yes. (*ibid.*, Watkins' evidence)

This form of self-censorship was explicitly encouraged within the education office. In 1859 when Lowe became Vice-President, he ordered that the practice of marking objectionable passages was to cease and that reports should simply be returned to inspectors who must make them conform to instructions.[8] Along with the returned report an inspector would receive a copy of the 1861 minute and an intimation that unless it was altered the report would not be laid before Parliament (*ibid.*, Lingen's evidence, answer 90). The situation was summed up by Lingen, '... Here is the Minute, stating what the report ought to be; here is a report sent in; here is the judgment of the Committee, that it does not conform to the Minute; the Inspector says, "Why?"; the answer is, that we do not consider it good policy, or for the interests of the service, to tell you; ...' (*ibid.*, answer 111). The stress on self-censorship was the main defence of members of the office to charges of autocratic behaviour with respect to this issue, as they maintained that an inspector, by making the changes himself, had given his consent to them (*ibid.*, questions 93–102). Thus Lowe indicated that, whereas previously reports had been printed omitting passages struck out by the Vice-President (*ibid.*, 56), the reason for the Declaratory Minute of 1861 was, '... my reluctance to strike out anything myself, ... I thought it might raise a controversy between the Inspector and the office, and that he would say, as I believe, in some cases he did say, that the context was interfered with, by striking out portions; and that the meaning of what remained was altered ... (*ibid.*, Lowe's evidence, answer 699).

Any inspector who criticized the department was held to be insubordinate. Therefore, a refusal to make the alterations which had been officially requested could call into question an inspector's suitability for their post. As one witness stated, 'I considered that the Department having laid down rules for his guidance, it was his duty to conform to them; if he was unable to conform to those rules, he was not a gentleman of the intelligence required for the office he held. If, on the other hand, he was able to conform to them, and did not do so, then it was quite right that his report should be laid aside as unfit to present to Parliament' (*ibid.*, Lingen's evidence: answer 744). The picture which is emerging of the relationship between inspectors, their reports and the Committee of Council office is that of an informal censorship, often carried out by the inspector himself, either at the explicit instigation of the department or as a result of previous experience of the operation of criteria of acceptability. Formal methods of censoring were only invoked when these informal methods had broken down.

Yet, given that the office maintained that they did not censor 'facts' (*ibid.*, Lingen's evidence, questions 41–42) it is necessary to confront directly the nature of these 'facts' in order to give a more adequate consideration of the material. Some of the evidence to the 1864 Committee shows that what were accepted as 'facts' could sometimes disagree with the department's policy and that if they came within the terms of such a disagreement then it was felt to be legitimate to suppress them.

Question 117: I understand you to admit that the reports were not presented if any of the arguments contained in the Inspectors' reports contradicted the policy of the department?

Answer: Yes, that is true as regards argument only; if an Inspector had reported a matter which he had observed, whether it was for the policy of the department or against it, that would not come within the scope of the minute.

Question 118: But if he pointed out those facts by showing how they confuted the policy of the department, that inference would be objected to?

Answer : Yes, I think so. (*ibid.*, Lingen's evidence)

Therefore 'facts' could be incorporated into arguments in favour of the department but not against it. Yet the distinction between what counted as a 'fact' and what counted as an argument is unclear. An example of this is in the discussion of suppressed passages from an 1861 report,

Question 612:   What I wish to know is, why you think this passage, for instance, was intended to harass the department — 'The schoolmistress at Conway is the best infant teacher in my district, admirably suited for her duties in every respect, and deserving of the greater credit because she is not certificated, although she is aided by pupil teachers.' How can you imagine that was intended to harass the department?

Answer 613:   Taken with the rest, it appeared to me to be a certain case picked out at a rather critical time of the discussion to show this — here is the best teacher of a particular class in my district who is not certificated.

Question 615:   The sting of the passage lay in its being offered at a critical time, when the particular policy to which it referred was under the consideration of Parliament?

Answer :   ... Its referring to a single teacher seemed to me to lend it a certain character of unfairness, and that unfairness was aggravated by the particular time at which it appeared.

Question 616 :   It was a statement of fact?

Answer :   It purported to be a statement of fact, and that the fact was so, I have every reason to believe.

Question 617 :   Therefore, it was your opinion that the Inspector who stated that inconvenient fact at an inconvenient time, showed an inclination to harass the Department?

Answer: Yes; ... (ibid ., Lingen's evidence, a further illustration lies in the discussion in questions 124–131 of Lingen's evidence).

This illustrates that acceptable reports were those which were appropriately expressed in relation to department policy. The knowledge which they provided about schooling in nineteenth century Britain was that in terms of which money was paid. For it was held that, 'You cannot ..., in the practice of a department separate the Inspector's report, which is part of the official communication, from the general responsibility of the Committee of Council in making the grant' (*ibid.*, Lingen's evidence, answer 144).

In this chapter I have attempted to outline some of the intricacies of the web of relations of knowledge/power which are illustrated by the relationship between the Committee of Council on Education, the staff who operated under its auspices and the rest of the social world. I have been emphasizing that the papers of the inspectors and the Committee of Council cannot be equated, in any simple sense, with 'reality'. This is *not* to say that either the inspectorate or the education office were engaged in providing 'false' accounts of schooling; but rather to stress that the relationship between these accounts and the world to which they refer is complex and must be understood in terms of the purposes for which they were developed — that is, the structuring of elementary schooling aimed at producing social relations amongst working class people, which would be compatible with industrial capitalism. To paraphrase an argument used by Foucault in another context, but which is of relevance here: the categories used to present this 'knowledge' were not lying in a state of nature ready to be picked up by the perceptive observer, they were *produced* by the construction of a systematic form of state intervention.

Notes

1 Neither can they explain why it was that official action was targeted at improving the social status and formal identity of teachers; yet, attempts by teachers to further this by professionalizing the occupation were firmly restricted, in so far as these attempts involved a shift in the control of the structuring and content of the occupation from the state to teachers themselves.

2 Examples were Sir John Sinclair of the Board of Agriculture — a precursor to the new mode of government – who supervised the compilation of the Statistical Survey of Scotland 1791–9; Henry Brougham, leader of the Whigs 1815, instigated Select Committee on Education of the Lower Orders of the Metropolis in 1816, attempted to introduce a Bill, in 1820, based on its findings; James P. Kay; Lord John Russell; Palmerston; Francis & Leonard Horner. Myers (1970) notes that Kay, Russell and Landsdowne drew up the recommendations for government action from the Select Committee Report of 1837–8.

3 Sir John Sinclair, educated Glasgow, Edinburgh and Oxford supervised its compilation.

4 It is not necessary, for the purposes of my argument, to enter into the debate about the precise nature of the relationship between protestantism and capitalism, which surrounds Weber's work. For a full account of this see Marshall, 1979, 1980 and 1982.

5 For a more detailed account of its contemporary significance, see McCrone *et al.*, 1981.

6 *1864 Committee*: iii. Report indicated that an increase in the number of schools inspected had led to an increase in the volume of individual reports, therefore printing of these was discontinued in 1858. It was resumed in 1859 for sale only, and finally stopped in 1861.

7 *1864 Committee*: Answer 19 (Lingen's evidence). The report had contained remarks about the comparative morality of Catholic and Protestant countries.

8 However, the practice continued till 14 February 1862 when Lowe, having by chance discovered that reports were still being marked, sent a formal minute ordering its cessation.

PART 2:
The Features Explored

In the last chapter I argued that the mechanisms for regulating schooling established a hierarchical network of official relations. This organizational form reflected the image of society with which the educational 'experts' and state officials operated. It was during the process of institutionalization that the strategies which were directed towards structuring social relations to make them compatible with an industrial capitalist social order became 'neutralized' programmes of state power. In the next four chapters I shall be exploring in detail what was involved in implementing these programmes. At the same time, through this exploration, I shall also be investigating specific features of the social map of truancy.

Chapter 4

The Organization of Schooling

Introduction

The notion of a 'correct' space for schooling is essential to the social map of truancy. But how did this emerge and what is the significance of the way in which it was organized? Within discussions of schooling at this time little attention has been paid to the fine detail of the physical organization of schools. This is partly because of the way in which schooling itself has been taken for granted among historians of Scottish education, but it is also because of the lack of attention that has been given to spatiality. As I have argued, space isn't simply a background against which social life takes place. Social formations are also spatial formations (Soja, 1981). Therefore we need to give attention to the ways in which these interact and to the politics which are enmeshed there.

Between the late eighteenth century and the mid-nineteenth century there was an architectural flourish of new functional types of building which in design and scale, combined the intellectual concerns of the period with technical innovations such as those in ventilation, fire-proofing, drainage and water supply. At the start of the period Markus (1982) notes that there were a few types of building, primarily based on the country house, the church and derivatives such as guild halls. At its end there were dozens of new ones, including railway stations, art galleries and museums. Given the compartmentalization of living which accompanied industrialization (Thompson, 1974), this development is hardly surprising for as Markus points out, 'The typological explosion is an important mechanism for vastly increased specialization of role and function in society' (p. 16).

One aspect of these more general architectural developments was the development of special designs for schools. These illustrate the importance which was placed on the structuring of educational space both amongst educational theorists and amongst those involved in state regulation of schooling. Indeed, early state grants on education were restricted to the provision of school buildings. As I shall show here, it is by paying attention to the fine detail of the spatial relations of schooling that we can begin to understand the force, and appreciate the implications of the more general argument concerning the ways in which state activity can structure and regulate the minutae of social life. I shall demonstrate this firstly by examining the way in which schools were to be structured internally and showing how disciplinary relations of social order were constructed as an *educational* necessity. I shall then extend this discussion in order to explain the way in which the links between schools and their local communities were characterized within state documents. In so doing, I shall be providing a preliminary to my discussion of social identity which is extended throughout the rest of the book.

From Social Order to Educational Necessity

What were existing schools like? 'The earthen floor, in which there are numerous large holes, is all over so uneven that it was impossible to steady a chair on it. There are no desks, except the master's, which is broken. The children write on the forms, kneeling on the floor, which is often so puddled, through the imperfect roof, as to render this impossible. There is no blackboard, and a few small maps are soiled by the damp of the wall and the smoke' (LIV, 1860, p, 232). Considering this example of the kind of school which regulation was directed towards eradicating, it is understandable that state activity was initially focused on the physical arrangements of schools. The early direction of state aid was towards building grants which were aimed at encouraging warm, well-ventilated schools. This could be seen as signifying an enlightened concern for the physical well-being of pupils and teachers. However, this would be simply to apprehend the surface of a more profound official view of the way in which spatial organization would pre-dispose people to types of action.

In this respect the impact of early psychological theories such as 'associationism' was important. Developed by David Hartley in the first half of the eighteenth century, 'asssociationism' was influential amongst people such as Jeremy Bentham, James Mill, William Allen (of the Lancastrian school movement) (Markus, 1982) and educational 'experts' whose thinking was germame to state intervention into schooling. A fundamental tenet of this theory was that environmental stimuli could cause physiological changes. It was held that the ideas which formed the mind were the result of these changes and that the patterning of the stimuli were important in determining the way in which ideas were 'associated'. Their proper patterning was believed to be essential for a child's mental development and the organization of the school environment was crucial for this.

Advocates of particular educational theories were therefore generally also advocates of an associated organization of educational space. Indeed, prior to the setting up of the Committee of Council on Education there were already a number of school plans around. For example, Jeremy Bentham's educational ideas were expressed spatially in his plan for a Chrestomathic school (or school of useful knowledge). The building was to be twelve-sided and to have six radial segments of pupils arranged in concentric circles. The master was to be in the centre with, placed in a ring round him, six monitors who were each to be in charge of a segment of pupils. The seating was to slope up towards the edge of the building which was designed to have high windows in order to prevent external distractions. The children attending the school would be seated according to individual attainment, with this being measured by a system of continuous competitive testing. Although the school was never built, the theme of central supervision with hierarchical arrangements, involving the use of monitors, was to figure prominently in the later organization of school buildings.

Infused within these arrangements were disciplinary relations based on the principle of panopticism. The panopticon was a development of Bentham's derived from a system of workforce organization which had been developed by his brother Samuel in eighteenth century Russia. A design principle which was also to be used for prisons and asylums, it was based on a system of continuous observation.

> ... at the periphery, an annular building; at the centre, a tower; this tower is pierced with wide windows that open onto the inner side of the ring; the peripheric building is divided into cells, each of which extends the whole width of the building, they have two windows, one on the inside, corresponding to the windows of the tower; the other, on the outside, allows the light to cross the cell from one end to the other ... By the effect of backlighting, one can observe from the tower, standing out precisely against the light, the small captive shadows in the cells of the periphery. (Foucault, 1979, p. 200)

Disciplinary relations were therefore founded on an architectural form which facilitated the automatic functioning of power relations through the arrangement of space. Visibility and segmentation were to help to generate an internalized control of individual behaviour. Integral to disciplinary relations has been what Foucault has described as the 'relay of power' (*ibid.*, p. 174). The relay is a variant of the panoptic principle: the invisible observer who has the continuous possibility of seeing the detailed actions of those under surveillance. Since they never know whether or not, at any particular moment, they are being watched, those under surveillance always behave as if being observed. Continuously operating, both vertically and horizontally, within a network of relations, a sufficiently discreet relay can increase the effects of a disciplinary mechanism without hampering the activity to be disciplined.

One version of this which was developed within schooling around this time, was the monitorial system. This system was operated by using older children to teach younger children. There were two main types: that developed by Andrew Bell, a Scots army chaplain, while he was superintendent to a male orphan asylum in Madras in the late eighteenth century; and that developed by Joseph Lancaster, a quaker, who set out his ideas in 'Improvements in Education' (published in 1803). Markus (1982) argues that Lancaster was probably more influential in Scotland, although both systems were important. In England, they were operated within the two main organizations through which state funding was channelled. These were the National Society, which favoured Bell's system, and the British and Foreign Schools Society, which favoured Lancaster's version. Both variants were designed to enable the maximum number of children to be taught with a minimum number of supervisors and were therefore relatively cheap to operate. (Bell, for example, argued that under his system one master could deal with 1000 pupils [Markus, 1982, p. 215]).

With Bell's system the pupils stood in the centre of the room, arranged either in squares or in U shapes during most of the teaching. The children were positioned according to their progress through a system of 'place capturing'. Desks for use in writing lessons faced the wall and were placed against it. In contrast, with Lancaster's system the centre of the room contained fixed benches and writing desks placed in parallel rows. The edges of the room were free, but the floor was marked with semi-circles so that individual classes could stand facing their monitor who would be placed at the wall to take the lesson or to work from a work card on the wall. The master's desk was on a raised platform on the central axis of the room, and the floor sloped upwards from there so that everyone within the room was visible to him. Under these conditions, discipline was rigid and teaching was directed at conveying 'facts'. For this reason early adherents such as David Stow (who set up a model infant school in Glasgow in 1828) gradually moved away from using this system and developed alternatives. Initially state authorized school plans incorporated designs which would be appropriate for teaching under these systems. However, the monitorial system was not particularly favoured by education officials because its rigidity and methods of rote learning limited the extent to which it was successful at appropriate identity formation among pupils. It was gradually to be displaced by the forms of organization favoured by state officials.

I have been stressing that state intervention was directed towards the development of disciplinary relations as integral to schooling. However, the mechanism of regulation *for* schooling was external *to* schooling. Its success was dependent on an ability to generate and perpetuate internalized definitions of action amongst people, such that what would generally be defined as a 'good' school would be synonymous with a school which conformed to Committee of Council minutes. The construction of a 'good' school was, first and foremost, the construction of a specialized space which would make possible the correct upbringing of the younger members of the poorer classes. Just as there was, at this time, no uniformity of space for schooling so, as I have illustrated, there was also no generally held view as to what ideal spatial arrangements might be. An arrangement of rows of desks with a space at the front for the teacher as opposed to, for example, the placing of desks round the walls with a space in the centre for the teacher, had to be explained and illustrated to those applying for state grants towards the building of schools.

As I have indicated, a major part of the initial work of the education office was to regulate the use of state funds which were provided for building schools, in order to ensure that designs would conform to the stipulated requirements. The scale of this administrative task meant that procedures needed to be rationalized. As part of this process wording which made state inspection a necessity and which restricted aid to schools 'for the education of the poorer classes' (XL, 1840, *Letter of Appointment*, p. 12) was incorporated into the standardized deeds for buildings. School inspectors were to convey to the education office information about the detailed plans for schools and teachers' houses in particular applications. It was officially recognized that buildings would

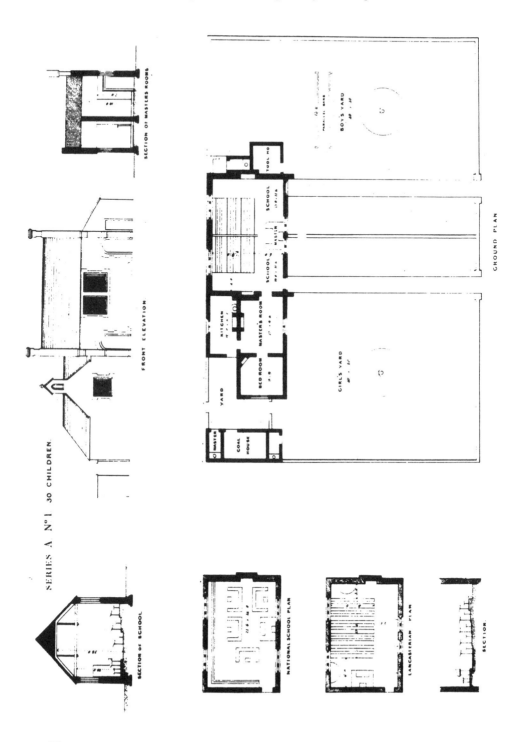

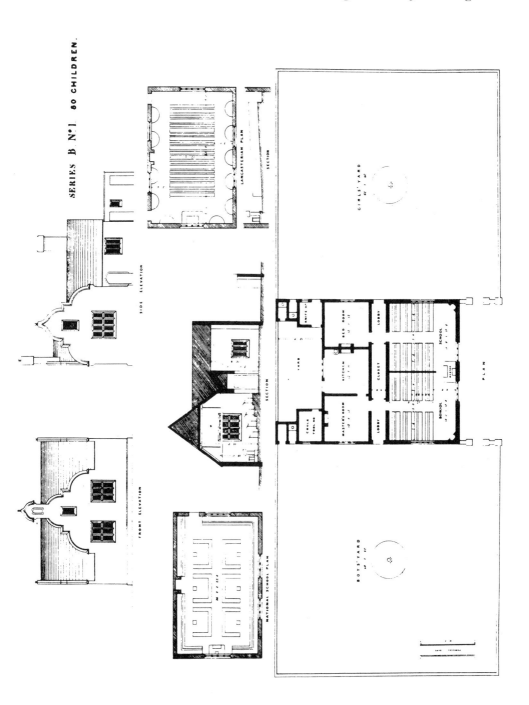

*No. 1.

A School for 48 Children of one sex, in 4 Classes; with a Class-room having a Gallery capable of containing two of the Classes.

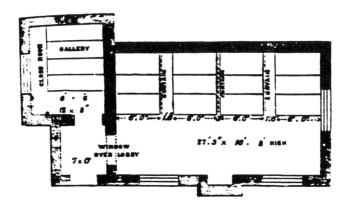

No. 2.

A School for 48 Boys and Girls, in 4 Classes; with a Class-room having a Gallery capable of containing two of the Classes.

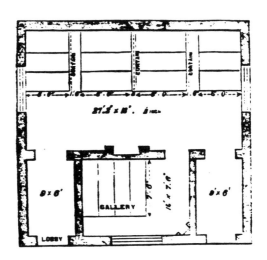

*The capacity is stated in each case *exclusively* of the class-rooms, because on certain occasions (such as school festivals, public examinations, solemn admonitions, and the like, it is desirable to have the means of seating *all* the children *together*. At the same time, as the class-room with its gallery is always equal to the accommodation at least of two classes, it may be reckoned as so much *additional* space available for most purposes of ordinary instruction. The Building Grants of the Committee of Council on Education are calcualted at so much *per square foot* of area in the school-room *and* class-room, and *not* at so much *per child accommodated*. The amount of such grants is not affected therefore, by any assumed standard of capacity.

No. 3.
A School for 72 Children of one sex, in 4 Classes; with a Class-room having a Gallery capable of containing two of the Classes.

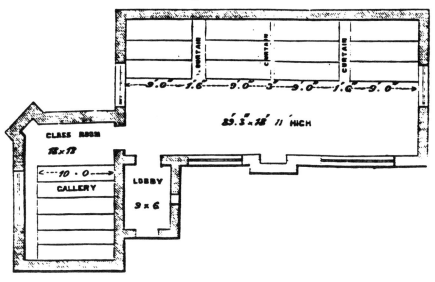

No. 4.
A School for 72 Boys and Girls, in 4 Classes; with a Class-room having a Gallery capable of containing two of the Classes.

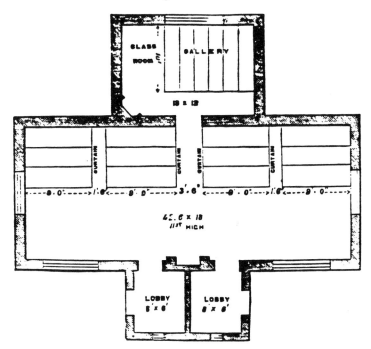

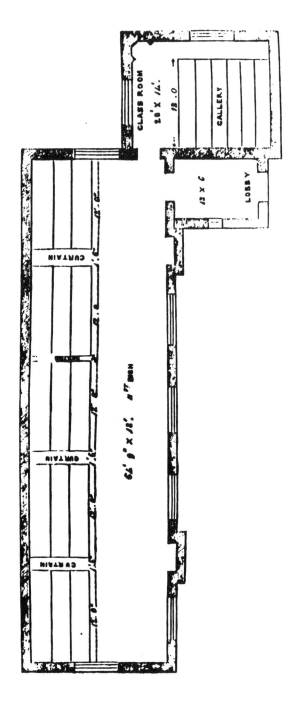

No. 5.

A School for 120 Children of one sex, in 5 Classes; with a Class-room having a Gallery capable of containing two of the Classes.

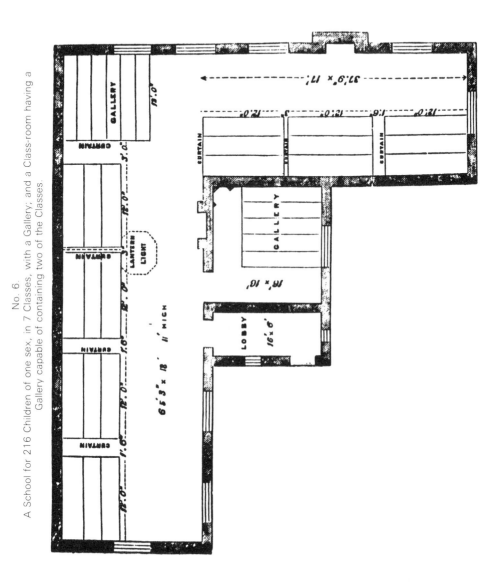

No. 6.

A School for 216 Children of one sex, in 7 Classes, with a Gallery; and a Class-room having a Gallery capable of containing two of the Classes.

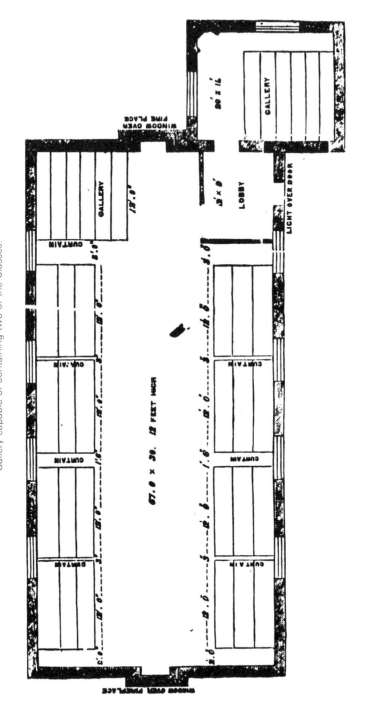

No. 7.

A School for 240 Children of one sex, in 8 Classes, and a Gallery; with a Class-room having also a Gallery capable of containing two of the Classes.

not all immediately conform to the regulation plans, so a certain amount of leeway was permitted provided that the existing design was compatible with the operation of state approved teaching methods. Alternatively, it had to be possible for any necessary alterations to be made in order to fit in with these teaching practices (XX 1841, *Supplementary Minute*, p. 12). The official plans and the explanatory documents were published in order to provide a standard against which existing schools were measured and a model for the construction of new schools. Each plan was presented with possible alternative classroom arrangements, according to the teaching system which was to be used there (XX 1841 'Minutes ... Relative to the Plans of School-Houses', 20 February 1840, p. 3). These were the mutual instruction or monitorial system and the mixed method, which combined simultaneous teaching (using a separate class room in which a class would be taken to say their lessons together) with a modified monitorial system involving the use of paid monitors.

As I have emphasized, the key to the automatic functioning of power relations within the panoptic principle was the possibility of constant supervision: the invisible observer; the totally visible object of the gaze. The relay of power, a hierarchical mutation of this, operated through the classification of levels of participants and the mutual visibility of those on adjacent levels. 'The main end to be attained is the concentration of the attention of the teacher upon his own separate class, and of the class upon its teacher, ... without obstruction to the head master's power of superintending the whole of the classes and their teachers' (XLI, 1854–5, *Memorandum Respecting the Organization of Schools*, p. 83). By the 1850s the mixed method, which was believed to be less rigid than the monitorial system, was being officially promoted. This was reflected in different spatial interpretations of the panoptic principle within authorized school designs. It was no longer necessary for the whole school to be completely visible to the master in charge at all times. It was only necessary to have, constantly available, the possibility of his viewing key segments of the school. What Foucault has described as the cellular dimension of disciplinary relations meant that classes of pupils were the responsibility of their immediate teachers; total visibility of the pupils was therefore only a necessity for the person in charge of each particular group.

The delegation of authority and responsibility involved in such arrangements would provide an encouragement to people at each level to internalize the prescribed norms of behaviour.

> The common schoolroom should, therefore, be fitted to realize
> ... the combined advantages of *isolation* and *superintendence* ...
> The best shape ... is an oblong. Groups of desks are arranged
> along one of the walls. Each group is divided from the adjacent
> group ... by an alley, in which a light curtain ... can be drawn
> forward or back ... but not so as, when drawn, to project into
> the room more than four inches in front of the foremost desk.
> (*ibid.*, pp. 83–4, my emphasis)

The architecture of discipline: continually visible segments enabling the master to look down the room and see the assistants in charge of each group, while the finer detail of the interior planning meant that the width of a group was to be no greater than would allow the assistant to encompass the pupils with one glance. '... extra space, ... is not only superfluous, but injurious' (XXI, Part 1, 1859, p. xvl). An economy of space would be both cheap and efficient.

This control of communication by sight also meant the control of communication by sound: a structure of noise and silence. 'The timetable of a school should be so arranged that classes *engaged in occupations comparatively silent* (...) may always be interposed between the classes that *are reading or receiving oral instruction*' (XLI, 1854–5, *Memo respecting etc.*, p. 84). Though scholars were divided into classes, the coordination of pedagogic action would impose an internal rhythm and this would generate the overall unity of the school. The synchronization of order which Thompson (1974) has argued was integral to the way in which industrial production was being organized at this time, was also incorporated into the organization of schooling. An institutional consequence of this was the introduction of the school timetable. Anarchic communication, such as copying and whispering, were forbidden in this tightly ordered environment of regulated action. An efficient school, which would be able to counter the influences of a child's class background, would be an organized setting with individuals appropriately classified and in their allotted place. As a result, it would be possible to keep them constantly occupied with the business of schooling. A badly organized school, that is to say, one not adhering to the Committee of Council minutes, would inevitably be a badly disciplined school (XLIV, 1850, *Gibson 1848–49*) which would not be able to inculcate the required habits into the scholars.

What was being advocated was a unified system of disciplinary relations which encapsulated all participants. Throughout the network of relations, the vertical and horizontal operation of the relay of power would enable the system to be self-sustaining. For while the teacher had authority over pupils, to the extent to which they did not conform to this authority, the pupils revealed an inefficient teacher. Similarly, though the headmaster superintended the teachers, their conduct could indicate to an inspector, the low level of the master's efficiency. This is why Foucault (1979) has described the relay as, '... both absolutely indiscreet, since it is every-where ... and constantly supervises the very individuals who are entrusted with the task of supervising; and absolutely "discreet", for it functions permanently and largely in silence' (p. 177).

The classification and particularization of space was epitomized by the precise way in which it was detailed, counted and allocated. '... no group of benches ... should be more than 12 feet wide ... An allowance of 18 inches on each desk ... will suffice ... a space of three inches will suffice for drawing and withdrawing the curtains' (XLI, 1854–5, *Memo etc.*, p. 84). This facilitated the classification of people which, in contrast, promoted the generalization of *individuals* in terms of the particular formal identities which were an implicit part of this process. The counterpart of this detailing of objects was therefore an absence of concern with the detail of individual people with whom schools were to deal. The explanation for this lies within the moral topographical theories which underpinned discussions of education at this time. For schooling was not primarily to be concerned with helping multi-faceted people to achieve their full individual potential. Individuals were of interest only as the constituents of a class of the population — the future carriers of the problematic moral topography of a social grouping. As such, though the relay of power facilitated the surveillance of individual pupils, they were seen as objects to be fitted in to the regulated system of schooling, not subjects participating in their own development.

This official model which was being expounded through state regulations represented an idealized version of schooling. A version which reflected a vision of the contribution which schooling could make to the production of a society in which different groups of people would know their 'correct' place and the behaviour appropriate to that place. The material taught in schools was to be linked with the 'condition of workmen and servants' (XLI, *Minute 11 April 1839*, p. 2).

By emphasizing that this model was being promoted I am not however precluding the possibility that in some schools a particular teacher might encourage an able male pupil to work towards university, as the 'lad o' pairts' tradition implies happened in Scotland. This was not, though, the aim of state intervention, it therefore would not count as an indication of an efficient school. Indeed, this could possibly have been considered as a contra-indication, in terms of the minutes, since it would involve individual tuition; and teaching methods which involved individuals working to their own pace, with the teacher offering random assistance, at his or her own discretion, were rejected. Such practices, it was argued, generated, '... an Air of extreme Languour and Listlessness, and produced among the other Classes a Degree of Restlessness which interfered with the general Order and Quiet of the School' (XXXIII, 1842, *Gibson, 1842*, p. 219). It was maintained that instruction could be paced at the level of the group in schools where teaching methods were based on the strict classification of pupils according to attainment. This way of operating, it was believed, would promote a discipline which pupils would internalize (XLIV, 1850, *Gibson 1848–49*) and this would encourage them to adhere to their school class's modal level of activity.

The architecture of discipline, the visible indicator of the relay of power relations, was designed to structure social action. More than this, though, I am arguing that it was informed by a belief that it would permeate through to the structuring of thought. If sufficiently well enforced, the internalized discipline promoted by this structure would even allow sections of pupils to spend short periods without tuition, without resulting in the kind of disciplinary problems which occurred in badly organized schools when children were not being taught directly (XLV, 1857–58, *Gordon 1857*, p. 677). It was the mutual reinforcement of the organization of thought/action which would enable disciplinary relations to be produced and reproduced.

This is further illustrated by the significance of classification. Today it seems self-evident that schools should be divided into classes. Yet inspection reports contain discussions of the difficulties which schools had in conforming to this method of organization because of the '... comparative novelty and strangeness of the organization recommended' (XLII, 1854–5, *Cumming and Wilson, 1854*, p. 719). In other words, the necessity of classes was not always self-evident. An argument had first of all to be made in its favour. I have pointed out that classification and counting were central elements of a new genre of knowledge which was being propounded at this time. As Hacking (1981) has argued, though any new classification might have a clearly describable rationale, the *fact* of the classification and counting was internal to a new practice. Jones and Williamson (1979) have shown that in discussions of education the population was generally classified in terms of people's principles and habits. At the level of the school, classification was advocated as both a means of presenting knowledge and a way of engendering different mores among the pupils. It was interwoven through the network of school relations, at every level reaffirming the object-status of those to whom it referred.

Classification facilitated the surveillance of the individuals who constituted the group, and so made the inspection of a school easier. Inspection of a school consisted of the assessment of the *classes* within that school. Although individuals were selected for examination by the inspector they were considered to be *examples* of their class. The rigor of the classification within a particular school, together with the performance of the pupils examined, were taken to be indicative of the efficiency of a teacher, and therefore of the school (XX, 1841, Instructions, see Appendix). At a deeper level, classification was the basic unit of the pedagogical relation, since it was a core component of what was to be defined as good teaching practice. This was to consist of the teacher analyzing and classifying the constituents of an object and then the pupil reconstructing that object. Analysis and synthesis of work, graded in terms of its difficulty, would encourage a child to systematize memory, classify facts and understand 'related laws' (XX, 1841, *Minute on Constructive Methods of Teaching Reading, Writing, and Vocal Music*).

Ways of teaching, such as imitation, which would not actively engage a child's attention, were rejected since it was only through understanding the interpretation which the school was to present as correct, that children would be able to take what they had learnt beyond the confines of the schools in which they were taught (XLIV, 1850, *Gordon 1849*). This had been a problem about which philanthropic visitors to schools in England had complained (Jones and Williamson, 1979). These visitors were shocked that when they visited schools where children would be prepared to recite the ten commandments for a penny, they could see no evidence of the children either following the commandments in their daily lives, or even having understood them.

The systematization of thought, an apparently unexceptionable educational tactic for, after all, this is the basis for communication and understanding, had, as its shadowy corollary, a foreclosure on other ways of thinking and behaving, since only one mode of systematization would be acceptable. Knowledge was to be what the school presented as knowledge, and, as parents who objected to the part of the curriculum which involved their daughters scrubbing school floors, were to discover, alternative views were taken to be indicative of ignorance (LIV, 1860, *Woodford, 1859*, p. 235: XLIX, 1861, *Woodford,*

1860, p. 217). The material to be taught and the way in which it was to be taught were to be compatible with the overall purposes of regulating schools. That is to say they were to be compatible with the encouragement of authority relations which would reinforce the structure of a social world in which the interests of a few would be presented as the interests of many.

The moral value of instruction as much as, and often more than, its intellectual worth was stressed by the inspectorate (XLVII, 1856, *Gordon, 1855*). Indeed, the approach to educational theory and teaching practice of the Swiss educationalist Pestalozzi was advocated precisely in terms of its disciplinary effectiveness: '... yearly Reports have always spoken in the highest terms of the advantages ..., among which, besides the all-important one of a good handwriting acquired in a comparatively short time, the habits of order and cleanliness which it promotes have always been conspicuously mentioned' (XX, 1841, quoted from *1831, Genevese Commission on Primary Schools in Minute on Constructive Methods etc.*, p. 21).

Classification in schools was, then, a means of utilitarian control. It was held to be both economic, in that it made it possible to teach larger numbers with fewer intermediaries between pupils and head teachers as well as being quicker than other methods. Further it was efficient, since it incorporated both an overt and a hidden curriculum. Classification is therefore an example of the way in which, as Foucault (1979) has indicated (p. 176), relations of power did not operate alongside of pedagogical relations, but rather they were incorporated into them. In this way they enhanced the efficiency of teaching. This way of structuring pedagogic relations generated new problems for it required that pupils in a class have a particular pattern of attendance. This pattern of daily attendance for a set number of hours during particular weeks of the year was to become considered as *regular*. Other patterns, in consequence, were marginalized as *irregular*.

The process of imposing one pattern was not considered to be a difficulty within the regulations, since it was argued that properly organized schools would be attractive places for parents to send their children, so such schools would be attended according to the state-imposed rhythm. Once at school, habits of 'regular' attendance by the pupils would be promoted by good teaching. A poorly attended school was therefore taken to be indicative of a need for better organization (XXXIII, 1842, *Gibson [Appendix on Dunbar and Haddington] 1841*; XLIV, 1851, *Woodford, 1850*). This argument was used not only at the level of pedagogic practice, but also at the level of school management.

For example, the way in which the collection of school fees was organized was taken to influence attendance. Advance payments, rigidly and punctually enforced were seen as promoting 'regular' attendance (XXXIII, 1842, *Gibson, 1841*). Common practices, such as the weekly payment of fees, were strongly criticized on the grounds that they meant '... weekly engagements for attendance at schools; this leads to much irregularity. If the first day of a week be lost from any cause, or if it is foreseen that it will be a broken one, the child is kept away by the parents ...' (XLIV, *Woodford, 1850* , p. 741).

In respect, then, of organization and the use of anatomo-political techniques, the space created for state-regulated schooling was one form of the deployment of biopower. As such, it instigated the issue of the relationship between particular schools and the 'problem' of attendance, since the level and pattern of attendance in a school were taken as indices of the efficiency with which a teacher implemented the model procedures of the Committee of Council minutes. To this extent, attendance, considered as a problem of inadequate schools and teachers, was a temporary difficulty which would be resolved by strictly following state regulations. However, as the degree to which such practices as class teaching could be implemented was dependent on the uniformity of the pupil's attendance, a teacher's defence against a poor inspection report was frequently given as the type of community in which the school was sited (LII, 1854, *Woodford and Middleton, 1853*).

There was, therefore, a constant tension, for the problems of habits and lifestyle with which schooling was designed to deal were also given as the explanation for its failure to operate successfully. This fundamental ambiguity which generated the contradictory themes of 'inadequate schools' and 'inadequate environment' as explanations for the problems of systematizing schools, was inherent in the particular formation of a system of state-regulated schooling which was based on an incorporation and expansion of existing provision. The foundations of the 'problem' of attendance were being laid through the necessity of an inspector deciding on whether the difficulties of a particular school were caused by an 'inadequate teacher' or a 'problem community'. The basic assumption that certain environments would not be conducive to successful schooling permeated the language of inspection reports, where poverty, attendance patterns and attainment in school were frequently linked (*ibid.*). Thus, some schools were held to be good *though* their pupils belonged to the poorer classes (LII, 1854, *Middleton 1852*) while others were held not to be good *because* their pupils belonged to the poor.

Schools and Their Communities

The tight order of the state-regulated school was indicative of the belief of an elite grouping that the social world outside of the school was, for certain sectors of the population, characterized by disorder. As I indicated earlier, the creation of new forms of industrial organization were undermining traditional relations of authority, particularly those rooted in the family. Indeed, J. F. C. Harrison has noted that, 'No period in British history has been richer in movements for radical and social reform than the decades 1830–1850' (1973, p. 179). He lists: political reform, Owenite socialism, Chartism, trade unionism, factory reform, cooperation, anti-Poor Law agitation, secularism, the struggle for an unstamped press, friendly benefit societies, workers' and adult education, temperance, phrenology, vegetarianism, universal peace, the Anti-Corn Law League, anti-state church campaign, millenarianism, machine-breaking and agricultural riots.

It was also, in Scotland, a period in which there was a major redistribution of the population (Flinn, 1977). Rapid urbanization during the first three decades of the century had meant that by the early 1840s a third of the people lived in towns of over 5000 inhabitants.

Industrialization was one factor contributing to population movement, but others were also involved — for example, the waves of emigration (early 1830s, late 1840s, 1850s) and heavy Irish immigration in the 1840s were related to failures in the potato crop; landlords in some areas shifted tenants to shore districts in order to work at lucrative kelping; and of course the Highland Clearances had a radical impact on the distribution in certain areas. Internal migration was also important, and though inter-regional movement was light, movement *within* regions was more extensive. Therefore, though some parishes increased their population, only in the Lowlands did in-migration mean that the population grew faster than the natural increase.

On a superficial level, these changes led some critics of the provision of parochial schools to point out that in some areas with a large population there might be no parochial school, whereas in areas where the population had diminished drastically, a school might be only partially full (Myers, 1970, p. 40 quotes one source estimating that a result of the 1843 Disruption was a doubling of the number of schools). At a deeper level, the belief that an ordered environment meant the eradication of problems was the counterpart of the view that social problems were problems of a world which was not strictly enough organized. State organization of schooling was the means of dealing

Population of Scotland by Regions 1801–1901: Percentage of Total Population

Year	Far North	Highland counties	North-east	Western Lowlands	Eastern Lowlands	Borders
1801	4.3	15.2	13.7	20.6	34.6	11.5
1811	3.8	14.4	13.1	22.8	34.3	11.5
1821	3.9	14.0	12.8	24.4	33.6	11.2
1831	3.9	13.1	12.7	26.6	33.2	10.4
1841	3.7	12.0	12.2	30.2	32.3	9.6
1851	3.5	10.8	12.1	32.1	32.1	9.4
1861	3.4	9.5	12.0	34.6	31.5	8.9
1871	3.1	8.5	11.8	37.0	31.6	8.1
1881	2.7	7.7	11.2	39.1	31.7	7.6
1891	2.4	7.0	10.8	41.2	31.7	6.9
1901	2.0	6.3	10.3	44.2	31.3	5.9

Derived from Flinn, M. W. (Ed.) (1977) *Scottish Population History*, Cambridge, Cambridge University Press, p. 306, table 5.1.3 based on census data.

Urbanized Proportion of the Total Population

Census	Percentage of total population in centres of 5000 or over	Percentage increase over previous decade	Percentage of total population in centres of 1000 or over
1801	21.0	—	
1811	24.2	29.4	
1821	27.5	31.7	
1831	31.2	28.2	
1841	32.7	16.2	
1851	35.9	17.3	
1861	39.4	16.2	57.7
1871	44.4	23.6	
1881	48.9	12.8	
1891	53.5	17.6	
1901	57.6	19.7	74.3

Source: *ibid*.

with these. By creating a *certain* structure in a world where uncertain relations were held to threaten existing order, schools were to be constituted as places of safety — havens which would secure future generations from these external dangers.

Spatially, one way of securing a school's exemplary status as a purveyor of a healthy and morally correct way of life, as well as ensuring its accessibility to the population, was the stipulation by the minutes that the school had to be in a central location which was free from the dangers of moral and physical pollution (XL, 1840, *Plans of School-Houses, 1840*). Draughts, dampness, overcrowding and poor ventilation were frequent complaints of working class housing generally at this time (Gauldie, 1976). They were also endemic in many schools. Since problems of the environment were considered to be essentially problems of the habits and life-styles of the poor (Jones and Williamson, 1979), the improvement in school buildings would also be a means of revealing to the local population the kind of action which would make possible the eradication of these problems in their homes. For schooling was seen as 'part of a compact and comprehensive scheme for the amelioration of a particular district ...' (XXXV, 1845, *Gibson, 1845*, p. 157).

The school playground was considered to be a buffer between the school and the community. 'In the absence of a school playground, the street becomes the resort of the children after school hours; ... they meet with vicious men and women, and with children of their own age, who have been corrupted by vicious parents, or other bad example, or even children trained to desperate courses by thieves ... ' (XL, 1840, *Minute, 20 February 1840*, p. 32). It was not simply to be a place of recreation. This view was criticized by inspectors who complained about people who failed to understand the 'educational' function of the playground and who thought that any vacant adjacent ground could substitute for this (XXXIII, 1842, *Gibson, 1842, (Aberdeen & Fordyce)*, p. 215). It was to protect the children from undesirable influences while at the same time helping to extend the teacher's influence beyond school hours. By watching or participating in the children's activities a teacher could find out about their characters and in so doing, extend the moral influence of the schoolroom (XL, 1840, *Minutes, 20 February, 1840*).

At the same time, the dangers of the external environment posed a threat to the security of schooling, therefore the creation of a safety zone to which children could be attracted was not enough. If schools were to provide an ordered setting, there has to be a means of ensuring that the order of the school would radiate outwards and become conterminous with that of the community. What had to be avoided was either contamination by the turmoil of the environment or the school remaining an island of appropriate relations within chaotic surroundings. There was, then, an inherent tension in the relations which schools were to have with their locality: the strategy of schooling as an intervention aimed at crystallizing relations of authority was fraught with ambiguity.

Teachers were to encourage children to spend as much time as possible with them to 'increase the beneficial influence which his own more eleveated mind' (*ibid.*) would have on their thoughts and habits in order to counteract the 'effects of evil example at the child's home' and provide 'better than paternal care' (*ibid.*). Constructed as a disciplinary mechanism, structured through new forms of power relations, school-ing undermined older relations of authority — that is, those of the family — yet, at the same time, it was precisely in terms of familial relations that it was legitimated. This paradox will be discussed more fully in chapter 6. For the present I shall only note that the creation of this disciplinary regime, part of the restructuring of socio-economic relations which was involved in the separation of 'work' from 'home', carried within it a particular view of an ideal *form* of family life: an ordered domestic sphere under maternal supervision, with the father providing for the household's overall security through participation in work outside the home. The further away that particular home environments were from this ideal-typical notion of family life, the more difficult but more important was the role of the school.

Regulation enabled state mediation between relations of the family and education and was instrumental in structuring them in accordance with a particular view of the sexual and social division of labour. (David, 1980, argues that this *sustains* the sexual and social division of labour. However, as I argued earlier, state regulation had a dynamic anticipatory dimension. Therefore what is being dealt with here is *production* as well as reproduction.) Systematic state involvement enabled the development of schooling as a technique for rendering visible and therefore potentially accessible to change, the minutiae of habits and beliefs of large sections of the population.

The encouragement of children to spend time outside school hours in the vicinity of the school was extended to the encouragement of communication with the parents to secure a continuity in methods of dealing with the children by coopting parents to support the work of the school through their actions in the home (XX, 1841, *Instructions to Inspectors, 1840*). Teachers who visited the homes of their pupils to find out more about them were held up as exemplary in inspection reports (XLIV, 1850, *Gordon Report, 1848–9*). These visits were double-edged for they both facilitated the consideration of the particular circum-stances of individual children and made it possible to attempt to influence relationships in the home in favour of the institutional and hierarchical demands of schooling (*ibid.*).

This attempt to mould relations within the family and, at the same time, to structure their links with the school provided the bedrock for later discussions about the rights and duties of parents in respect of education. The incorporation of the family was a logical extension of the panoptic principle. Put another way, the problems of providing a correct upbringing for a class's juvenile members, as constructed in the moral topographical arguments, necessitated the structuring of what Althusser has referred to as the family-school couple (Althusser, 1972). Together, the family and the school were constitutive of what was held to be the appropriate environment for children. The extent to which it was acceptable for children to work outside the home was dependent on the financial circumstances of the family, that is, it was viewed as a necessary evil for poor families. 'Good' parents, it was held, would endeavour to have their children attend school whenever possible. Problem parents would not, though they were held to be a temporary problem, since it was argued that once children had experienced the benefits of state-regulated schooling they would come to recognize its value and, as the parents of the following generations, would encourage their off-spring to attend (XXXIII, 1842, *Gibson, 1842*).

The stress on the importance of family-school harmony in ways of dealing with children was a fundamental aim of state schooling. There was no ambiguity about the nature of this link: the tune was not to be called by the family but by the school. This was illustrated by the problem of school fees. Fees were usually a teacher's only income. This gave the teacher a vulnerablity to the community in their locality which contravened the state view of appropriate relations between the two. For while the official view was that the teacher ought to be regarded as an authoritative figure in a community, inspectors complained that in some areas parents regarded themselves as doing the teacher a favour if they sent their children to school and paid their fees. This was compounded by instances of parents trying to influence what went on in schools by threatening to withdraw their children or withhold payments of fees if their demands were not met.

Suggestions for securing the authoritative balance, such as the deduction of wages at source, from the wages of workers and their subsequent payment to the teacher by the employer were only feasible in some cases. (Carron Iron Works and the mining stations at Sauchie and Barrowstowness were mentioned favourably for having this type of arrangement. [XXXII, 1846, *Gordon, 1846*; L, 1847-8, *Gordon, 1847*]). The suggestion from inspectors was that teachers were sometimes dealing with this by falsifying their returns, claiming to receive fees which they ought to have been paid rather than those which were actually realized, since without a minimum of fees they would not even be eligible for a grant (LIV, 1860, *Woodford, 1859*). There was, then, a twist to the problem of encouraging uniformity of school organization by providing a model to be copied: the impression of following the regulations might be managed sufficiently to pass an inspection without the rules necessarily being followed when the inspector was no longer there.

The creation of a specialized space for schooling was part of the compartmentalization of living which was crystallizing at this time. Based on the principle of panopticism, the focus on discipline made possible the structuring of problems of the social order as problems of education. When visiting a school, an inspector would have to decide whether difficulties were caused by the school — therefore possibly lowering or withholding the grant until matters were changed, or whether they were owing to circumstances beyond the school's control; in which case full money would be given and possibly sympathetic bending of the rules.

The discussion so far has been based on the claim that the setting up of a model of what a good school ought to be like made it possible for a state agency to structure the organization of schools. What are the implications of the discretion mentioned above, and the exceptions which were recognized to the rule that no plans could be accepted which precluded the possibility of, at some stage, being brought into line with education office requirements? These exceptions underline the significance of schooling as an area of life under control; for they were to be made in 'poor and populous places' (XXXVIII, 1844, *Grants in Poor and Populous Places, 22 November, 1843*). For it was in such areas that it was seen as most vital that a foothold of disciplinary influence should be gained. The reason, it had earlier been argued, was that '... there is a large class of children ... I mean pauper orphans, children deserted by their parents, and the offspring of criminals and their associates; ... (from whom) the thieves and housebreakers of society are continually recruited ... (and who have) filled the workhouses with ignorant and idle inmates' (XLI, 1839, *Letter from Russell*). Put another way, schools were to be substitutes for home environments which were held to be inadequate either because of an absence of authority relations of the family or because existing relations would not provide for the correct upbringing of children since the parents were outside the law.

Unsupervised schools would do harm to children from adequate home backgrounds ('poor but virtuous parents'), for others any school would be better than no school as the children could not come to any more harm in school than out of it. Once accepted for some form of financial aid the school managers could be put under pressure to make changes. (A series of minutes was passed which made the initial process of accepting grant applications more flexible – 2 April 1853 (England and Wales only); 20 August 1853; 14 July 1855 extended grants to deal with improvements to old premises. Also XLVII, 1856, *Circular to Inspectors, 7 August 1855*, p. 34).

The significance of the regulation of space is therefore reinforced rather than undermined. For this flexibility indicates that the implementation of regulation would be mediated through the exigencies of particular situations and that it would be increased in areas which were held to be particularly threatening for social order. The creation of a specialist space for schooling made possible the structuring of particular formal identities through which the relations of a class of the population were to be structured. For the disciplinary organization was designed to enable pupils to learn their place in the wider social order and to understand that it was ultimately beneficial as well as necessary for that order to take a particular form. In other words, structured as an *example* to the local community, the discipline of the school-room was to foster a disciplined way of life. The hierarchical organization of schools was presented as both a *means of engendering* appropriate social relations within the population, and a *reflection* of such relations. 'The class supplies in its own way occasions of duty, discipline and struggle, which are the very type of those that shall turn up in the future progress of life' (XXXIII, 1857, *Gordon, 1856*, p. 644).

A major facet of the implementation of the programmes of power which I discussed in chapter 3 was the production and structuring of a specialized space for schooling. The outline which I have given of what was involved in doing this is basic to any attempt to understand the social map of truancy for it reveals the creation of an ordered setting where people and actions would be under authorized control, and the way in which this control was to be extended to the family. I have suggested, during the course of the discussion that the creation of this space carried with it the structuring of particular social identities. For example, new forms of authority relations, based on discipline, were to restructure older relations of the family. In conjunction with one particular form of the family, schooling was to structure the lives of the juvenile members of the working class and consequently to sustain a social order compatible with industrial capitalism. A child not at school was therefore out of place, not merely failing to learn appropriate relations of authority, but participating in a world of disorder, beyond control.

Chapter 5

Professionalism and Teaching: Programmes and Strategies

Introduction

The construction of mechanisms designed to regulate schooling was, as I have argued, an aspect of more general activities within the state which were directed towards the production of a stable social order. An important consequence of this has been the generation of an officially sanctioned version of normality and the marginalization of alternatives to this. It is through this process that deviance is produced. For this reason my account of the production of knowledge refers firstly to the social map of normality set out in chapter 1 and secondly to the social map of deviance which I described there. An important result of the organization of a place for schooling being based on a theory of moral action was that it involved setting an agenda for acceptable behaviour for those who were located in schools.

In this chapter I shall look at the way in which state regulation contributed to the production of the formal identities of those who were to operate schools, that is, the teachers. For the formal identity of teacher refers to a key agent of the disciplinary regime and is therefore an important feature of the social map of the child. In doing this, I shall be exploring discipline as, '... the specific technique of power that regards individuals both as objects and as instruments of its exercise' (Foucault, 1979, p. 170). Teachers were strategically sited between state officials and those sectors of the population whose social relations were to be restructured by schooling. An illustration of tensions inherent in this position is the ambiguous identity of the teaching occupation.

Teachers were officially considered to be agents of the state and state action involved officials in mobilizing 'professionalism' as a resource for the improvement of the status of teachers. There are parallels in this process with features of Weber's characterization of the state as being able to exercise a monopoly over the legitimate and organized use of force within a given territory. For official mobilization of professionalism involved claiming, on behalf of the state, a monopoly of the legitimate authorization of the specialized knowledge and competence involved in 'professionalism'. When made by members of an occupational group, this kind of claim is a distinctive feature of a profession (Friedson, 1975). By means of this, entry to it can be controlled and its market position secured. However, the autonomy of a profession is *relative* to relations of state power since this autonomy is *granted* by the state to an occupational grouping. It was the failure of teachers to achieve this autonomy which has led to teaching remaining of uncertain professional status.

For the purposes of my argument it is important to distinguish two aspects of the authority claim of 'professionalism': firstly, it involves a claim to a particular *social status*, that of the 'professional'; secondly, it involves a claim to a monopoly of the legitimate employment of specialist resources of knowledge/power in social relations which have, as a focal concern, the particular knowledge/skills from which the given professionalism is derived. Which is to say that it is also a claim to a *political resource*. By making this distinction, I shall be able to explain more clearly the contradiction which was embodied in professionalism as a programme of state power. This contradiction meant that, although the teachers' programme of professionalism followed the pattern of other occupations, the programme of state power to maintain teachers as employed functionaries pressured the professional association of teachers in Scotland into a trade union identity.

I shall begin my discussion of this when I look at the professional programmes which were embedded within state discourse. For these were to be a means of underpinning the incorporation of teachers as state agents. Here I maintain that state action in relation to teaching helped to structure it as an occupation carried on by people trained to hold an authoritative position within the officially promoted organization of schooling. As part of this a career structure was developed which specified the relationship which was to be encouraged between the school, as personified by the teacher, and the community of which it was to be a part. The state programme was directed at the status of teaching. It involved a concern with the siting and training of teachers and with the use of the examination as a mechanism for raising their status as well as for certifying their specialist knowledge.

However, as I shall show, this programme of professionalism embodied a contradiction. This will be displayed in the final section of this chapter. For professionalism was used as a resource by teachers within their struggle for autonomy. This struggle was directed towards resisting their incorporation as state functionaries and towards challenging state claims to legitimate authority in issues of education. Unlike the state programme, which focused on the social status of teaching, the strategy of teachers also involved a claim to a political resource and was therefore directed at the promotion of *both* aspects of professionalism. By drawing attention to the way in which teachers rejected being identified as state agents and acted to resist incorporation, this section illustrates a dissonance, generated by the success of the state programme of professionalism between the state-structured formal identity of teacher and the informed identities of some of the people involved in teaching. However, before doing this I shall need to explain what the occupation of teaching was like prior to state intervention. To do this I shall draw directly on the historical research which has been carried out on Scottish teachers by Myers (1970).

Teaching

As an example to the local community in terms of moral topography, the school was to provide for the correct upbringing of the juvenile members of the lower classes. For '... there is tendency in the occupations connected with some of the branches of industry ... to impair the character of domestic education among the labouring classes; and the remedy was looked for in the school' (XLV, 1847, Gordon Report on Edinburgh and Glasgow Normal Schools, p. 526). Since it was, 'a place not merely of instruction, but of general education — as appropriating in fact, somewhat more of the office of the parent. It followed that the general character and manners of the masters became to the promoters of schools a matter of still greater interest than before; and the same could be, at once, discovered and formed, or in some degree influenced, in the Normal school' (*ibid.*).

I have already indicated that prior to the intervention of the state the social identity of teachers was more fluid, for 'teacher' was an umbrella term, referring to people of varying status with a wide range of backgrounds. This is reflected in the range of teacher incomes. Myers (1970) has argued that university professors, burgh and academy teachers, a few adventure school teachers and a very few parochial schoolmasters had incomes which were equivalent to those in middle class occupations such as clergy, doctors and lawyers. These would constitute the top income group and those within it would earn about £100 and over per year (*ibid.*, p. 86). He maintains that most parochial, some subscription, sessional and non-parochial teachers would have lower incomes than this, earning around £50 to £100 a year, which would be equivalent to a lower middle class income. Although one contemporary description of the salaries of parochial teachers stated,

> The salary of the master is fixed at a sum not less than the value of one chalder and a half of oatmeal [a chalder was a dry measure equivalent to about 3490 litres], nor more than the value of two chalders — the value being determined by the average price of grain throughout Scotland in the 25 years preceeding and amounting at the present time in the one case to 25l. 13s. 4d., and in the other to 34l. 4s. 4d. The salary is payable by the heritors [local landowners] ... In parishes of great extent, the salary may be apportioned among two or more teachers; in which case it is raised to the value of 3 chalders (51l. 6s. 7d.)... (XXXV, 1845, Gordon, 1845, p. 168)

Nonetheless, '... the bulk of the Scottish teachers would have been struggling to survive at a lower class economic level, while striving to attain a socially middle class position' (Myers, 1970, p. 86). For people in this last group earnings could be well below the £50 level. For example, a General Assembly Education Committee enquiry into schools in Scotland at this time found that for those schools reported as offering an income of less than £35 a year there was an average income of £19. They found that from fifty-four of this group the annual income possible was reported as being less than £10. For 322 it was between £10 and £20, and for twenty-eight was between £20 and £35. 'From this pittance the teachers have, in very many instances, to provide the accommodations of a school-room and dwelling-house for themselves; and, in others, a free school-room is the only advantage of the kind which they possess' (XXXV, 1845, Gordon, 1845, p. 175).

In comparison, the income of a minister in 1834 had the range of £150 –£500 per annum, with an average of about £200. The average wages in 1850 for a farm labourer were £23–£30 per annum; those for skilled workers were about £52 per annum. Generally speaking then, a teacher earned more than a farm worker and an unskilled labourer, and about the same as or less than artisans, skilled factory workers and small businessmen (Myers, 1970, p. 47). It is not clear what the levels of pay were for women who taught since Myers does not make a gender distinction. Although he notes that, according to contemporary observers, female pupil teachers tended to come from higher social classes than males.[1]

The level of income which was generally possible from teaching therefore, often meant that teachers also had other occupations. For example, in rural areas the person who taught at some times of the year might have a different occupation at others, such as during the harvest. Alternatively, in districts too poor to support a teacher, someone, such as a pupil from another school, would sometimes go and teach. Parochial teachers were often also expected to be heritor's clerk/session clerk. These jobs did not involve much work (for example, the heritor's clerk would attend meetings of the local landowners and these took place about once or twice a year) and could offer a little extra income (about £3 a year according to Gordon, *ibid.*).[2] Frequently trainee ministers would teach during the vacations of their divinity courses and after they had finished their courses they would teach while waiting to take up a permanent church appointment. This happened to such an extent that it was suggested at one point that the divinity session should be altered as it fell when schools were best attended, and when older scholars and other adequate substitute teachers were hardest to obtain (XLIX, 1861, *Middleton*, 1860).

The diversity of this social grouping can be illustrated further by looking at their experience prior to teaching. Scotland had a reputation for having proportionately more teachers with university experience than other parts of Britain. However, though this may have been the case, its impact is difficult to ascertain. For example, though Davie (1961) claims that a third of parochial teachers had been through college, Myers (1970) points out that this high figure is related to the large number of 'stickit ministers'. These were candidates for the Ministry who taught part time in parish schools while attending university, and full-time while awaiting a parish appointment. Further, it should not be assumed that the significance of attending university in nineteenth century Scotland was the same as it is in the twentieth century. Students would go to university young (for example, some went at 12) and spend time doing what would today be considered as secondary school level work: the emphasis was on having *attended* university as much as, if not more than, graduation. (See *ibid.* for a more detailed account; also, McCrone *et al.*, 1981.)

The teaching jobs with the highest status were those in burgh schools, Dick Bequest schools and parochial schools. These had security of tenure at a time when most teaching jobs were on a short term contract basis. These posts tended to be held by those with higher qualifications, that is, graduates and those who had attended university. It has been estimated by Myers (1970) that in the 1860s a third to a half of parochial teachers had some university experience. There was also some teacher training provided by the established church, though this was neither widespread nor systematic. Thus, a model infant school was established in Glasgow in 1826–27 to which was added, in 1831, a juvenile model school; both were set up to train teachers, and by 1838 they had trained about 200 (XLII, 1854–5, Woodford, 1854, p. 684). The General Assembly's Education Committee also provided some teacher training in the Edinburgh sessional school where, from 1826, they sent teachers who were appointed to their Highland schools. As with the situation in the universities, teacher training in this period differed from its later form, in that there was no training programme for training consisted of the teachers observing 'the most approved methods of teaching' (*ibid.*). Further, teachers attended only for as long as they felt was either necessary or convenient (*ibid.*).

It is not possible to give exact figures for the number of people teaching in Scotland at this time. However, it has been estimated that in 1815 there were about 2000 and that by mid-century the figure was approximately 5000 (Myers, 1970).[3] Part of the dramatic increase in numbers can be attributed to the Disruption of 1843 when a section of the established church broke away to form the Free Church of Scotland. This was because teachers in parochial schools had to be affiliated to the established church. Therefore immediately after the Disruption schools were set up in which those teachers who were in sympathy with the Free church, could work. One writer (Saunders) has estimated that this doubled the number of schools. Although figures should be treated with caution, it would seem fair to say that the impact of what little training there was available is likely to have been minimal. If contemporary commentators are taken into account then it is possible to get an impressionistic idea of the range of the standard of teachers at this time. It seems that they were an amorphous group, in terms of pre-teaching experience ranging from graduates through 'stickit' ministers, local widows and spinsters running so-called dame schools in their kitchens, disabled soldiers and failed business men, holding schools in lofts and sheds (Myers, 1970).

This variability of the extent to which teaching constituted a distinct occupation was to be the target of state policy in the regulation of teaching. 'Formerly the parochial schoolmaster might be picked up wherever he could be found, and provided the presbytery by private examination found him qualified to teach the branches required to be taught in the particular parish, his previous occupation or training was of no consequence' (XLVII, 1856, *Cumming & Wilson, 1854*, p. 601). State inspectors were instructed to ask questions about a teacher's other occupations. This meant finding out both about their occupation prior to their current appointment, and about any which was contemporaneous with it (see questions 114–6 in Appendix). Restrictions on the activities of a teacher were introduced so that it became permissible to engage in only a limited range of other occupations without affecting the eligibility of their school for financial aid.[4] But teaching was promoted as a distinct occupation primarily through the mobilization of professionalism as a programme of power.

Professional Programmes

This mobilization of professionalism and the incorporation as state agents of those who taught, were central to state activity in structuring the formal identity of teachers. The official fostering of a power-form which is derived from claims to specialized knowledge and competence should not be seen as an indication that the programmes which I have already discussed were being supplanted. Rather it needs to be understood as involving the mobilization of professionalism as a resource for the improvement of the social status of teachers. Consequently it was *supplementary* to the fundamental programmes which were embedded in the construction of the mechanisms for regulating schooling.

A profession involves specialized knowledge and skills which are learned by means of formal training; it has a service orientation, as well as a self-regulated ethical code. Within the literature on professions, professional prestige and autonomy are assumed to flow from the specialized competence and the service orientation. However, Larson (1979) has argued that writers have often simply accepted the assumptions implicit in the ways in which professions present themselves, instead of critically examining them. By unquestioningly importing the self-justification of professional privilege into the sociological ideal-type, such accounts end up by merely reproducing the preferred self-image of professionals.

Most approaches to professions derive their ideal-type from the medical and legal professions and they neglect to consider the extent to which programmes of professionalism may involve competing claims to territorial competence. For example, in relation to the medical profession, midwives and doctors contest the legitimacy of each others' territorial claim over women in childbirth. In other words, there is a failure to identify 'profession' as involving areas of contested legitimacy. This is linked with the stress which is given within this work to a functional relation with 'central social needs and values'. There is a focus on the knowledge and service dimensions, and a tendency to assume that professions have a neutrality in respect of the class structure in which they are placed. However, 'The ideal-typical approach seldom takes account of the concrete historical conditions in which groups of specialists have attempted to establish a monopoly over specific areas of the division labour' (*ibid.*, p. xiii).

In contrast, Larson has pointed out that, 'As it rises, an occupation must form "organic" ties with significant fractions of the ruling class (or of a rising class); persuasion and justification depend on ideological resources, ... special bodies of experts are entrusted with the task of defining a segment of social reality, but this trust is also to be understood within the broad confines of the dominant ideology' (*ibid.*, p. xv). Professionalization is a process through which particular groups attempt to structure and control markets for their services and, thus, to translate the scarce resource of their expertise into the scarce resources of social and economic rewards. This process, which began in the nineteenth century, and which involved *collective* social mobility for particular occupational groupings was thus implicated in the structuring of a new kind of social inequality, based on a system of credentialling and involving *individual* mobility within an occupational hierarchy.

> By 1860, or thereabouts, the elements of professional standing were tolerably clear. You needed a professional association to focus opinion, work up a body of knowledge, and insist upon a decent standard of conduct. If possible, and as soon as possible, it should have a Royal Charter, as a mark of recognition. The final step, if you could manage it — it was very difficult — was to persuade Parliament to pass an Act conferring something like monopoly powers on duly qualified practitioners who had followed a recognized course of training and passed recognized examinations (Reader, 1966, quoted in Myers, 1970, p. 174).

The central components of the programme of professionalism in the mid-nineteenth century consist of: (i) an association specifically concerned with (ii) the demarcation of specialized knowledge and competence; (iii) the regulation of a generally recognized means of acquiring these, that is, training; (iv) the provision of the means of publicly displaying this through examination and certification; (v) the setting of general standards of conduct; and (vi) the claiming of monopoly powers of practice for qualified practitioners.

State action in relation to teachers can be seen as demonstrating a concern with all except the first of these components. There were several ways in which official action to structure the formal identity of teacher promoted professionalism. For example, through a concern with the correct siting and the provision of specialist training for teachers. The promotion of this was furthered by the introduction of the examination as a mechanism for raising the status of teachers, through certifying their specialist knowledge. The possession of this was to become a pre-condition for someone being able to teach.

As I argued earlier, since types of conduct were held to be linked to features of an environment, state intervention into schooling was constructed in terms of a concern to create a particular space for schooling. The architectural features of the state-planned schools, based on the segmentation and visibility of the participants in schooling, would predispose people to approved moral action. Within this space the correct upbringing for the juvenile members of the poorer classes was to be provided. This schooling was directly to structure the behaviour of the immediate participants, and indirectly to structure that of the community in which it was sited. For schools were to be both a model for and a reflection of appropriate social relations.

Training Teachers

The wide biographical range and poor calibre of teachers and candidates for teaching posts (XLV, 1847, *Gordon, Report on Edinburgh and Glasgow Normal Schools*) can be understood, in moral topographical terms, as a problem of sites which would enable teachers to be correctly trained. There were two main sites officially considered to be appropriate for this: the elementary school itself; and the Normal school, which today would be referred to as teacher training college. Within the elementary school, 'the employment of pupil teachers is seen to have certain incidental advantages ... The master, in supplying their instruction in its later stages, finds an opportunity of improving his own knowledge. ... And, from the increase of teaching power, the school-room has an appearance of improved order, industry and discipline — though this might be as well mentioned among the designed and chief uses of the pupil-teacher system' (XLIX, 1861, *Gordon, 1860*, p. 23–4).

This is the self-sustaining hierarchy of a disciplinary regime: aimed at teaching pupils, the school was also to produce pupil teachers who, by their presence, would improve the teacher. A five-year apprenticeship, the pupil teacher system would incorporate older pupils through an annual grant. In this way it would encourage those who might otherwise leave, to extend their schooling and to participate at a higher level in the hierarchical relay of power relations. (Those who successfully completed apprenticeships could be employed as assistant teachers (Minute 23 July 1852) with an annual stipend of £25 for males and £20 for females, and could take a certificate of merit after another three years.) Nevertheless, the system of pupil teachers was primarily aimed at recruitment for Normal school and at the end of this apprenticeship, it was argued, these pupil teachers would have been sufficiently prepared to enable them to be candidates for this. The intention was that at the end of their apprenticeship people would sit a public examination, conducted by an inspector, in order to get a Queen's Scholarship — a grant for attending Normal school (usually £20–£25).

It was a condition of a pupil being accepted into the apprenticeship that their home background was vetted to make sure that it was in accordance with what was being promoted within schools. If it was not acceptable then the pupil could be required to board in an approved household (XLV, 1847, *Regulations Respecting the Education of Pupil Teachers and Stipendiary Monitors*, 21 December 1846). Nonetheless, the trainees tended to remain in the local community. One drawback of this was that they would not, therefore, have access to the 'cultural setting' (XLV, 1847, *Gordon, Report on Edinburgh and Glasgow Normal Schools*) which was necessary for them if they were to be able to fulfil the exemplary role which it was officially maintained that teachers ought to fulfil (*ibid.*). Officially it was argued that, 'the first, and very often the last point of their career at which they are brought into intimate and domestic contact with persons of superior cultivation, and are obliged to conform to a higher standard of manners and habits, is in the normal college' (LI, 1854, *Circular Letter to Inspectors*, 26 November 1853, p. 28). To have this access teachers would have to train outside of their local environment within the Normal school.

The regime of the Normal school was to be an extended version of that which was to be created in elementary schools. Ideally, it was to constitute what Goffman (1968) has called a 'total institution', so that all aspects of a trainee's life could be visible, and therefore accessible to alteration, during their period at the establishment. Although Edinburgh and Glasgow Normal schools were not residential their time-

TIMETABLE FOR EDINBURGH NORMAL SCHOOL

APPENDIX III.

NO. 1.—TIME TABLE FOR THE NORMAL STUDENTS, Edinburgh, February 1847.

Hours	Monday	Tuesday	Wednesday	Thursday	Friday	Saturday	Sunday
A M							
6–7	Dress and put rooms in order.						
7–8	Private study and preparation in Library.						
8–8	¹Prayers—Psalmody; Scripture reading and exposition; Prayer.						
8–9	Breakfast.						
9–10	²English Reading and advanced Geography.	¹McCulloch's Course; special attention to the subject of Reading; Bible Lesson of the day given by Rector, or one of the Students.	²English Reading and Etymology.	¹McCulloch's Course; special attention to the analysis of sentences; Bible Lesson of the day given by Rector, or one of the Students.	¹Lecture on Pedagogics; Themes prescribed, and Exercises returned, with Comments; Physical Geography, with use of Globes.	⁵Sacred Music.	¹Bible History and Doctrine, 9–10.
A M P.M.							
10–3		See Elementary School Time Table.					
3–4	¹Latin Rudiments, Delectus, and Caesar.	¹Senior Students: Virgil, and Adams' Antiquites. ²Junior Students: Elementary Grammar and Geography.	¹Latin Rudiments, Delectus, and Caesar.	Same as on Tuesday.	Same as Tuesday.		
4–6	Dinner and Recreation.						
6–7	⁴Gaelic Students with Master; the others at private study.					Private study.	
7–8	³Euclid {Senior Section, Book IV.—Algebra, Trigonometry. Junior Section, Book I.—Arithmetic, Algebra.					Private study.	
8–9	Supper.						
9–9	¹Prayers.						
9–10	Private Reading; ¹occasional revisal of Latin Rudiments by Junior Students.						¹Abstracts of Discourses given in and revised.
10	Retire for the night. Gas extinguished at 11.						

¹Denotes that the Lesson or Exercise is conducted by the Rector.   ²Head Master.   ³Mathematical Tutor.   ⁴Gaelic Tutor.   ⁵Singing Master.

Source: XLV 1847

tables reveal that students' time was almost totally regulated, leaving little free time.

It is fundamental to total institutions that the barriers which ordinarily separate sleep, work and play are broken down. This increases the pressures for conformity in all spheres of existence.

> First, all aspects of life are conducted in the same place under the same single authority. Second, each phase of the member's daily activity is carried on in the immediate company of a large batch of others, all of whom are treated alike and required to do the same thing together. Third, all phases of the day's activities are tightly scheduled, with one activity leading at a prearranged time into the next, the whole sequence of activities being imposed from above by a system of explicit formal rulings and a body of officials. Finally, the various enforced activities are brought together into a single rational plan purportedly designed to fulfil the official aims of the institution ... When persons are moved in blocks, they can be supervised ... one person's infraction is likely to stand out in relief against the visible, constantly examined compliance of others'. (Goffman, 1968, pp. 6 −7).

Along with the allocation of duties and economic rewards in such places, come the allocation of character and being (*ibid.*, p. 111).

This was an important difference from the situation in the elementary school which was specifically involved in the *compartmentalization* of areas of life and, in particular, the separation of education from 'life'. The elementary school was designed, not only to socialize pupils but also to attract others in the locality to its ambit. Although it was aimed internally at its pupils, externally it was concerned, in a more general way, with the wider social world. This was why the notion of total institutions for providing elementary schooling was specifically rejected (XLVII, 1856, *Correspondence of Committee of Council*, 8 December, 1855, p. 30). In contrast, the Normal school had one aim: the training of teachers, not simply to occupy the teaching role during school hours, but to epitomize appropriate behaviour in their whole way of life. Normal schooling was, then, to structure the social identity of teachers by moulding the in-formed identities of people teaching in accordance with the official model.

As models for the communities in which they worked, teachers were to take the example for their own behaviour from outside these localities. Most teachers, especially after the extension of training and recruitment to pupil teachers, came from areas considered to have moral topographical problems. By definition, therefore, they were held to have had the upbringing which schools were to attempt to alter. It was therefore important to remove trainee teachers from such local influences. There is a remarkable parallel here with people sent to Reformatories and Industrial Schools for, along with the candidates for Normal schools, they shared the characteristic of having home environments which were thought to be unsuitable for appropriate identity formation. Environment was considered to be so influential that children from areas where there was little possibility of mixing with those whose mores would be acceptable to the authorities, would, it was believed, be involved in the least acceptable behaviour. The behaviour itself was seen as a sign of such an environment. For these children, residential schooling provided a solution, by isolating them from the problematic surroundings, and therefore enabling the teacher to act 'in loco parentis'. Because of the amount of surveillance possible, it was suggested that children from these establishments would be ideal to become future teachers. XL, 1840, p. 22.

The insistence on a specialist space for the correct formation of teachers was important both for consolidating the state version of what constituted good teaching and for crystallizing particular positions for teachers and pupils within the hierarchical relations of the disciplinary regime. The status of teachers outside schools would, it was held, be improved by these measures (*ibid.*). In order to assess the implications of this in terms of the social identity of teachers and the professionalization of teaching it is necessary to consider the disciplinary strategy of the examination.

I pointed out in chapter 4 that within a disciplinary regime, an internalized control of 'correct' individual behaviour was promoted through the visibility of social action and the segmentation of space. These are also techniques which enable discipline to be articulated through judgments about the normality of social action. Officially appearing first not in individual schools, but in the *system* of schooling, the examination was a technique for reinforcing the power relations embodied in the architectural arrangements of schools. It extended their automatic functioning beyond the level of a particular institution. Examinations were fundamental to the knowledge and competence claims of professionalism and it was through this that they operated to legitimate relations of authority.

The impact of the normalizing judgment embedded within the examination needs to be understood firstly in relation to segmentation.

In the short interval between 1839 and 1855 (by this date, the Committee of Council insisted that all teachers in state-aided schools were to be part of this hierarchy) there was a shift from the amorphous grouping of people referred to by the umbrella term 'teacher', to a clear career structure for the members of the teaching profession. No longer simply teachers, but certificated teachers who were graded as first, second, or third class, registered teachers, assistant teachers, Queen's Scholars, pupil teachers — first to fifth year, stipendiary monitors — first to fourth year. Each title indicates a position within the network of the schooling system, duties to be carried out within a particular school, and knowledge and skills which an individual would be expected to have. Segmentation meant that they could be immediately compared by positioning trainee teachers, both vertically and horizontally, within the network of relations which constituted the schooling system.

Secondly, it should be understood as facilitating visibility since it made it compulsory that people's occupational profiles should be signified in a clear relation to the system of schooling. Although the inspector's visit to a school could be seen as a form of examination, it differed from this new mutation which was involved in the ordering of teachers. When inspectors visited schools they examined samples of classwork, not individual performances; there was no set syllabus to be covered and there were no carefully demarcated stages for working through it; written records were minimal. In contrast, the examination as a means of assessing trainee teachers, consisted of written questions related to a formal syllabus which was divided into stages. The written answers were marked by the inspectorate. A formalized knowledge displayed in a written record, answers to exam questions provided proof of the transference between teacher and trainee of what was to be known (Foucault, 1979, p. 187). Initially the setting of examinations for pupil teachers who were apprenticed to teachers in elementary schools, was aimed at assessing the efforts of the *teacher in charge* in giving them proper instruction (XXXIII, 1857, *Circular to Inspectors*, 4 March, p. 34). The results provided visible evidence of that which would otherwise have to go on trust. Poor results were seen as a reason for curtailing a teacher's participation in the training of pupil teachers (XLV, 1847). In fact the category of 'stipendiary monitor' was to enable teachers not considered competent to train pupil teachers, to have some assistance.

The content and structure of each stage of training was organized according to the regulations outlining the official view of efficient and economic schooling. Necessary knowledge for working in grant-aided schools was to be transferred to the trainee teachers in order for them to display it in the examination. This gave the inspectorate, teachers and future employers necessary knowledge of their future employees: for it was to become a condition of receiving a grant that a school should employ trained teachers. In this way the nexus of power relations constituting the system of schooling operated to construct a particular 'knowledge' appropriate for teaching within that system. Through the examination this gave rise to a new 'knowledge' about the participants within the system, so making candidates' knowledge and knowledge of candidates visible beyond the immediacy of a given institutional setting. The examination is a fundamental feature of professionalism. The examination certificate, laying claim for a candidate to a particular position within the system of schooling, and stating its holder to have a particular degree of competence, is the public display of the knowledge/power coalition of the examination. It is both legitimated by it and legitimator of it: a good teacher is trained; a trained teacher is good (XLVII, 1865, *Gordon, 1855*, p. 574; XLIX, 1861, *Middleton, 1860*, p. 245).

It was no accident that the training institution for teachers was referred to as the Normal school, for it is an essential feature of the techniques of discipline, of which examination is one, that they enable the construction of a norm; in this case, for teacher and taught. The written examination, a technique which acknowledges individual performance by means of classifying and quantifying it, offered a new precision in the statement of an individual's capacity to teach (first class, second class, third class) which, paradoxically, curtailed individuality (XLIX, 1861, *Cumming, 1860*), and encouraged uniformity in teaching (XLII, 1862, *Woodford, 1861*). The syllabus presented to trainees was approved knowledge for teachers which, through the medium of the examination, was to become knowledge against which teachers would be judged as competent or otherwise. Effective, because of its simplicity (Foucault, 1979, p. 170), the examination combined hierarchical observation and normalizing judgment in a coalition of power relations and knowledge relations (*ibid.*, p. 184). This self-perpetuating regime was instigated by the state and underpinned by financial rewards which increased according to the degree of participation in the system.

	Pupil teacher	**Stipendiary monitor**
At the end of first year	£10.00s	£ 5.00s
second year	£12.10s	£ 7.10s
third year	£15.00s	£10.00s
fourth year	£17.10s	£12.10s
fifth year	£20.00s	—

At the end of each year a teacher was to be paid for pupil teachers, at the rate of £5 for one; £9 for two; £12 for three; and £3 additional for every further monitor.

Teachers would get a grant towards their salary if they completed
1 year of Normal school and gained certificate of merit £15–£20
2 years £20–£25
3 years £25–£30

(XLV, 1847, *Regulations Respecting the Education of Pupil Teachers and Stipendiary Monitors*, p. 5)

Training requirements might be temporarily relaxed, for example, for those already teaching when state regulations came into operation. But the necessity of examination, the means of positioning in the system, rendering visible and immediately measurable in terms of a norm, remained constant. The category 'certificated' referred to those who were examined and trained; the category 'registered' was for those too old to take training, that is, those aged 35 and over, their examination being simpler and the assessment being pass or fail only (LI, 1854, *Minute* of 20 August 1853).

Considering that inspectors had been complaining about the lack of abilities and the unsuitability of many teachers, this formalization of what was necessary to be a good teacher, the controlled apprenticeship, the rigorous measurement of individuals, in short, the professionalization of the occupation of teaching, could be understood as a benign improvement. After all, how can one have effective schooling without effective teachers? Surely it is the examination, set by those who know, which reveals the truth of a candidate's knowledge? Yet, it must be remembered that it was *one particular* interpretation of 'necessary knowledge for good teaching' which was being disseminated in this way: it was knowledge sanctioned by those holding authoritative positions within an embryonic system of schooling. A system which was being structured to marginalize the ways of life of some groups and to aid the ordering of social relations in a world which a particular group of strategically located people viewed as problematic.

It is a characteristic of disciplinary power that the techniques involved in its exercise obscure its functioning while rendering visible those at whom they are aimed (Foucault). This becomes clearer in the case of teachers if we contrast the insistence by the education office on the need for the training and examination of teachers with the refusal to operate these techniques within the upper echelons of officials, at the level of inspector and above (see chapters 3 and 7). What is more, the rigid classification of identities lower down the hierarchy, the restrictions on the work which teachers could or could not do, was in direct contrast to the flexibility of those at the top, where senior education officials were not prevented from holding other posts as well (Bishop, 1971, p. 73).

At the same time as the use of the examination was being extended to assess untrained teachers, a certain imperfection was being revealed in this elaborate scheme — there were complaints that those who passed Normal school examinations were not necessarily able to teach. These complaints were sufficiently widespread for a probationary period to be introduced. It was ruled that no certificate of merit as a teacher would be given to anyone from a training school until they had been in charge of the same elementary school for two years and had been inspected twice during that period (LI, 1854, *Minutes*, 20 August, 1853, pp. 23–7; LXXIX, 1852–3, *Minutes*, 10 December, 1851, p. 9; XLIV, 1851, *Letter* of 20 November, 1849, pp. xxxiv–v). The written examination might guarantee the transference of a particular knowledge from teacher to taught, but it could not guarantee that those taught would themselves have the capacity to transfer that which they knew. What it could do, though, was to locate individuals in a nexus of power/knowledge, structure a professional, formal identity for teachers and, through its financial links, attract those from outside the state-regulated sector of schooling into its ambit. By doing this, professionalism, as a programme of power, was aimed at the incorporation of teachers as state agents.

Strategies for Autonomy

However, this programme embodied a fundamental contradiction. For it was based on promoting the status of teachers, this status having been gained through approved training and being evidenced by certification. It was therefore derived from their specialized knowledge and competence in the sphere of schooling. However, as I have argued, professionalism also constitutes a political resource. When teachers themselves attempted to draw on this in their strategy for self-determination, and when they disputed issues of knowledge with state officials, relations of class power in the form of state control quickly re-emerged.

Several other occupations had managed to gain professional status for themselves in the early nineteenth century – architects, civil engineers, accountants, actuaries, as well as the lower branches of the more traditional professions of physicians and barristers — that is, apothecaries, surgeons, vets, lawyers (Reader, 1977). Each of these occupational groupings had their own associations. The status of these associations in relation to both the state and their own occupational group was crucial in determining the success or otherwise of the project of attaining recognition as a profession. This can be illustrated in the case of teaching which, in the 1980s, is still of uncertain professional standing.

At the same time as the state was attempting to structure the formal identity of teachers, there were moves amongst teachers themselves to improve their social and economic status by means of professionalism. They argued that low pay, poor prospects and insecurity meant that generally the standards of applicants for teaching posts were low. They felt that teachers were seen as inferior to the middle classes and drew, in their arguments, on the model of the rise of surgeons from barbers, in their expression of a desire to be treated as more than skilled tradesmen.

Some teachers therefore engaged in activities which were concerned with the generation of the components of a profession which I have already outlined. In 1807 the Burgh and Parochial Schoolmasters' Widows' Fund was set up and from this came the Scottish School Book Association. In the 1830s and 1840s several associations of teachers emerged. An Aberdeen group had come into existence in 1838, and the Glasgow Teachers' Association established in 1846 had about fifty members and tried to broaden its contacts. However, none of these were as systematic or as widespread movements as the EIS was to become. On 18 September 1847 a group of other associations amalgamated at a meeting of over 600 teachers in Edinburgh High School, to form the Educational Institute of Scotland (EIS) (see Myers, 1970, p. 168, for a more detailed account of this. My discussion of EIS is based on Myers' work.) The EIS aimed to improve the social and economic status of teachers, to raise the standard of entrance to the occupation and, by doing this, to foster their specialist knowledge and competence as a resource for the development of educational policy. This was because there was anger among teachers that their views were treated with indifference by the state, and that teachers were not prime candidates for the inspectorate (*ibid.*). The EIS was therefore concerned with professionalism both as a social status and as a political resource.

In so far as it was concerned with social status, the aims of the EIS were, in some respects, compatible with those of the state. Both were involved in working up a body of knowledge, setting standards of conduct and conferring qualifications on teachers. However, whereas the EIS wanted to become ranked as an independent profession (*ibid.*, p, 113) and was mobilizing professionalism as a resource in this enterprise, state action was targeted at locating teachers within the system which was emerging from the implementation of state rules. Therefore Committee of Council regulations were directed at raising the status of teachers but *also at placing a ceiling on this*. Indeed, part of the reason for stressing the importance of the strict regime of the Normal school was to reduce the risk '... of the superior instruction of a normal school tempting to aspire beyond a schoolmaster's calling' (XLV, 1847, *Gordon, Report on Edinburgh and Glasgow Normal Schools*).

In aiming to remove the state-imposed limits on their professionalism, members of the EIS were displaying a dissonance between the state-structured formal identity of teacher and the informed identities of teachers engaged in the promotion of teaching as a profession. This dissonance was fostered by a basic contradiction in state policy since at the same time as promoting a programme of professionalism which involved structuring teaching in terms of officially legitimated knowledge/competence, it was also promoting programmes of class power which were embedded in the mechanisms for intervention into schooling. To the extent that alternatives such as professional power did not cohere with the fundamental programmes of class power their legitimacy was denied. In other words, the legitimacy of professional power in relations of education was contingent on its harmony with class power. Teachers' strategies for developing their occupation were based on attempts to employ professionalism as a political resource, and to assert its primacy over other power forms. The essence of this dissonance then was a dispute between two different forms of power.

This is illustrated by the issues which arose concerning the role of the EIS. There was debate among some members of the EIS over whether they should aim at taking over the role of the Committee of Council in Scotland (Myers, 1970, p. 231). However, other members felt that this would restrict the autonomy which they wanted from the state, and therefore would remove their ability to be an independent organization representing teachers. Nevertheless, the EIS did aim to take over some functions which the Committee of Council developed. An important instance of this was the examination of teachers. In Scotland, the Dick Bequest operated examinations in its area in the North East and the Committee of Council brought theirs into operation in 1847. Both these offered financial rewards and were highly regarded among the inspectorate (*ibid.*, p. 227). The EIS introduced an entrance examination which, after 1847, new members were required to have passed before being admitted. The diplomas awarded as a result of this were ranked. However, the EIS certificates failed to achieve the recognition to which the Institute had aspired. One reason for this was that those who had joined the organization before the ruling about an entrance examination, did not have to sit an examination in order to receive a membership certificate. Myers suggests that by December 1847 there were already 1300 members, with another 200–300 applications still to be considered. By 1851, when it received its Royal Charter it had about 1800 members. So most EIS certificates were indicative of membership rather than of a particular level of knowledge and competence displayed in an examination.

Further, the EIS Royal Charter only recognized their *capacity* to examine and evaluate teachers. There was no inducement or regulation provided to encourage teachers to sit its exams or school managers to require its certificates. It follows from this that in their strategy of obtaining professional autonomy from the state the EIS were trying to attain control of the formal mode of legitimating knowledge for teachers, having failed to secure either the monopoly of the means of doing this (examination linked with certification and funding) or the confidence of significant groups in the validity of their attempts in this enterprise. Indeed, Myers has argued that the EIS was disliked by patrons, school managers and clergy because it lacked ties with the church and because its examination and certification system was an attempt to rival that of the state, and it was the state system which involved financial aid. This, along with the primacy given by education officials to class-directed programmes over the use of professionalism as a political resource, explains the failure of the EIS to gain acceptance for their examinations and certificates.

By 1855, when the EIS approached the Committee of Council directly with a request for control over examination and certification of teachers, only about twenty to thirty candidates had actually sat their examinations. The Committee of Council sent a memo to them in April of that year, refusing their request. From then until the 1870s, by which time the EIS had lost all hope of obtaining a monopoly licensing power,

Myers indicates that there were never more than two candidates per annum for the EIS examinations (*ibid.*, p. 238); the exception being 1858 when hopes of getting recognition were raised, there being twenty-five candidates that year, ten of whom sat the examination. It is difficult to find figures with which to compare this but by 1865 the Argyll Commission found 1708 teachers who held Committee of Council certificates (*ibid.*, p. 230), and throughout this period an increasing number of teaching posts required candidates to hold Committee of Council certificates, since these were a condition of financial aid from the state.

Although they could to some extent exploit a basic contradiction in state programmes, teachers were ultimately unsuccessful in their strategy of professionalism. The functions which professional associations fulfilled for other occupational groupings were, for teachers, fulfilled by the state. State policy was directed at giving teachers knowledge and proof of this when they had attained it, but control of that knowledge was to remain firmly beyond the grasp of teachers themselves. Teachers were to be agents for the transmission of state-approved schooling, but were not held by the state to be suitable people to consult on matters of educational policy. Ultimately, their professional association was relegated, by the state, to the status of a trade union and was thus denied representation on school boards which were set up after 1872 (*ibid.*, p. 433).

In conclusion then, in the early stages of state intervention into schooling, problem teachers were often given as the explanation for problem schooling. State action was aimed at erasing this by structuring normality in relation to the formal identity of the teacher. This involved the construction of state agents with professional status but with tight restrictions placed on the possibility of them employing professionalism as a political resource. However, the in-formed identities of some people who were involved in teaching led them to resist incorporation by the state, thus rejecting the role of state agent in favour of attempting to structure that of independent professional. The failure of this strategy does not undermine the importance of recognizing the distinction between that which official policy envisaged teachers as being and their own interpretation of this. Rather it underlines the strength of programmes of power which are institutionalized, in the production of particular forms of social relations and in the constraint on action aimed at negotiating alternatives to these. Their location between state officials and the population whose social relations state-structured schooling was aimed at regulating, meant that teachers were key figures. However, I have argued that the aim of schooling was to structure relations outside the school. As can be seen from the social map of the formal identity of child and that of truant, social relations of the family are central to the discussion of relations external to the school. It is to the significance of these which I shall turn in the next chapter.

Notes

1 In England and Wales the Committee of Council were reluctant to make capitation grants to mixed schools under a mistress. Initially they assumed that a mistress could not handle boys over 8 or 9. They compromised and offered money — at the girls' rate for capitation grant — in April 1854 (Minutes 1853–4, p. 30). It has not been possible to examine the details of gender relations in the teaching occupation here. Work on these for this period in Scotland remains to be done.
2 This was allowed for in state rules if the population was under 400 (XIII, 1854–5, Woodford, 1854, p. 703).
3 He bases his estimate on the *Digest of Parochial Returns 1819; Church of Scotland Educational Committee Educational Statistics 1833* and *Report of 1850*; Kay-Shuttleworth, *Public Education* (1853); LIX, 1854, *Abstract of Returns Relating to the Population and Number of Schools in each of the Counties, Cities and Burghs, Scotland (according to the Census of 1851)*; Saunders, *Scottish Democracy*.
4 Four occupations were specifically mentioned: secretary to the Benefit Society of the village or parish (minute 20 February 1840). This was to encourage meetings to be held in schools rather than in taverns. Office of session clerk (Circular to Inspectors, relating to minutes of August and December 1846 and July 1847); heritor's clerk, in parishes of under 400 inhabitants (not applicable to those training pupil teachers or receiving augmentation to their salary); day teachers who also taught at night had to be relieved of some of their schoolwork by pupil teachers on the day of a night school being taught (minute 1 March 1855).

Chapter 6:

Schooling the Family

Introduction

Schooling was a biopolitical technique for intervening into areas of popular life. By describing it in this way I am maintaining that it involved, 'new methods of power whose operation is not ensured by right, but by technique, not by law, but by normalization, not by punishment but by control, methods that are employed on all levels and in forms that go beyond the state and its apparatus.' (Foucault, 1981, p. 89). In this chapter I shall argue that state regulation of schooling was implicated in the institutionalization of the 'normal' family and, consequently, in the institutionalization of family relations which I have described on the social maps displayed in chapter 1. State papers indicate that schooling was to be aimed at creating spheres of moral training which would be distinct from, and therefore would supersede the kind of upbringing which was viewed as inherent in a class. In discussions of this they reveal the concerns which underlay the creation of schooling as a *normal* activity, at certain times of the day and year, for children.

Social action was talked about there in terms of its relationship to particular formal identities. I have explored that of teacher and shown how state regulation promoted the structuring of this in the form which was to come to be considered as normal. Forms which did not conform to the state model were considered as problematic and came to be defined as abnormal, mistaken, inadequate. As part of this process of normalization, there emerged an ideal notion of the school, the family, the population and relationships between these. This became the measure against which behaviour was judged. Implicit in this were the mores of a social order predicated on the dominance of industrial capitalism: distinct spheres of responsibility, congruence of norms, activities regulated by the clock, rationalistic attitude to money, its accumulation and expenditure. Yet, as I have indicated, the process of industrialization did not take place uniformly over the whole of Britain and, as Corrigan (1977) has pointed out, attempts to regulate the populace could often precede any direct impact of this process. It follows from this that any attempt to develop a uniform system would encounter variable situations. The definition of these as problems and the official response to them highlight the constituents of the formal identities.

The relay of power, expressed in the architecture of the school and designed to encapsulate participants within the school, operated through visibility and segmentation. Since this was part of the attempt to generate an internalized control of individuals' behaviour, there was a further aim of their encapsulation *out* of school. Behaviour outside of school was taken to be indicative of both the *necessity for* and the *success of* the local school in perpetuating approved relations of authority. Therefore social relations were both embedded in and formed by this new type of organization. As such, wider social relations were not simply the background setting for the systematization of schooling. These relations deepen the significance of the themes within official papers.

Discussions of attendance in inspection reports embody these issues since school attendance is at the interface of the school and the wider social environment. As I have been arguing, these reports were dealing with the application of one particular model of schooling in a world in which various forms co-existed. In the last chapter I discussed dissonance between the formal and informed identities of teachers and which was generated internally by the success of the state programme of professionalizing teaching. In this chapter, in contrast, I am concerned with a different type of dissonance, that deriving from forms of social relations which were external to the state model, and against which this was being imposed. Discussions of problems for the model and the varying solutions outlined in the reports were part of the construction of a paradigm of the 'normal' in educational knowledge and knowledge of deviance.

The impact of schooling on the sexual and social division of labour has been discussed by David (1980) in her account of schooling in England in the late nineteenth and the twentieth centuries. David has drawn attention to the neglect of work on relations *between* schooling, the family and the economy in her argument that the 'family, and the education system are used in concert to sustain and reproduce the social and economic STATUS QUO ... they maintain existing relations within the family and social relations within the economy ...' (*ibid.*, p. 1). Important as it is to stress the relations *between* these spheres, there is a need to go further and emphasize the significance of state activity in structuring schooling as a medium for *producing one particular form* of these relations as a norm and gradually marginalizing the other forms which co-existed.

In this chapter I shall show the way in which the official definition of schools as substitutes for, or supplements to, inadequate parenting, marginalized the in-formed identities of specific groups of parents, as well as family relations which involved particular forms of the social division of labour. In doing this I shall be explaining the way in which state regulations, by embodying one version of the scheduling of social identities, were also propagating a version of the structuring of social time. As I shall explain, the content of the curriculum reinforced the impact of the structure of schooling in altering certain forms of social relations. In particular it was aimed at fostering 'correct' identity formation of future parents. That is to say, it was generating what was to come to be officially considered as 'normal' parenting and concomitantly to promote a particular definition of appropriate family relations. That people whose ways of living were being rendered deviant by state action did not passively acquiesce to this, is illustrated by the refusal of some parents to accept the legitimacy of state definitions of education. In conclusion, I shall return to a discussion of the significance of this argument for an understanding of the social maps displayed earlier.

Problem Parenting

State regulated schooling operated to make social relations which were officially defined as inappropriate into institutional problems. This occurred because the organization of schooling presupposed one scheduling (Gurvitch, 1964) of social identities. This involved parents being providers, children being dependent and school coming prior to work. Attendance at school according to the officially prescribed pattern and adherence to the rhythmic order which was part of this were therefore constituent features of the formal identity of pupil. These rhythms, I have maintained, were based on a scheduling of social identities which was compatible with industrialization. Yet, in the Britain of 1851, 'half the population still lived in small rural communities and the largest single occupation was agricultural labourer' (Anderson, 1978, p. 16). Older rhythms were therefore still very important and, even late in the nineteenth century, in Scotland large sectors of the urban population moved to rural areas in periods of harvest, when agricultural work was plentiful. So although numerically designated time was important in one setting, it co-existed with an older way of classifying the temporal, involving a different form of social scheduling — one circumscribed by seasons and tasks. In other words, the situation was characterized by what Gurvitch (1964) has referred to as a 'hierarchy of time'.

The variable pattern of life involved differing forms of the social division of labour. In its older form, the social division of labour had as its core, the family as a unit of production. Therefore members of the household would be an income resource. This older form of the social division of labour with its pattern of school attendance which varied in frequency and duration, became a problem to the extent that the new rhythms of the state-regulated school were elevated as a norm. This was revealed in official discussions through the development of the themes of parental poverty, habitat and occupational grouping. It is through these that the role of the 'problem parent' can be traced.

Poverty was an issue of importance for schooling because it was held that it was from the poor that the criminal classes were recruited (XXXIII, 1857, *Cumming and Wilson*, 1856, p. 667). A distinction was made between poverty as a problem of inadequate income (XXXIII, 1842, *Gibson*, 1842, p. 216), a difficulty against which 'worthy' people struggled, and the 'problem of poverty'. This was a mismanagement of money explained in inspection reports as the result of faulty mores. These derived from the lack of schooling of the parents in a household. '... the main cause why parents do not send their children to school is poverty, alike their fault and their misfortune. It is their fault that they expend in drunkenness sums of money which would enable them to spare the early labour of their children, and to support them in school for two or three years longer than their usual stay. It is their misfortune, that in very many instances being uneducated themselves, they know nothing of self-denial, of prudence, and of domestic economy. They neither know how to save money nor how to spend it' (LIV, 1860, *Wilkinson*, 1859, p. 275). Higher wages were not, therefore, considered to be a solution to this problem for '... in the larger towns the higher the wages they receive, the lower in general is their domestic condition; the richer they ought to be, the poorer they really are' (LIV, 1860, *Wilkinson*, 1859, p. 275).

The reason for this, it was argued, was that their lack of schooling in correct behaviour would lead parents to squander the money; and that it would further encourage children to go to work early rather than attend school.

> For some time past, the iron-miners have enjoyed a very high rate of wages from 3/- to 7/- and averaging 5/6 per day. This is more than enough to supply the usual comforts of families in their condition; the remainder forms a temptation to intemperance ... A police court established in the town ... convicts, at an average, in twenty cases per week, for riot, assault, or other misdemeanours incident to a state which so happily conjoins ignorance, obscurity, and every opportunity of vice, with what may, in their condition, be termed affluence ... At the same time, the high price of boys' labour in the mines is a lure to the neglect of their instruction; and the ill lesson is taught, by something like experience that education is little if at all wanted to secure all the comfort and prosperity which is desired. (XXXII, 1846, *Gordon Report on Airdrie, 1846*, p. 438).

Higher wages would therefore only exacerbate difficulties.

The problem of poverty was, then, an indication that mores between the home and the school were incompatible. Though it was recognized that there was no necessary harmony between the mores of the wealthy and those which schools were designed to propagate, this was not considered to be a problem. For elementary schools were not aimed at this sector of the population. They were aimed at those people who might have to spend long hours in their place of work and who therefore would be limited to the extent to which, even if they wished to do so, they could instil correct moral and religious principles into their children.

> ... intellectual instruction, which, in more favourable circumstances, might perhaps have been considered, with propriety, the teacher's primary aim, must now be regarded as subordinate, and mere auxiliary to moral and religious culture. His paramount object should now be so to adjust and apply these respective departments of instruction as either to prevent or to remedy the evils necessarily resulting from the neglect or violation of parental duties. (XXXV, 1845, *Gordon* 1845, p. 154).

Without this, these children would be at risk of being snared by the problem of poverty.

Just as the problem of poverty was indicative of the need for schools, so parents' occupational grouping and habitat were held to be keys to understanding kinds of children, attitudes to schooling, and likely consequent problems (XXXV, 1845, *Gordon Report on the Deficiencies of Elementary Education in Scotland*, 1845). In their analysis of educational discourse in the nineteenth century, Jones and Williamson (1979) noted the persistence of topographical accounts of the social world. I am extending their argument here when I maintain that, in so far as an explanation was offered of the way in which characteristics of an area could predispose people to types of action, this was done through a discussion of occupational grouping. It was claimed that,

> The children of an entirely rural parish are quiet, orderly and attentive, but intellectually not very quick ... Those of the fishing villages are comparatively self-reliant [This was taken to indicate a problem, since it was argued that they could manipulate their parents.] ... The children of the mining population are naturally tinged with the insulated and peculiar ideas which their parents may happen to have acquired in their contracted field of observation, and they are so tenacious of their prejudices as to be scarcely manageable if they are crossed ... The children of the manufacturing population exhibit the various character of towns' children generally ... (XLII, 1862, *Woodford* 1861, pp. 200–1; see also, XXVII, 1866, *Scougal*, 1865, pp. 329–30).

To the extent that the allocation of tasks among members of a community did not follow the pattern which was presupposed by the state-regulated school, there was a clash of the scheduling of identities. This was sharpest in the case of occupational groupings where work was not restricted to parents, but where all members of the household participated, especially if it was task-oriented and governed by seasons and weather (XLIX, 1861, *Woodford*, 1860, p. 214). For instance, the work of the fishing population was marked by these characteristics. The men fished, the children were expected to collect bait (XLII, 1862, *Woodford*, 1861, p. 200) and, at certain times of the year the population would migrate from their villages to the main ports where the women used the centralized facilities for curing the catch (L1V, 1860, *Middleton*, 1859, p. 259). The division of labour among the agricultural population followed a similar pattern, with the people in the poorer sectors, that is cotters (for a description of this way of life see Cameron, 1979), changing location once a year. This was known as the 'moving term'.

Geographical mobility was, in itself, a problem for a system which presupposed a fixed population, and for explanatory categories which dealt with people as *either* urban *or* rural. It was held to be particularly difficult to get mobile groups to accept the officially desired relations of authority. For example, collier families who were migratory were believed to be unsympathetic to education. 'A remarkable difference of character in this respect is exhibited by those of the collier families, which are not migratory, and which have profited in their sense both moral and intellectual, by long experience of the blessing of steady industry' (VL, 1847–8, *Gordon*, 1847, p. 331). But, more specifically, for these groups schooling was an activity which was traditionally interspersed with periods of wage-earning so that at certain times of the year local schools in some places would be closed altogether. In rural districts, winter was held to be the season for schooling (XXXIII, 1842, *Gibson*, 1842, p. 216; LIV, 1860, *Middleton*, 1859, p. 258) particularly for older children, whereas spring and summer were the seasons for younger children who were too small to attend during the harsh winter weather (XXXIII, 1842, *Gibson, 1841*, p. 64). This pattern was sufficiently extensive for inspectors to organize their visits in relation to this (XLII, 1865, *Cumming*, 1864, p. 277; XXVII, 1866, *Black*, 1865, p. 292) and for early inspection reports to distinguish average attendance in schools in the summer from that in winter (XXXIII, 1842, *Gibson*, 1842, pp. 225 and 250).

In mining and manufacturing districts there also existed a form of the social division of labour in which children were considered as contributors to the maintenance of the household, although the rhythms differed from those which I have already described in that they were not dependent on seasons and the weather. They were dependent on the expansion and contraction of the production of particular firms and industries (XXXII, 1846, *Gordon*, 1846, pp. 413 and 438; LXXX, 1852–3, *Woodford*, 1852, p. 787; LII, 1854, *Woodford*, 1853, p. 985; LII, 1854, *Wilkinson*, 1853, p. 1057; XLII, 1865, *Gordon*, 1864, p. 224). In state papers this was dealt with on two levels. On one level, it was an issue of the correct relationship between the labour market and the school. At this time the necessity of schooling was a matter of dispute with some people believing that the idea of schooling for all children was wildly impractical (see Myers, 1970; and David 1980, for a fuller discussion). Children were an important source of cheap labour, although their employment was subject to restrictions in some industries (see Best, 1973). Myers (1970) points out that factory inspector reports in 1857–62 in Scotland show a fall in male adult labour by 18 per cent while male child labour increased by 53 per cent and female child labour by 78 per cent (p. 6). Adaptations such as half-time schooling and evening schools were negotiations between what were held to be the exigencies of the labour market and the necessities of having a schooled population. In rural areas equivalents to these concessions to patterns of working were that the timing of vacations was linked to the timing of the harvest or the moving term (LXXX, 1852–3, *Woodford*, 1853).

The extent to which it was acceptable for schooling to accommodate to local conditions was limited though, for there was a danger that the local population might introduce their own variations. By doing this there was a risk that they might reverse the relations of authority which the regulation of schooling was structured to foster. Thus, vacations might be extended spontaneously by local people and as a result children might not return to school promptly at the official close of the harvest vacation. This created a self-reinforcing problem:

> In consequence of the thin attendance, classwork goes on very languidly for weeks, and the knowledge of this fact becomes an excuse for not attending sooner. I visited a parish school three weeks after it was nominally re-assembled, and found not one of the first class present. While the excuse for almost every alternate child's appearance was that he came only 'last Monday', 'yesterday', or 'this morning', making it pretty clear that a considerable proportion of the attendance even at that time was due to the intimation of the visit. (XLIX, 1861, *Woodford*, 1860, pp. 214–5).

There was a danger that such faulty habits of attendance would 'spread, by the mere force of custom or the contagion of example ...' (XXXII, 1846, *Gordon Report on Airdrie, 1846*, p. 438). Further, such a threat to appropriate relations of authority between the home and the school might raise the possibility of this also happening *within* the family. For children could take the opportunity to choose to be absent from school, refusing to return unless their parents agreed to provide an explanation for their absence which would be acceptable to the school (XLII, 1862, *Woodford*, 1861, pp. 200–1). The problem of making concessions to local customs was, then, the problem of establishing the dominance of a form of authority relations which would restructure local mores sufficiently for them to cohere with the uniformity of a national system. In short, by altering inappropriate parenting state-structured schools would erase the mores which resulted in the problem of poverty as well as erasing the faulty mores which were associated with particular occupational groupings and habitats. Consequently, faulty relations of authority — those involving the failure of parents to acquiesce to the school and the failure of children to acquiesce to their parents — would disappear.

The wage-earning of children was discussed as both necessary and an evil, in so far as it interfered with the rhythm of the state-regulated school (LIV, 1860, *General Report*, pp. XX–XXI). Along with illness, it was held to be a legitimate reason for absence. That is, absence from the regime of the school-room was legitimate if it implied presence in that of the workplace, or confinement at home because a child was ill. Otherwise, neglecting school was considered to be a bad habit indicative of ignorance of good habits and therefore of problem mores (XLII, 1865, *Gordon*, 1864). What was important about the relationship between the labour market and the school, was that children should be in designated school space during designated school time.[1] A schedule of identities such that a child could be a worker as well as a pupil was only indicative of inappropriate family relations if that child was a worker *rather than* a pupil during designated school time. Therefore, insofar as the issue of child labour was considered to be an avoidable problem, it was an issue of appropriate parenting. Work was somewhere children were sent by their parents who, if they were 'good' parents, would only do this if their own earnings were insufficient to maintain the family; otherwise they would want their children to attend school (XXXIII, 1857, *Wilkinson*, 1856; XLVII, 1856, *Gordon*, 1855).

The age at which children could be employed was circumscribed by the extent to which legislation restricting the employment of children could be evaded. The Mines Regulation Act 1860, for example, restricted the employment of boys under 12 to only those aged 10 and over who could produce a teacher's certificate to the effect that they could read and write. Without this they would have to attend school for a minimum of three hours daily, for two days weekly. However, though some (XLV, 1864, *Gordon*, 1863, p. 247) claimed it increased attendance, others (XLV, 1864, *Woodford*, 1863, p. 257 and XLII, 1865, *Jack*, 1864, p. 260) did not agree, arguing that they found evasions. To the extent that these evasions were seen as a problem of 'our industrial condition' (XLVII, 1863, *Middleton*, 1862, p. 160), which required young people to be employed as cheap labour, it was seen as unsolvable. But insofar as evasions were related to discussions of parenting the solution was held to be quite clear: the problem of child labour was dealt with here as a problem of *parental ignorance*. It was maintained that absence from school was '... aggravated by every fresh demand for juvenile labour, and seems likely to grow with the material prosperity of the country, until parents ... become sufficiently enlightened ...' (XXXIII, 1857, *Wilkinson*, 1856, p. 676).

Though it was often argued that good schools attracted pupils, it was recognized that this was circumscribed by the operation of the labour market and the social division of labour generally. As I have argued, the rhythms of certain occupational groups were, *by definition*, problematic since they differed from that of the school. The target, though, was not simply their difference: it was the habits of life which were implicit in these groupings that schooling was to aim at altering. This was because it was only the state-structured school which could provide for the correct upbringing of the population. Officially it was expected that parental relations of authority would be compatible with those which were being embedded within schools. To the extent that this was not the case, schools were to erase the incompatibilities. This process was defined as being concerned with 'making good deficiencies in parenting'. Attendance which did not conform to the officially promoted pattern in terms of either rhythm or duration was therefore taken to be indicative of poor or problem parents (XLV, 1847, *Gordon Report Edinburgh and Glasgow Normal Schools*).

The main aim of the state-regulated school was to provide training in correct principles and habits, the teaching of skills such as reading and writing was seen as a subordinate part of this (XXXV, 1845, *Gibson*, 1845, p. 154), for it was argued that it was habit which constituted education.

> ... very many of the Adventure schools cannot be considered of any value as means of education. Naturally enough, they are very ill-attended; and they produce a habit in that respect, which remains when better schools have come to be established in their place. If they qualify to read and write, and do the simpler operations of arithmetic, this is the utmost that can be said of what they do. In short, a great part of this class of schools is not to be acknowledged as supplying so much of the mentionable means of education. (XLV, 1857–8, *Gordon*, 1857, pp. 688–9).

Since problematic groups were believed to have passed through a series of stages on their way to becoming a problem, schooling was a means of providing approved stages through which future citizens would pass. It follows that the state model pre-supposed that schooling was an activity which would take place prior to wage-earning activities, and would be full time. This was especially important since '... in the daily resort to school, there is a lesson of constancy and regularity: obedience to the Master's rule disposes to the observance of other rules human and divine: ... the intercourse of the young at school is regulated by the same maxims which are applicable to conduct in society at large' (XLV, 1847, *Gordon, 1846* , p. 395). 'Good' parents would either already have established such relations within the family or would follow the example set by the school.

If children attended school according to either a different frequency or duration to that which was integral to the state promoted pattern, they were considered as neglecting school. This was therefore taken as indicating a possible dissonance between relations in the school and those in the home. In other words, it was a sign of problem parenting. Problem parents were those whose pattern of living conformed to alternative rhythms to those fostered in the school. School rhythms were defined as 'regular' whereas alternatives came to be equated with 'irregularity'. Such parents were either inadequate or bad, depending on whether they were unable or unwilling to secure the conformity of their child to state promoted norms.

The provision of the possibility of schooling was held to be the solution both to the difficulties of people being unable to obtain schooling and to those people who did not want schooling (LII, 1854, *Cumming and Wilson*, 1853, pp. 989–90). A lack of interest in schooling was seen as a direct consequence of a lack of experience of schooling. 'Of the indifference it is, perhaps, not well to speak much, when it is the direct consequence of the privation which it is desired to remove' (XXXV, 1845, *Gordon Report on Deficiencies etc.*, 1845, p. 172). For schooling, it was maintained, would enable people to recognize their best interests and to understand that these lay within the form of the social order which was to be propagated by the school. It was not that to be within a particular category meant that people would auto-matically be treated as problems, but rather that membership of a category provided an automatic explanation for any failure to adhere to the prescribed relations of schooling. Such was the extent to which it was seen as indicating *potential problems* that it was remarked on if no such problems seemed to exist, '... the population is agricultural in part, and in part engaged in fishing occupations; money is scarce, and wages are low; notwithstanding these drawbacks good schools exist' (LII, 1854, *Wilkinson*, 1853, pp. 1054–5).

A problem parent was therefore one whose children's work provided a necessary contribution to the maintenance of a household and which conflicted with the patterns of schooling that the state was fostering. That is to say, children of problem parents were involved in a scheduling of social identities which meant that they were, for example, workers during the time which the state had designated for them to be pupils. Problem parents were therefore those who failed to recognize the primacy of the order of schooling, or who failed to assert authority over the behaviour of their children which was in agreement with that of the school.

Institutional Problems

I have argued that the activity of schooling was often patterned according to older forms of social relations. How was it that the model pattern which the state was promoting came to be accepted as desirable even at the lower levels of the institutional hierarchy? It was not simply that state officials started to discuss these previously unproblematic matters as difficulties which a state designed system would have to overcome. Nor was it that those providing schooling saw the state model as self-evidently desirable. Rather regulations and the form of what was to count as efficient and economic schooling meant that different patterns of attendance became *institutional* problems. There were several ways in which this occurred.

Financially, the payment of government grants required that a pupil attend school for a minimum of 176 days throughout the year (with an allowance of sixteen days for absences on top of this). Grants were paid for teaching assistance, in the form of pupil teachers or stipendiary monitors. If a school had an insufficient number of pupils who met this attendance requirement, it could call into question the need for the teacher to have assistance (since this was calculated in relation to the average attendance), and therefore could jeopardize the annual grant. Pedagogically, it was a hindrance to class teaching, the state's approved form of efficient and economic teaching. It was difficult to pace work at the level of a group whose membership did not remain constant for more than a short period of time, and teachers claimed that children forgot what they had learnt while they were absent. There was a possibility that a teacher and school could be defined as inadequate if there was a lack of class teaching and if the school's performance was poor (XLIX, 1861, *Woodford*, 1860, p. 218). These same social relations which state-regulated schooling was to alter, and which were being rendered problematic *for* schooling, were used as a defence by teachers to explain the limited effectiveness of schooling, especially in respect of attendance (XLIV, 1850, *Gordon* , 1848–9, pp. 575–9). By drawing the attention of inspectors to the way in which problem parenting hampered their work teachers could defend themselves against charges of inadequacy.

This also raised problems for inspection. There was, of course, always the issue of whether children would be present at the inspection visit (XL, 1852, *Woodford*, 1851, pp. 660–1); LXXX, 1852–3, *Middleton*, 1852, pp. 805 and 811). But, aside from this, the assessment of a school which an inspector made during his visit was based on examining some of the children as *examples* of their class. The form of this assessment therefore presupposed that there would be classes to be sampled. An inspector then had to decide whether a given performance could be explained by the attendance pattern of the children (L, 1847–8, *Gordon*, 1847, pp. 331–2; XLV, 1864, *Gordon*, 1863, p. 243), or the teacher's capacity to teach (XLIX, 1861, *Middleton*, 1860, p. 237), and to what extent the teacher's ability affected attendance (XXXIII, 1857, *Gordon*, 1856, p. 640). Paradoxically then, the external social relations which schools were to help mould, were often given as an explanation of the limited effectiveness of the operation of the state model of schooling.

The dissonance between the in-formed identities of children and the formal identity of pupil which was embodied in state regulations was taken as indicating either of two possibilities. These were that a teacher was not conforming to the state model of a 'good' teacher or that parents who lacked experience of good schooling were, as a result, not organizing their life in such a way as to encourage their children to conform to the officially fostered rhythm of schooling. In order to counter the charge of inadequate teaching, teachers would draw the attention of state officials to the ways in which problem parenting hampered their work. The ways of living which were seen as likely to indicate problem parenting were those which involved the organization of work tasks along non-industrial lines, the working of long hours within industrial organizations and those circumscribed by poverty.

The Content of Schooling and Normal Family Relations

But a model of correct social relations was not only embedded in the structuring of schooling, it was also a feature of the content, especially within the industrial curriculum which was officially promoted at this time. For by promoting the correct identity-formation of future parents this was to be the means of propagating future appropriate family relations. Officially, it was argued that by providing a curriculum which was related to the main occupations in an area, certain advantages would follow. Firstly, children would be trained to habits appropriate to their likely future occupations. Secondly, employers would come to recognize the value of a period of schooling. Thirdly, this would also lead to local people recognizing this and therefore attendance would improve. It was assumed that children would follow the occupation of their parents (XLIX, 1861, *Gordon, 1860*, pp. 228–9). Ideally, the content of the curriculum was to involve the teaching of knowledge which would combine correct mores and habits with future usefulness (XLIV, 1850, *Gordon, 1848*, pp. 567–8).

However, creating links between school subjects and local forms of labour could be difficult if the industry in a parish were so simple that no previous instruction was required or so diverse that it could not be encompassed within the schooling provided (L, 1847–8, *Gordon, 1847*, pp. 329–32; XLVII, 1856, *Gordon, 1855*, p. 574). Despite these difficulties, attempts to link the labour market and the curriculum were officially encouraged, with special grants being made available to promote the teaching of what were generically referred to as the industrial subjects. These grants covered school field-gardens, workshops for trades, school kitchens and wash-houses (LI, 1854, *Circular to Inspectors*, pp. 55–8). Industrial subjects included agriculture, which was encouraged in some Highland schools (XLVII, 1856, *Gordon, 1855*); and geology, minerology, bookkeeping, navigation, technical drawing, agricultural chemistry and mechanics which were offered in schools in various districts (LlV, 1860, *Gordon, 1859*). Inspectors were specifically told to make enquiries about industrial subjects and reports remarked favourably on those schools which related subjects to the occupations in an area (XLV, 1847, *Gordon, 1846*). In so far as schooling was seen as a preparation for the outside world, it was viewed as ideally taking place *prior* to people taking on the identities of worker and parent. As a result of this separation of schooling from 'work' and 'life', the school activities of children were defined, not as wage-earning work but as education.

Though schooling was to be relevant to a person's future identity, at the outset a distinction was made between schooling and training for a particular occupation. '... there is much in the industrial that ministers to general culture. Were it not so, it may be doubted whether industrial instruction would have obtained a footing in the schools at all, because the other is justly deemed more essential ... and because the knowledge of trade or craft comes, of necessity, at a later season' (XLV, 1847, *Gordon, 1846*, p. 397). Training was therefore not the aim of schools for particular craft skills could only be acquired in the workplace (LI, 1854, *Annual Grants Day Schools of Industry, Circular to Inspectors*, pp. 55–8). The teaching of industrial subjects, 'consists always of some general notions of the subject or the principles of that occupation, and is never ... accompanied with any manual practice' (XLV, 1847, *Gordon, 1846*, p. 397). This was because, with the exception of districts where one kind of employment predominated, or where there were 'class schools' connected with factories and mines (for example, XLVII, 1856, *Gordon, 1855*, pp. 574–9), it was recognized that the precise future role of boys could not be identified.

The aims of the industrial curriculum were distinguished according to the category of children at which it was directed, and this affected its content.

> The true test is ... whether the children are placed under industrial instruction as part of an ordinary education in school, or whether they are so placed in the absence of all other means on their part of learning to gain an honest maintenance. In dealing with this latter class, manual work must stand before book work ... So far as industrial occupation is mixed up with other lessons of children IN ORDINARY SCHOOLS, it is of a general character, and is not intended to furnish the learners with special means of livelihood' (LI, 1854, *Letter from Lingen to Bellairs*, 12 November 1853, p. 58; but also XXXIII, 1857, *Grants for Promotion of Schools Wherein Children of the Criminal and Abandoned Classes may be Reformed by Industrial Training*, 2 June 1856).

It was stressed that 'The object of industrial (*as part of ordinary*) instruction should be ... to fit the learner for doing his best in life, not to prescribe definitively his sphere in it' (XL, 1852, *minutes, 1850*, pp. 55–8).

The greater the dissonance which was held to exist between the social identities of children categorized according to their particular social backgrounds and the formal identity believed to be linked with backgrounds defined as appropriate, the greater was the intensity of industrial teaching. The poor and the criminal were therefore distinguished from working class people generally, in that their schooling was to be occupationally oriented as well as morally appropriate. For working class people moral appropriateness was sufficient.

It was not that there was no distinction made between the poor and the criminal (XXXIII, 1857, *Cumming and Wilson, 1856*), but rather, because both groups were taken to be indicative of problem habits they were conflated in institutional practices. (For example, the wording on the certificates enforcing compulsory schooling for these categories of children did this. [XLV, 1857–8, pp. 19–22].) This was what made possible statements linking the establishment of pauper schools to the reduction of juvenile delinquency in particular districts (LIV, 1860, *Gordon, 1859*). Children whose upbringing would, it was considered, not encourage them to accept the rule of state authority, that is, those from the criminal classes (outside the law) and those from the abandoned classes (without parental authority) had no appropriate model of authority relations and therefore needed special provision. This was designed, 'not to give an instruction transcending the real needs of this class of people, but to give that which they do need more effectually ...' (XLIV, 1850, *Gordon, Report on Sessional Schools 1848–9*, p. 551, quote from General Assembly's Education Committee memo of 1842 to the Committee of Council).

The impact of the structure of schooling was to be reinforced by its content. This was to be made relevant to what were understood to be the social identities of people at particular social levels. By doing this, it was argued, school would become more interesting to the pupils and, as a result, they would attend according to the officially promoted pattern (XLIV, 1850, *Gordon, 1849*, (Appendix A, Female Orphan Asylum, Aberdeen); XXXIII, 1857, *Gordon, 1856*). It would therefore become more efficient at inculcating into children behaviour which was considered to be appropriate to working people and would be able to 'supplement the deficiencies, to correct the errors, or to counteract the positive evils of their home education' (XXXV, 1845, *Gibson, 1845*, p. 154).

The difficulties which existed in identifying the precise future occupation of boys were not believed to be a problem in relation to girls. For them the situation was different since there was an *assumed homogeneity* about their *primary* future identity which it was thought would be within the home. In consequence, the extent to which a child was *primarily* prepared to become a worker or to become a parent was gender related. Though men, women and children participated in work activities and there was a qualified acceptance of child labour by the state, the definition of what would be relevant for a child's future life presupposed, not only a separation of work from home, but that men would be identified as workers and that women would be identified as servicing the needs of men and children within the domestic sphere. For example, one inspector, reporting on a visit to a school in which the pupils were involved in providing meals for unmarried workmen, noted that, 'The proprietors here aim at improving the social condition of their workmen in a way which, as yet, has been very little tried in Scotland, — by a very special training of the young females for the duties of domestic life that probably awaits them' (XXI, Part 1, 1859, *Special Report on Female School of Industry at Eglinton Iron Works, 1858*, p. 235). It is apparent then that though schooling was to structure relations in the home and therefore influence both boys and girls (LI, 1854, *Circular to Inspectors*, August, 1850, p. 57), relevant schooling for boys was dogged by uncertainty about their precise future occupation, but this was not the case with girls.

Because of this vision of the appropriate identity for girls the content of their schooling was seen as necessarily to be restricted in comparison with that for boys.

> ... the lessons of the school for both sexes are less suited to the one sex than to the other. For example, are there not portions of some of the reading lesson books, which would have no place there, if the books were compiled exclusively for the formation and the information of the female mind, — while there would have been no need for any corresponding omissions, if the books were exclusively for males? 'C'est une étrange chose que la science dans une tête de fille' ... (XLIX, 1861, *Gordon, 1860*, p. 226).

The industrial curriculum was given a priority in discussions of schooling for girls since, 'while the period of school attendance was the same for both sexes, it was not requisite for the female to proceed so far in the different literary branches ...' (XLV, 1857, *Gordon Report on Edinburgh and Glasgow Normal Schools*, p. 536). A good school mistress, it was maintained, would not simply teach sewing and knitting but would also make her female pupils, 'scour and sweep the school, dust the furniture, make and keep the fires, and clean the stoves or grates' (LI, 1854, *Circular to Inspectors*, August, 1850, p. 57).

I have stressed that state intervention into schooling was concerned with the structuring of diversity in order to produce uniformity. There is always a danger, when basing an argument on official discourse, of colluding with it. I have tried to avoid this by drawing a distinction between formal and in-formed identities, by stressing that the new model of social relations contained contradictions which generated conflict within it, and by emphasizing that the very *necessity* of state intervention into the structuring of social relations implies the continued existence of alternative definitions of appropriate social relations external to the authorized forms. This is illustrated by the challenges which were presented to official definitions of appropriate knowledge for girls.

Generally speaking, so far as the industrial curriculum was concerned, the greater the emphasis on the 'practical' as opposed to the 'theoretical' aspects of a topic, the less likely it was that local people would accept either the knowledge-claims of the teacher in this sphere, or that it was even the legitimate province of schooling at all. (For example, this problem was noted with the introduction of subjects such as agriculture into schools. [XLIX, 1861, *Gordon, 1860*, p. 229]).In the case of the industrial curriculum for girls there were instances of mothers who questioned the official definition of good education for girls. Such women were held to be exhibiting a 'very foolish prejudice' in their objections to their daughters scrubbing school floors. Their claims that their children were sent to school to be taught and not to be servants of the school-mistress were taken by officials as evidence of their ignorance (LIV, 1860, *Woodford, 1859*, p. 235).

These parents considered the domestic curriculum to be a waste of time and their refusal to accept its definition as education led to cases where local mothers would approach the school to enquire about the payment which their daughters were to receive for undertaking this work. In some districts,

> the parents ... refused to let their girls 'waste' the school time in learning to sew. They wish to go on with their other education first, saying that 'they can get a while at sewing afterwards when they are more able to profit by it.' In one case a deputation of mothers waited upon the chief promoter of a department for needlework to inquire what was to be allowed to their daughters for their sewing, referring to what they got for hoeing, weeding, and gathering bait and the only answer that could be given to this inquiry prevented attendance ... (XLIX, 1861, *Woodford, 1860*, p. 217).

This lack of agreement between parents and officials as to what was education and what was work could lead to parents rejecting school as the appropriate place for their children, and as a result to them withdrawing their children from school.

This indicates that definitions of social action were not based on any universal consensus. Further, it is clear from opposition to the industrial curriculum that schooling was not always viewed as offering children an enlightened preparation for their future and as rescuing them from having to participate in wage-earning work. Choosing between sending a child to school and sending them to work was sometimes a choice between sending them to do the unpaid work which authorities called education and sending them to do wage-earning work for employers.

Yet the official construction of school as the place for education; of education as that which the state defined as such; of teacher as educator and pupil as receiver of knowledge; meant that activities of pupils within school could not be defined as wage-earning work, even though, as in some industrial schools, the children's activities could earn money which was used to reduce the costs of running an establishment. As an official report of one school stated,

> The best means ... of training to future usefulness must, it appears, be more or less set aside for such work as will bring in money for defraying the expenses of the establishment ... The girls, besides assist in house cleaning, washing and cooking, according to their age and strength; are kept very much at knitting and needlework; and, as this is also made to PAY, the teachers have frequently stated to me that the amount of work required, and the number of hours necessary to obtain it from girls so young or so unpractised as many of them are when admitted, are so great, that with the other things to be done, and the time needful for recreation, *they have too little time for their education otherwise.* (XLIX, 1861, *Woodford, 1860*, p. 219. Capitals, emphasis in original; italics, my emphasis).

This may well be an extreme example; nevertheless it underlines the way in which action was officially defined in relation to its institutional setting.

In my argument here there is no intention of romanticizing the working conditions of children in paid employment. The conditions of work and their implications for the quality of children's lives have been sufficiently documented for there to be no question of this being the issue (see Best, 1973). Rather, what I am drawing attention to is the way in which action was officially defined in relation to its structural setting and that this reinforced a compartmentalization of home, school and work. As part of this reinforcement and its consequent structuring of what were considered to be appropriate family relations, alternative ways of living were not only constituted as problems, but were taken as signifying ignorance. Knowledge presupposed social relations which were compatible with those of the school.

The constituents of the formal identity of parents which appear on the social map of the formal identity of child (that is, the 'normal' in educational knowledge), and the feature of 'problem families' which appears in the map of the formal identity of truant (that is, knowledge of deviance), should be understood, then, as deriving from patterns of social relations which nineteenth century state regulated schools were aimed at altering. They were produced by the official authorization of one specific model of schooling as 'correct' and normal, and by incorporating one particular model of 'correct' family relations into the industrial curriculum. At the same time as promoting *the family* as fundamental to the production and maintenance of social order, state action was undermining the relations of actual families by marginalizing alternative versions of family relations. These were those which involved temporal rhythms and a form of the social division of labour which did not accord with the officially authorized pattern of schooling. This pattern formed the core of the state *system* of schooling which was formally introduced in 1872. By this time, alternative patterns of social relations, seen as indicative of inappropriate parenting, had become entrenched as institutionally problematic for a system which embodied correct/normal social relations. This was what made it possible for problems of the state system of schooling to be taken as indicative of problematic family relations.

Notes

1 In his work on England, Hurt (1979, p. 204) argues that there was little protection for children working outside school hours. He notes that 'Under the Elementary Education Act, 1876, it was possible to prosecute an employer if the child's work interfered with his efficient education. The act, invoked solely against those who employed children during school hours, proved something of a broken reed.'

Chapter 7:

The Emergence of the Individual

Introduction

By discussing the institutional action outlined in the diagram in chapter 1 I have been able to explore the pre-conditions for the features of the two social maps which also appear there. In so doing, I have emphasized official concern to teach the mass of the population to know their place, within the state promoted order of social relations. I have underlined the significance of relations of class and gender in these features. But the argument needs to be taken further, for the maps with which I am dealing are concerned with the coalescence of these themes, concerning relations of space and time, in the production of the *individual* social identities of 'child' and 'truant'.

To argue that official discourse dealt with social order as the central purpose of schooling is not necessarily to claim that this provides a *total* understanding of the impact of schooling. Indeed, as I pointed out earlier, official reports indicate that some parents regarded schooling as important because it provided tuition in skills to which children might otherwise have little or no access — for example, reading, writing and arithmetic (XLIX, 1861, *Woodford, 1860*). This was a reason for opposition to the introduction of subjects which dealt with skills which children could obtain from other sources. In other words, what schooling was to be about and the way in which it was to operate were matters of controversy. For, co-existing with the belief that schools should keep people in their allotted place, there was also a view that schooling could and should offer children *opportunity*, even if this opportunity was circumscribed by the basic tenets of a particular definition of social order. Schooling was, then, Janus-faced, and both aspects must be examined in order to reach an adequate understanding of discourse on truancy. There are two distinctive features being introduced in the view of schooling as providing children with opportunity: the concern with individual children, and the instigation of the notion that schooling can be understood in terms of opportunity.

A major shift in what schooling was to be about and how schools were to be assessed took place during the 1860s. This also involved a change in the kind of knowledge which schools would convey both about pupils and to them. What underlay this was an administrative programme to increase the efficiency and economy of regulating schooling. It meant that knowledge of schooling was no longer to be knowledge of the performance of classes of a school, and schooling was no longer to be primarily concerned with locating classes of the population. Rather, knowledge of schooling was to become based on the performances of individual pupils, and schooling was to become concerned with the provision of opportunity for individuals to achieve a better position within the hierarchy of school assessment. Implicitly, as I indicated in chapter 3, this hierarchy was taken as a reflection of the wider social world. The components of my argument here need to be distinguished from those of the 'lad o' pairts' tradition in Scotland which was discussed earlier, as referring to the theoretical possibility for any bright male child to gain access to university. This myth referred to the possible success of talented individuals. The discursive shift with which I am concerned here, in contrast, dealt with schooling as offering the possibility of achievement for *all* pupils, not simply those boys who were defined as being clever.

From the start, a concern with economy and efficiency had been basic to the construction of state regulation. By the 1850s and 1860s the rigour of the enforcement of the Committee of Council's minutes was being called into question. In part this was a reflection of governmental concern over the rapid rise in state expenditure on education at a time when the government was trying to reduce expenditure generally. In 1833 expenditure had been £20,000; in 1846 it was £100,000; in 1859 it was £668,000 (Wilson in Humes and Paterson *op. cit.*). The solution to these difficulties was held to be an increase in the precision of the collection and measurement of data about schooling. The main aims of the alterations were an increased standardization of inspection, of the assessment of a school's relationship to the minutes and, associated with this, an assessment of the school's grant-earning capacity. The first means of doing this will be discussed in the next section. It involved a stricter enforcement of the regulation that teachers should collect what the education office defined as necessary school statistics. This was done by developing a further mutation of the panoptic principle which took the form of promoting the use of one version of the school register. The way in which this register was kept was incorporated into the definition of an efficiently organized school. This was the way in which the 'avalanche of numbers' became manifest at the level of the school.

The second measure was the Revised Code of 1862 which instituted the measurement of the results of elementary schooling by means of the individual written examination. The notorious system of payment by results was an integral part of this and was developed as a solution to the problem of ensuring the cost-effectiveness of regulating schools. Inspection was no longer to be carried out by selecting a few *examples* from each class, for examination. Instead, each pupil was to be examined in what were referred to as the 'Standards'. These were aptly-named since they instituted a *standardization* of forms and levels of pupil performance. This produced a hierarchy of attainment which was to be linked with the duration of school attendance and the ages of pupils. By extending visibility and segmentation beyond individual schools and into the *system* of state-regulated schooling, the register and the Revised Code were aimed at eradicating 'problem schools' both from state aid and from the social world.

Registers

Today the use of the school register is taken for granted and, as I indicated earlier, it is often the only source of figures about attendance which is kept as a matter of routine. Yet, in the nineteenth century, its usefulness was by no means self-evident to those involved in schooling. An argument first had to be made for both the necessity and the particular form which the classification and counting of school attendance was to take. The use of the register was not unique to Committee of Council schools, neither was it their innovation. For example, the episcopal church provided its schools with registers (LII, 1854, *Wilkinson Report, 1853*, p. 1048). The Dick Bequest Schools in the North-East of Scotland had them and, though it was extremely rare, some parochial teachers also kept daily attendance registers, and some kept books containing details of their pupils such as, name, age, stage of progress at time of entry, degree of progress made, and the character which they displayed in school (XXXIII, 1842, *Gibson Report on Aberdeen and Fordyce, 1842*, p. 217). However, what I am arguing here is that it was through the *systematic* action of state education officials that the register was to become a necessary part of the definition of what it was to run an efficient school.

Panoptism, as I have explained, was fundamental to the state model of schooling. Deriving from key features of the architectural model of the panopticon, its core components were visibility and segmentation. In a panopticon the organization of physical space ensured that those within it were constantly visible to observers. As a result of this constant possibility of supervision, power relations would function automatically. Inspectors, as state agents, were to collect data about schools according to that which it was officially defined as relevant to know. In the early stages of inspection, knowledge of individual pupils was not encompassed within this definition of 'relevant'. In assessing schools inspectors would select pupils from each class in order to examine them as *examples* of their class. The performance of these pupils would enable the inspector to assess the efficiency of the teacher and therefore that of the school.

However, in terms of the precepts of panoptism, the problem with this was that inspection visits occurred, at their most frequent, only once a year. It was only during these visits that a school would be *immediately* visible to government officials. Though it was possible in this way to inspect the spatial organization of a school directly, the temporal patterning of school relations was less accessible. The written record was to be a means of overcoming this by making significant features of a school's year *mediately* visible to inspectors. In particular, the register was to provide a constant record of attendance throughout the year, therefore making it easier for an inspector to assess the relationship of a school's performance to the efficiency of a teacher. It did this by extending the organization of space and time in the school on to a level of administration which would make its patterns visible beyond the immediate spatial/temporal location of the individual school. Based on the classification and counting of attendance, the register was the visible manifestation of the 'avalanche of numbers' (see chapter 3) at the level of the school. As such, it was intrinsically linked to the belief that an initial step towards the solution of a problem was its quantification.

The problem which was being pursued at this time constituted a reversal of earlier official concern with the way in which a school could affect a neighbourhood; for an inspector needed to be able to judge the way in which a particular neighbourhood affected attendance and schooling. Registers were held to be an indication of a well-managed school, a measurement of its problems and an encouragement of its pupils to attend.

> Some have not introduced daily marking, for the very reason that renders it more desirable and important, namely, the great irregularity in the attendance of the children. When this irregularity is greater than usual, the obviously best course, both for the character of the teacher, and with the view of showing the necessity on the part of the managers for trying some corrective means, is to ascertain and show by a well-kept daily register the actual amount of it, and with what class of scholars and under what circumstances the defalcation chiefly lies. Indeed, the registration alone of irregularity has, in many schools, gone far to correct it. (XLII, 1854–5, *Woodford, 1854*, p. 707; also XLII, 1862, *Gordon, 1861*, p. 206).

From the outset of regulation it had been ruled that the keeping of a school register was to be a condition attached to awards of financial aid from the state (LXXIX, 1852–3, *Correspondence on School Registers*, p. 50). However, even though particular figures were necessary for the calculation of state grants (*ibid.*), there was no clear definition provided as to what were to count as important school statistics. It was only when a capitation grant became available in England and Wales (XLI, 1854–5, *Minute, 2 April 1853*; see also, Wilson, *op. cit.*, pp. 98–9) as a means of spreading state influence by encouraging 'regular attendance' among the 'poor and populous' areas that the inadequacies of existing forms of registers became an object of systematic concern. This was because the conditions of the grant required children to have 176 days' attendance per year (though there was an allowance of sixteen days for absences i.e. 192 days in total). Though the grant was confined to England and Wales, the impact of the concern with registers was not so confined. For inspectors advocated that the counting of individuals, a prerequisite for the capitation grant, should be incorporated into the assessment of schools in Scotland as a means of improving both registers and attendance.

What was the prevailing situation to be altered? Inspection reports reveal that there was no uniform interpretation of what it was to keep a school register. For example, sometimes registers might simply consist of a catalogue of enrolments with occasional indications of the payment or non-payment of fees (XLI, 1854–5, *Woodford, 1854*, p. 707). 'The daily attendance, the ages, dates of entering and leaving, the payments of school pence are, in some cases, not all entered, and the averages are not taken uniformly for the same periods of time' (XLII, 1862, *Gordon, 1861*, p. 206). There were further difficulties in that, because schooling was often interspersed with other activities, some schools reported having an entirely different set of pupils at different seasons, yet methods of recording this meant that its extent was difficult to gauge (XXXIII, 1857, *Woodford and Middleton, 1856*, pp. 620–1).

This problem was increased by it being rare for a register to distinguish children who were leaving finally from those who were transferring to another school. For this reason information about the frequency with which children changed school was sparse. One result was that this made the overall duration of a child's schooling difficult to assess.

> ... it remains to be ascertained how long in general the pupils have the benefit of ... [school instruction], not only how many years, but for how many months in each year they ordinarily attend. ... a large proportion of ... schoolmasters in schools under my inspection have been less than three years in the situation which they now hold. They cannot from personal knowledge state how many children have been three or four years at school; and the registers are so commonly considered the property of the individual schoolmaster, that when a change takes place there is no record to exhibit the fact. (LII, 1854, *Cumming and Wilson, 1853*, p. 989).

These difficulties were exacerbated by the fact that it was seldom possible to identify individual pupils and trace their subsequent progress from records (XXXIII, 1857, *Cumming and Wilson, 1856*, p. 661). From this we can see that just as problematic as the mobility of pupils was that of teachers since they often took their registers with them, leaving no record available in the school for consultation (XLIV, 1850, *Gordon, 1849*, p. 555)

> Some teachers employ forms of their own contriving; and these are sometimes upon loose sheets, showing for how brief an existence the record has been meant, and some are intelligible only to the teacher who keeps them ... signifying that they are considered as his own, and not as the property of the school. (XLII, 1862, *Gordon, 1861*, p. 206)

It was impossible to compile more general statistics since this lack of uniformity made it difficult to develop a more detailed picture.

Problems were further compounded by the variations in the methods of calculating entries (XLV, 1857–8, *Wilkinson, 1857*, p. 705). Inspectors complained that averages were often merely guesswork, or calculated from the highest month or quarter of a year's attendance (XXI, 1859, Part 1, *Middleton, 1858*, p. 238). Sometimes the figure would be higher than the highest weekly average.

> In two cases last year, that had an unusually suspicious look, I took time to calculate *the average attendance for the year*, from the 'Daily Register', and found it (in one case a little under, and in the other a little over) ONE HALF of what had been entered. ... (XXI, 1859, Part 1, *Middleton, 1858*, p. 239)

It was impossible to assess the extent to which such mistakes were genuine or were deliberate manipulations on the part of teachers to increase the amount of aid they would receive (XLIX, 1861, *Woodford, 1860*, pp. 214–15). But often registers were simply not available for inspection because many schools didn't keep them at all, but filled out official forms with estimates. '... I have been more than once told by teachers that the reason why they did not keep a register was, that the attendance was so irregular' (XLII, 1862, *Middleton*, 1861, p. 227). This was to become increasingly less acceptable for it was argued that, 'No one would believe, who had not made the experiment, how great is the difference of the result, in averages and other particulars, when taken from general impressions, and when calculated from actual entries (XLVII, 1856, *Circular to Principals of Training Schools*, 5 February 1855, p. 13).

The figures given in inspection reports were, then, frequently providing a veneer of precision, for there was no general agreement on either *what* should be counted or on *how* calculations should be made. Indeed there was a range of figures which were offered to inspectors. These included a selection from: the number actually on the books; the greatest number on the books in the previous six months; the number at the day of inspection; the average daily attendance during the previous six months; winter attendance (given in early reports); summer attendance (given in early reports); the greatest number present during the previous six months. But the figure which was given consistently for all schools was the number present at day of inspection, and even this would sometimes be an estimate. Such disorganization in a structure aimed at the systematization of schooling in particular, and the ordering of social relations generally, had to be tackled in order for there to be a closer control over the allocation of financial aid. Forms relating to state grants presupposed a regularly kept register as a basis for paying grants and also for general educational statistics concerning schools.

However, from the information available, discussions of such issues as the duration of attendance could only take place in the most general terms, sometimes focusing on the turnover of pupils in a school (XXXIII, 1857, *Gordon, 1856*, p. 639). Similarly, although there were frequent complaints in reports about short and irregular attendance, especially in the case of older pupils, the assessments of this were also impressionistic (LII, 1854, *Cumming and Wilson, 1853*, p. 1014; XXXIII, 1857, *Gordon, 1856*; *Woodford and Middleton, 1856*; XLV, 1857–8, *Cumming and Wilson, 1857*, p. 696). In short, though initially it was assumed that the keeping of accurate registers was an unproblematic requirement, inspectors found that, in their existing form, registers were an inadequate aid to regulation, for the information which they contained was generally based on estimates, derived from memory, calculated in a variety of ways and often either distorted by a teacher's misunderstanding of the meaning of 'average', or deliberately manipulated by teachers in order to get a larger state grant. Given that there was a belief among officials that useful knowledge was based on the order created by classification and counting, accurate knowledge of a school's efficiency and relationship to its local community could only be based on increasing the precision of the collection and measurement of data about attendance.

How did the shift occur from this situation of diversity to one of uniformity where the necessity and form of registers was to become self-evident? The form of the register which was to be fostered by the education officials was set out in specimens which laid down a minimum requirement for the keeping of approved figures.

Though the education office maintained that this form did not have to be adhered to if a school wished to keep other kinds of figures too, these particular figures were *required*. Therefore others would be variations on this core and would be seen *in relation to this*. But this in itself was not enough. Specimen registers had been published in the 1840s yet school statistics were still not generally kept in a standard form. The reason for this was that in the 1840s specimens (XLV, 1847, pp. 100–1) had been suggested by an inspector but their use had not been systematically incorporated into the assessment of what was to count as efficient. This was done in the 1850s by two methods: incorporation into the definition of an efficient school and into the definition of an efficient teacher.

SHOOL.

No. I.—REGISTER OF ADMISSION, PROGRESS, AND WITHDRAWAL.

(To be kept by the Principal Teacher.)

Name.	Index Number.	Date of Admission.		Age at Time of Admission.		Residence.	Occupation of the Parents.	Means of previous Instruction.	Whole time during which the Child has been at school before coming to this School.	
		Year.	Month.	Years.	Months.				Years.	Months.

Date of the Child's Admission to each successive Class of the School.

	1.		2.		3.		4.		5.		6.		7.		8.	
	Year	Month	Year	Month	Year	Month	Year	Month	Year	Month	Year	Month	Year	Month	Year	Month

Withdrawal.

Date.		Age.		Time in the School.		Class.	Assigned reason.	Proposed Occupation.	Signature of the Child.		Remarks.
Year.	Month	Years.	Months.	Years.	Months.				At the Time of Admission.	At the Time of Withdrawal.	

161

No. II.—CLASS REGISTER OF

(To be kept by the Teachers of each Class; to be verified, and

Number.	NAME (Of each Child in the Class, to be written in by the Principal Teacher).	From Monday the_____ Day of_____ to Saturday the_____ Day of_____.												Number of School Days.									Paid as School Fees.		
		M.		Tu.		W.		Th.		F.		S.		Present.	Absent.								£.	s.	d.
																Excused.									
		Morning.	Afternoon.	Morning.	Afternoon.	Morning.	Afternoon.	Morning.	Afternoon.	Morning.	Afternoon.	Morning.	Afternoon.	Present.	Sick.	Weather.	Circumstances of Home.	Poverty of Parents.	Other reasons.	Without excuse.	Total.				
I.	No. present daily																								
II.	Average No. present for Week*																								
III.	No. who have been present at all during the Week†																								
IV.	Average No. of Days attended by each Child present at all‡																								
V.	No. on Register§																								
VI.	Total Receipt by School Fees																								

* Add the totals of all the columns (Morning and Afternoon), and divide by ten.
† Count the names opposite to which there is *any* dot during the week.
‡ Divide the total sum of the columns of attendance by twice the number of names referred to in the last preceding note.
§ Count names ( ).

SCHOOL.

THE _____ CLASS.

the Totals collected into No. 3 weekly by the Master or Mistress.)

[Here follow Columns, similar to the preceding, for each of the other Twelve Weeks to complete the Quarter.]	Quarterly Total for each Child.				REMARKS on Studies and Progress of the Class during the Quarter.
	Number of School Days present.	Paid as School Fees.			
		£.	s.	d.	
					(Signed)_____
					Schoolm_____
					⎫
					⎬ Managers.
					⎭
					the Day of 186

Quarterly Results.

_____ II.

_____ III.

_____ IV.

_____ V.

_____ VI.

A separate register in this form will be required for each class. Each double page (including the shorter leaves between) answers to a quarter of a year. The attendance (morning and afternoon) should be shown by a pencilled dot; ink will cause blotting, and marks pricked in with a pin will show on each side of the paper. This register should always be kept under lock and key when not in use. The time table of each class should be entered in its register; a certain number of fly-leaves being left at the beginning for the purpose.

Efficient Schooling

Firstly, inspector reports were used to outline ways in which registration could become part of school routine. This was done through directly confronting the opposition of teachers who argued that the irregularity of pupils' attendance prevented registration from being worthwhile (XLII, 1854–5, *Woodford, 1854*, p. 707), and that, especially in large schools, daily registration of attendance was too time-consuming (*ibid.*, pp. 708–9). Official reports argued that where registration was properly integrated into a well-organized schooling routine, for example, by getting monitors and pupil teachers to mark daily registers simultaneously, with the master making a digest of these for the other forms to be completed, then the problems which teachers complained of would not exist. In this way, the calculation of figures which would provide a profile of a school's temporal pattern was presented as part of a properly organized school. Thus problems in getting figures were to be taken as indicative of poor organization (XLIX, 1861, *Woodford, 1860*, p. 218). Properly kept figures were to be both an indication of attendance patterns, and a means of fostering patterns which would be more compatible with the definition of regularity provided by the education office (XXXIII, 1857, *Woodford and Middleton, 1856*, pp. 620–1; *Gordon, 1856*, pp. 643–4). This was reinforced by the publication of letters from school managers and teachers, requesting clarification of the nature of attendance figures (XLV, 1857–8, p. 37). Replies set out methods of calculating figures and indicated that instructions would start to be published along with registers.

It is fundamental to my argument that the regulation of schooling involved the structuring of space/time and knowledge/action in such a way as to produce a theory and practice of normality which conformed to the state model and which marginalized alternatives. Indeed, the minimum attendance requirements set out by the education office were purposely set, 'at a point beyond common practice', as a means of fostering change in social behaviour. 'It never was supposed by their Lordships ... that every child in the school would fulfil the condition which depends upon ... attendance ... the Minute was framed upon the principle of encouraging improved practice' (XLV, 1857–8, *Letter from Lingen, 21 September 1857*). Thus, although 'common practice' could not be known in terms of the official form of measurement (XXXIII, 1842, *Gibson, 1842*, p. 216; LII, 1854, *Cumming and Wilson, 1853*, p. 989), it was *assumed* to be inadequate for the purposes of the education office.

The policy was therefore deliberately aimed at designating existing patterns as problems.

Though at this stage the specified necessary attendance level for individual children to earn a grant was not *directly* applied to Scotland, it nonetheless served to reinforce attendance as a pedagogical problem. For class teaching was the officially authorized mode of teaching and what could be taught, whether pupils would be classified correctly, or even whether they could be classified at all, were restricted by the extent to which they attended school. It was also reinforced as a financial problem since classification and performance were constituents of the definition of an efficient school.

The second way in which the keeping of state-approved registers was linked with efficiency was by incorporating it into the definition of an efficient teacher. This was managed by including instruction in the keeping of registers in the curriculum of Normal schools and setting a question on this in the second year examinations on School Management (XLVII, 1856, *Circular to Principals of Training Schools, 5 February, 1855*, pp. 13–14). Faulty exam answers were preserved and students who had not answered the questions on registers correctly were to have this recorded, even though they might have passed examinations in all other areas. Inspectors were then instructed to examine these people on all aspects of registration when they inspected the schools in which the students had taken up posts. The payment of their augmentation grant was dependent on the results of this (XLVII, 1856, *Circular to Principals of Female Training Schools, as to Answers Made by Students to Questions proposed in the Examination of December 1855, upon School Registers & Returns, 21 January 1856*; also *Circular to Principals of Male Training Schools etc., 22 February 1856*, pp. 14–18). It was not, then, that one version of what was to count as a properly kept register was directly imposed. But rather, that teachers were trained in the provision of information which would be useful to the education office. This particular version was directly related to the payment of grants and was incorporated into the definition of necessary knowledge for efficient teachers.

These changes meant that estimates and approximations would no longer be acceptable. Indeed, the circular explaining the capitation grant minute to inspectors specifically rejected approximations (XLI, 1854–5, p. 55). Instead, the tight organization of the school was to be extended to the keeping of school records. Random figures on scraps of paper were to be replaced by a Register of Admission, Progress, and Withdrawal; a Class Register divided into half-days, days and weeks; a Class Register divided into weeks and quarters; and an annual table divided into quarters. Officially, schooling was no longer to be a seasonal activity; rather it was to be an activity regulated and counted by clock and calendar time. The temporal counterpart of the strict classification of space, the register made it officially necessary to account for time: in other schools; in this school; in each successive class in this school; for the termination of time in this school; and for time spent out of school space on a school day. Just as there was an official categorization of particular space as belonging to schooling, so there was an allocation of time, in the form of the 'school day', and the 'school year'. This systematic accounting for time was designed to facilitate the development of a profile of patterns of schooling generally, as well as to develop a profile for individual schools.

But more than this, the focus on the precision with which data about schools were gathered made possible the emergence of the individual whose institutional profile could immediately be seen from the school record. For the basic unit of data was no longer to be the class, but the individual pupil. The Register of Admission, Progress and Withdrawal made visible an individual's school career (date and age of admission, previous instruction, duration of previous instruction, date of admission to each class in this school, age and date of withdrawal, duration of attendance, reason for withdrawal). This institutional profile located individuals not simply in the school, but in the wider social world, through the inclusion of the parental occupation and the child's proposed occupation. It thus would provide a record of the scheduling of social identities of those passing through the school, formalizing the demarcation of 'work', 'life' and 'school'. Further, children had to be categorized as being in a particular location during given segments of school time. Out of place meant out of sight of the authority relations of the school. The classification and counting of kinds of absence was a means of making officially visible, and therefore keeping within the network of authority relations, individuals who were not actually present/visible within the space of the school.

'... The presence of each child is indicated by a blank space ...' (XLVII, 1856, *Circular to Principals of Male Training Schools*, p. 16). The register was to constitute a reversal of the visibility of pupils within the school; absence from school was to be indicated by the presence of an explanation in the register. It was therefore to be a means of locating absences:

'... if absent without leave the letter A is placed in the space ...; if attendance has been prevented by circumstances at home, the letter H is written; if by sickness, the letter S; if by any other excuse received by the teacher, the letter X; or if leave of absence has been granted, the letter L is written; ... on every occasion the cause of a child's absence is *immediatley seen* ...'.

In this way, classification and counting solved the problem of visibility. It transformed the invisible into the visible and, through the categorization of absences, made it possible to distinguish acceptable from unacceptable. The emergence of attendance profiles for individual children, a prerequisite for the construction of individual subjects within official discourse, was then made possible by the form of the register which was officially promoted by means of direct financial incentives in England and Wales, and indirectly throughout Britain by its incorporation into definitions of efficiency in schooling.

Examinations

In nineteenth century Britain, just as now, the individual written examination was a controversial technique for assessing education. Early in this period it was an innovation which was used within a few, upper class settings such as Oxford and Cambridge or by a few occupational groups (such as apothecaries) who were attempting to secure the favourable market position of a profession by restricting entrance to that occupation. However, the use of this technique was gradually to expand during this period as it became enmeshed in a range of institutional sites and practices which reached all classes of the population. In part this expansion reflected the spread of successful examination candidates from upper class establishments into official positions within the state (Montgomery, 1965, p. 16). For example, both Robert Lowe (Vice-President of the Committee of Council on Education, 1859–1864) and Ralph Lingen (Secretary of the Education Department, 1850–1870) had Oxford backgrounds. After Northcote-Trevelyan in 1853 the principle of individual competitive examination was being promoted within the civil service.

The rise of public examinations at this time can be understood in terms of functional selection, educational expediency or social regulation (MacLeod, 1982). The first view equates the spread of examinations with a spread of meritocratic selection processes. The second takes examinations to be an extension of educational activity aimed at improving the transmission of knowledge. In particular this was an argument made during the nineteenth century by those promoting the use of examinations in middle and upper class schools (Roach, 1971). Both these views reflect the extent to which the technique of individual written examination encapsulated liberal ideals of competition and the allocation of individual reward according to merit. It had the advantage that it could be administered economically since one person could read standardized questions to a large number of candidates, as opposed to older methods of examination used within universities, where one student would be questioned by several examiners (Hoskin, 1982). Further, it produced results which were quantifiable and, as I have argued, the production of quantifiable information was an important aspect of state activity.

However, at the same time as promoting this technique for widespread use within elementary schools, the education office was one of the slowest parts of the civil service to comply with the use of examinations to assess its recruits, preferring to continue to recruit by patronage (Bishop, 1971, p. 73). Lingen argued, '... since rank and wealth held the keys to advancement socially, politically and commercially he saw no reason for the abolition of patronage' (Bishop, 1971, p. 41). To understand this and the significance of examinations in elementary schooling, the third interpretation of their role needs to be taken into account. This stresses that examinations codify the beliefs of particular groups and reflect an aim of these groups to produce or reproduce particular social relations.

By looking at examinations in this way, we can understand the profound impact which their institutionalization into elementary schooling was to have on the official construction of individual pupil identity and on our understanding of the role of schooling. In doing this, we are able to recognize the importance of the knowledge/power coalition within the examination which reinforces authority relations: what counts as knowledge is officially legitimated by the examination, a self-reinforcing technique which purports to define what it is to know. No longer was it to be sufficient for an individual to be subsumed within a class, located in a school. The examinations instigated by the Revised Code would facilitate the location of individual pupils within a *system* of schooling, making it possible to judge their performance beyond the level of the particular institution which they were attending.

Revised Code

What came to be known as the 'Old' Code had been drawn up in 1860. It was a summary and clarification of Committee of Council rules to date and was issued because of the volume of minutes which had built up since the Committee of Council's inception. As successor to the Old Code, the Revised Code had profound implications for schooling in Scotland. Despite this, historians of Scottish education have had very little to say about it and, to the extent to which they have said anything, it has been characterized by a lack of accuracy and coherence. The exception to this has been Wilson's examination of reasons for the delay in the full implementation of the Revised Code in Scotland (*op. cit.*). This neglect can in part be explained by the fact that the code was only fully implemented in Scotland for a very short time. It was introduced in Scotland in May 1864, suspended on 10 June 1864, and then suspended annually until the 1872 legislation (for a full discussion of the reasons for this see Wilson *op. cit.*). However, the new code had an important impact on schooling in Scotland because, though state grants continued to be paid under the Old Code, there was a constant possibility of it being extended to Scotland throughout the period until the 1872 Act. More significantly, the new code formed the basis for inspectors' assessments of schooling throughout Britain. Therefore, its importance lies in the way in which it structured the knowledge which was gathered about schools.

The code was a pre-condition of the generation of themes concerning individual opportunity and schooling within official discourse. It introduced a system of payment by results as a means of trying to ensure the cost-effectiveness of regulating schools. Within this system pupils were to be assessed individually by means of written examinations. Underlying it, were the findings of the Newcastle Commission on England and Wales. This had examined possible ways of extending 'sound and cheap' elementary instruction to all classes of the population. The commission's report of 1861 had concluded that there was a need to tighten up on the payment of grants, to standardize inspection, to simplify the grants system and to focus attention on slower rather than quicker pupils.

The new code was a means of reinforcing and extending the regulation of schools through the increased regulation of inspection. By rationalizing the system of grants being paid for buildings, teaching pupil teachers, augmenting teachers' salaries, books and apparatus, it shifted the financial focus from the *means* of schooling to the *results*. It did this by making payments direct to managers and conditional on the number and proficiency of pupils, the number and qualifications of the teachers, and the state of the schools. The new mode of inspection under the terms of the Revised Code helped to consolidate an authorized definition of a place and time for schooling as well as of what was to count as the effective transmission of appropriate knowledge. It therefore operated to crystallize the core form of what has come to be understood as basic education.

An important aim of the code was to pressure schools into enforcing a longer duration and more uniform patterns of attendance. With inspection being carried out in terms of the new code, alternative patterns of school attendance became problems of the inability to present pupils for examination:

> The number presented ... appears to fall greatly short of the average attendance, and it represents only those who, in the course of the year, had attended, however irregularly, for so many times as would amount to twenty weeks or more. Of the unpresented whose attendance had been of that amount or more, some had already left the school, more were only absent at the time, and some were unprepared. If compared with the number that attended in the course of the year for any length of time, the short-coming in the number presented would ... be very considerably increased. (XX, 1868–9, *Gordon, 1868*, p. 332; see also XXII, 1870, *General Report, 1869*; XXII, 1871, *Jolly, 1870*, pp. 318–19; XXII, 1872, *Gordon, 1871*, p. 83).

There were also problems of examination failure, '... the failures ... are sometimes very far from implying any fault on the teacher's part; they are simply the consequence of an attendance numerically sufficient, but extremely irregular' (XXII, 1867, *Gordon, 1866*, p. 302; see also XXV, 1867–8, *General Report, 1867*). The inability to present pupils and the failure of those who were presented both had implications for the level of grant which would be paid to the school. The linking of grants to the age of pupils made possible the emergence of the problems of 'late enrolment' and 'early leaving' (XXII, 1872, *Scougal, 1871*).

The code generated these problems firstly, by the reinforcement of the necessity of keeping a written record of individual pupils' attendance. It further consolidated the use of registers by directly linking the level of attendance to grant earned, in the case of England and Wales, and indirectly in the whole of Britain. It did this by stipulating a minimum attendance necessary for a pupil to be eligible for inclusion in the individual written examination. A development of mechanisms which were already in use in relation to teachers, the standardized individual examination was based on a set syllabus with demarcated stages which would provide a written record of individual performance.

The examination reinforces authority relations through the coalition of knowledge/power: what counts as knowledge is officially legitimated by the examination, a self-reinforcing technique which purports to define what it is to know. No longer was it to be sufficient for an individual to be subsumed within a class, located in a school. The examinations instigated by the Revised Code would facilitate the location of individual pupils within a *system* of schooling, making it possible to judge their performance beyond the level of the particular institution which they were attending.

EXTRACT FROM REVISED CODE

38. Schools may meet three times daily: viz., in the morning, afternoon, and evening.

....

40. The managers of schools may claim at the end of each year ...
    (a) The sum of 4/- per scholar according to the average number in attendance throughout the year at the morning and afternoon meetings of their school, and 2/6d. per scholar according to the average number in attendance throughout the year at the EVENING MEETINGS of their school.
    (b) For every scholar who has attended more than 200 morning or afternoon meetings of their school —
    (1) if more than 6 years of age 8/-, subject to examination (Article 48)
    (2) if under 6 years of age 6/6d., subject to report by the inspector that such children are instructed suitably to their age, and in a manner not to interfere with the instruction of the older children.
    (c) For every scholar who has attended more than 24 evening meetings of their school 5/-, subject to examination. (Article 48)

....

43. Evening attendances may not be reckoned for any scholar under 12 years of age.

44. Every scholar attending more than 200 times in the morning or afternoon, for whom 8/- is claimed, forfeits 2/8d. for failure to satisfy the inspector in reading, 2/8d/ in writing, and 2/8d. in arithmetic (Article 48)

....

46. Every scholar for whom grants dependent upon examination are claimed must be examined according to one of the following Standards, and must not be presented for examination a second time according to the same or a lower Standard.

....

(XLI, 1862,*Chapter 11, Grants to Maintain Schools,. Part 1, Elementary Schools*).

Knowledge of a teacher's capacity for conveying officially sanctioned knowledge to individual pupils was to be revealed by their pupils' display of what they knew to the inspector. The Standards, as these examinations were appropriately named, were to provide the basis for a new knowledge — one formed by measuring and counting — which was to be taken to indicate the *effectiveness* of schooling. In this way reports came to measure the performance of a school by counting that of the pupils. 'It has nowhere been officially stated, or implied, that the number of passes is the sole measure of a school's excellence, but it is one of the measures; and the school which obtains fewer passes is, *pro tanto*, the worse school' (XX, 1868 –9, *General Report*, p. 25). The individual examination was introduced as a more precise instrument of the measurement of schooling (XXII, 1867, *Middleton, 1866*, p. 325), by allowing for the assessment of the performance of *all* pupils it was to be a means of avoiding the dangers of teachers concentrating on a few children who might then be presented as exemplary in relation to the school.

It was not an innovation to schooling, although it was in so far as the pupils were concerned, for it was a technique used in the assessment of pupil teachers, and trainee teachers at Normal school. The associated pupil teacher's stipend and the Queen's scholarship were also based on payment by results. Inspection reports, since the inception of these particular examinations, had argued that there had been an improvement in standards of teaching. So, aside from their normalizing implications, surely the individual examination, the fixed syllabus and payment by results could at least ensure an eradication of problem schools and, consequently, a raising of standards of schooling among pupils generally? In this context, it might be expected that these measures would be welcomed by most people involved with schooling.

However, this was not the case, for large numbers of petitions were sent to Parliament to express the opposition of many people involved in schooling to the Revised Code (XLI, 1862). School inspectors also expressed opposition in their reports and were able to do this because the Revised Code was not official policy in Scotland. Several themes can be traced in both sets of documents. Firstly, the level of minimum attendance which was stipulated was felt to be unnecessarily high (XXVII, 1866, *Scougal, 1865*, p. 330; *Kerr, 1865*, pp. 302–3; *Woodford, 1865*, pp. 311–13). Secondly, there were objections to the specification of a particular duration and rhythm of schooling for grant eligibility. This, it was argued, would make it more difficult to allow for patterns of the social division of labour which involved schooling and income-earning work being interspersed (XLI, 1862[1]). Thirdly, the introduction of age as a factor in the classification of children was viewed as totally impractical, especially given the patterns of living of many people (XLI, 1862[2]). Such factors, it was maintained, were too far beyond a teacher's control for their efficiency and merit as a teacher to be judged on this. In short, a school might be penalized as a problem when the site of the problem might, either because of the patterning of local social relations or because of such contingencies as epidemics, lie beyond a school's control (XLI, 1862[3]).

The age/finance/attendance link was held to be too inflexible, narrowing the range of pupils which it would be financially beneficial to teach. Thus, it would discourage very young and older pupils since it had an implicit view that the norm for schooling should be continuous attendance above the age of 6 and under the age of 11. Whatever efforts a teacher might make with those who attended according to alternative patterns, they would not bring a financial reward to the school. These problems, it was argued, would be reinforced by the introduction of individual examination which dealt with a narrow curriculum and would be counter to the Scottish tradition of links between schools and universities (XLII, 1865, *Middleton, 1864*; XLI, 1862[4]).

These links meant that traditionally there had been the theoretical possibility for talented boys to go to university, whatever their background. However, this and arguments against the state requirement that there should be a record kept by schools of the means and occupation of parents (XLII, 1865, *Middleton, 1864*, pp. 272–7; XLV, 1864, *Woodford, 1863*, p. 254) should not be understood as a defence of an egalitarian past. For from the outset regulation grants for elementary schools had been class-based and schools were sometimes identified in inspection reports according to the class of the population which attended them (XXXIII, 1857, *Cumming and Wilson, 1856*, pp. 667–8; XLIX, 1861, *Gordon, 1860*, p. 224). The innovation of the Revised Code which clashed directly with the 'lad o' pairts' myth which I discussed earlier as figuring so importantly in the national tradition of Scottish education, was the identification of *individual children* in relation to class. The shift which the code facilitated by introducing the Standards concerned the possibility of achievement for *all* pupils, not simply those who were male and defined as clever.

To summarize, criticisms of the Revised Code highlight that it was rejected by many people since it would make it more difficult for teachers and school managers to negotiate between relations in the community and the state model of correct social relations. Official regulations were gradually making it less possible to adjust schooling to local communities; for they were aimed at adjusting relations in local communities to the implicit normality of state-structured schooling. This notion of normality was not based on a widespread pattern which already existed, but had its roots in the attempts to erase particular mores from groups of the population which were defined as social and moral problems, and was consolidated in an attempt to increase the efficiency of the regulation within the system.

Although I have indicated that many people objected to the mechanisms integral to the code, I have not yet answered the question as to the implications of the measures which were implemented in Scotland in relation to the official aims of increasing the efficiency and economy of schooling. Inspection reports indicate that, in these terms, there were problems with the measures, since they generated new forms of dissonance. For example, teachers would distort attendance figures if pupils might pass an examination but had insufficient attendance to be presented (XXV, 1867–8, *General Report, 1867*, p. xxlv). Teachers would pretend children were younger than they really were in order to present them for a Standard that they would definitely pass as opposed to one which they might fail (XXII, 1872, *Scougal, 1871*, pp. 126–7). Teachers would 'cram' children for exams (XXII, 1872, *Kerr, 1871*).

As money was not paid for individuals in Scotland, but a school's efficiency was assessed on this basis, teachers would avoid presenting children who might not pass (XXVII, 1866, *Black, 1865*; XXV, 1867–8, *Woodford, 1865–7*; XLII, 1865, *Jack, 1864*; XXII, 1871, *Hall, 1870*; *Middleton, 1870*). So inspectors started to demand explanations for non-presentation as selective presentation was so widespread and it could mean a good pass rate for a school with a poor presentation rate (XXII, 1871, *Jolly, 1870*; XXII, 1872, *Kerr, 1871*; *Scougal, 1871*). Reports argued that it was a mistake to assume that schools with the largest number of passes were providing the most education (XXII, 1870, *Kerr, 1869*, p. 386; XXVII, 1866, *Kerr, 1865*, p. 300; XXV, 1867–8, *Black, 1867*, p. 384; XXII, 1871, *Hall, 1870*, p. 296), since examination passes were a good measurement for the system but a bad one for education (XXV, 1867–8, *Woodford, 1867*, p. 421). Although a circular was sent to inspectors (XXII, 1872, 10 June 1871, pp. cxlv–cxv) and was aimed at curbing the practice of non-presentation, the problems of 'cramming' and the difficulty of verifying attendance figures remained.

But the significance of these measures is not simply that they set tighter controls on schooling, increasing the degree to which non-conformity was a problem, for there was another dimension. The individual written examination was a means of tightening control of teachers and inspection by restricting the definition of what was to count as efficiency in schooling. It constituted a new set of constraints through which teachers had to negotiate the presentation of their school. In so doing, it also made possible the construction of a new knowledge of normality, based on individual attendance and the age at which a particular stage of schooling would be reached. For there were six Standards and pupils had to be over 6 years old to be presented on the lowest (see also XXII, 1871, *Wilson, 1870*, p. 327; XXII, 1872, *Scougal, 1871*, p. 126). The register and the Revised Code, instruments for the measuring and counting of an individual's temporal experience, fostered the coalition of social relations of space and time in the emergence of the individual subject. This involved the emergence of an institutional profile for individual children which was silhouetted against a background of understandings which were class-based and gendered.

State-structured elementary schooling was no longer to be a mechanism for locating a class of the population, for generating and transmitting knowledge *of* a class and knowledge *for* a class. For the hierarchy of assessment of individual pupils which had been introduced into schooling was also a hierarchy for their individual achievement. What was to count as achievement within this context was, however, tightly circumscribed. Activities other than reading, writing and arithmetic were marginalized and those whose achievements were not encompassed by this model would not count as successful. The construction of individuals as subjects within schooling therefore helped to create another problem: the problem of ability. This was a problem of pupils who were less able to pass the Standards than their peers (XXII, 1867, *Gordon, 1866*) and who, because of this constituted a financial as well as a pedagogical problem for schools.

In contrast, for those pupils who could pass the examinations, they were to provide a means of personal progression within the hierarchy of attainment. In this way an apparent harmony between the formal identity and the in-formed identity of a pupil was to shift from being a pre-requisite for class members knowing their place to becoming the basis for individuals being able to achieve a better position. Problem attendance, in this respect, was to come to be seen as a barrier to the educational progress of children (XXII, 1867, *Gordon, 1866*; XXII, 1872, *Gordon, 1871*), progress, ability and achievement being defined in relation to the hierarchy of the Standards.

The tightening of control on inspection and expenditure and its consequent tightening on schools, made possible the emergence of an institutional profile for individual children, which was silhouetted against a background of class-based understandings. Paradoxically, this shift in focus to the *individual* as an *object* to be schooled in the Standards created the possibility of the emergence of the pupil as a *subject* who could *achieve* in the new hierarchy of attainment. In this way, not only could the problems with which schooling was structured to deal (that is, class mores) be understood as preventing efficient schooling, they could also come to be viewed as preventing the achievement of individual pupils. This was the way in which dissonance between the formal identity of pupil promoted by the state-structured school, and the in-formed identities of children officially expected to participate in schooling, became an individualized problem. That education officials were concerned to promote techniques of individuation, such as the written examination, and to judge working class children on this basis but were reluctant to have their own recruits judged in this way underlines the class bias and the limits of the 'individuality' being promoted.

Notes

1 XLI, 1862, *Petitions: Glasgow Free Church Normal Training College*, pp. 91–2; *Sub Committee, Free Church Education Committee*, pp. 101–2; *Presbytery of Elgin*, p. 127; *Presbytery of Strathbogie*, p. 77.

2 XLI, 1862, *Petitions: Free Church Kirkmichael*, p. 34; *Sub-Committee, Free Church Education Committee*, p. 101; *Education Committee, General Assembly, Church of Scotland*, pp. 107–9; *Presbytery of Strathbogie*, p. 77; *Directors Glasgow Free Church Training College*, p. 92; *Free Presbytery of Paisley*, p. 93; *Free Presbytery of Irvine*, p. 113; *Presbytery of Elgin*, p. 127; *Letter, Bishop of Edinburgh*, p. 20; *Memo, Rev. Presbytery of Glasgow*, p. 123.

3 XLI, 1862, *Petitions: Presbytery of Elgin*, p. 127; *Free Presbytery Turriff*, p. 139; *Aberdeen Synod of the Free Church*, p. 23; *Directors, Glasgow Free Church Normal Training College*, p. 92; *Sub-Committee, Free Church Education Committee*, pp. 101–2; *Education Committee, General Assembly, Church of Scotland*, p. 107; *Rev. Presbytery of Glasgow*, p. 123; *Presbytery of Dundee*, p. 34; *Presbytery of Strathbogie*, p. 77.

4 XLI, 1862, *Petitions: Glasgow Free Church Normal Training College*, pp. 91–2; *Sub-Committee, Free Church Education Committee*, p. 101; *Free Presbytery Turriff*, p. 139; *Free Presbytery Irvine*, p. 113; *Aberdeen Free Church*, p. 24.

Chapter 8

Conclusion

In contemporary Britain truancy is usually dealt with as a type of individual deviance. Yet, as I have shown, it has been produced socially. It is a result of the ways in which policies have been developed from political programmes and the ways in which they have been embedded in institutions. It's not that prior to state regulation schooling had no problems. Rather, it is that the particular issues which are today considered to be part of any discussion of truancy, have their thematic roots in the concerns which were institutionalized through the construction of a system of schooling. At the outset of the book I asked four questions. These were concerned with the programmes of power, the implementation of which was a precondition for the emergence of today's social maps. They were: Whose programmes? What were they about? How were they implemented? What have been the implications of this implementation?

In answering the first three questions I have maintained that state regulation of schooling was instituted in the nineteenth century, as a programme for class control, by an elite grouping with a shared understanding of the fundamental issues about the organization of social relations at that particular time. This programme became embedded in schooling by means of the activities of the education office and the school inspectorate. In the process it became 'neutralized' as a programme of the efficient and economic administration of regulations.

Schools were structured as mechanisms of discipline for the children of working class people. They were predicated on the necessity of producing and sustaining hierarchical relations of authority in an ordered social world. Diversity was construed as disorder, and consequently as threatening in so far as it could not be incorporated into the desired structure. Working class people were, by definition, a problem. This was why this form of schooling was aimed at them. The conditions which characterized their existence — long working hours and poverty — were dealt with as moral topographical problems which made them vulnerable to the possibility of slipping into the criminal class and, therefore, outside of social order. For long working hours were considered to indicate long hours in which appropriate familial relations of authority could not be enforced by parents. This raised the problem of an inappropriate upbringing for the future adult population. By providing a suitable location and a correct series of stages through which children would pass, state regulated schooling was to be the means of implementing these programmes. Fundamentally, this involved the structuring of social relations of space and time in a form which would promote a process of correct identity formation. This was done by creating an authorized place for schooling and structuring an authorized identity for those who were to operate schools, that is, teachers. The content of schooling was to reinforce these measures and, in so doing, was to facilitate the structuring of social relations, by means of regulating social relations in families.

As a result of state activity in establishing institutional parameters, the particular elements of normality which are featured on the social map of the formal identity of child were produced. However, social relations which did not conform to the official parameters of accept-ability did not simply disappear. Rather, as I have shown, they have been reproduced as deviance and have consequently made possible the production of the features which characterize the social map of the formal identity of truant. But problems for state regulation of schooling were not only those posed by the continuation of forms of social relations which 'good schools' were to alter. Importantly, they were also generated by contradictions *internal to* the state model.

The social maps under discussion refer to *individual* identities. Programmes facilitated the structuring of individuals as silhouettes against a background of class-based understandings, enabling the emergence of the problematic child. That is, a child whose relation to the authorized scheduling of social identities does not conform to the official model, and who therefore would not be able to progress through the official hierarchy of achievement. Put another way, official action enabled particular forms of *social relations* to be structured as *institutionally* problematic in such a way as to transform them into indicators of *individual* and *personal* problems.

I have used social mapping to trace the shift from varying patterns of attendance being a taken-for-granted aspect of varying ways of organizing social life, to the production of the *problem of irregular attendance*. The legislative 'solution', in the form of universal compulsion, which was enacted in relation to Scotland in 1872 marked the beginning of the erection of an official apparatus which was to be aimed at problematic individuals. This was to emerge from the institution of mechanisms such as: special meetings of the newly-formed school boards in order to deal with 'defaulting parents'; certificates issued by school boards in order to instigate prosecution of parents; the compulsory officer, who would visit the homes of absent children and report to the school board (Grant, *op.cit.*).

The relationship between knowledge and institutional action is one of *reciprocal interaction*. A particular 'knowledge' underlay the erection of an institutional structure to deal with problematic social groupings. The actions involved in this made possible the generation of a new 'knowledge' in terms of problematic individuals. This has become the basis for the construction of solutions based on institutional mechanisms targeted at individual subjects. In other words, the construction of problems and the structuring of solutions are *dynamically* linked. Indeed it is part of my argument that by looking at the implications of past policies we can understand the extent to which policies do not in any simple sense provide solutions but often generate other problems.

I will illustrate this in the final phase of my history of the present. For having displayed the pre-conditions of contemporary knowledge about 'normal children' and 'truants' my discussion would not be complete without some consideration of solutions offered in official documents on the basis of this. The initial statement of the reason for setting up the Pack Committee (*ibid.*, p. 1) set the report in the context of a concern about the links between truancy and delinquency. However, while in the nineteenth century state action was aimed at producing tightly ordered schools which would attract pupils and as a result keep them inside the law, in the twentieth century this is no longer the case. Rather it is the strict order of the classroom and the rigidity of the timetable and the curriculum which are officially held to drive 'problem pupils' to absent themselves from school, and which are seen as raising the possibility of children slipping outside the law. The issues which are involved in this can be characterized as a 'problem of continuity'.

In the nineteenth century the problem of continuity for schooling was the problem of effecting a series of *discontinuities* between existing forms of social relations and those which schools were to promote. This was to involve the compartmentalization of living: a separation of work, school and life; and the segmentation of schooling, both spatially, in its internal design, and temporally by the use of the timetable and the division of pupils' experience of schooling into stages. However, the success with which these discontinuities have been instituted has generated the contemporary problem of continuity, which is officially discussed as an issue of *transitions and links*. This is concerned with the *minimizing* or *erasing* of discontinuities caused by compartmentalization and segmentation. For example, there is the problem of the transfer of pupils from the primary stage of schooling to the secondary stage. This involves the question of the correct management of links between primary and secondary schools. The aim is to minimize the difficulties which 'problem' children may have in adjusting to the discontinuities inherent in their frequent shifts between different teachers which is a result of the subject-based division of labour among secondary teachers. Then there is the problem of the transition between school and work. This involves the correct management of links between the curriculum and industry (the provision of 'relevant' schooling and 'work experience'); and between schools and the careers service.

The issue of transitions and links concerns the difficulties which the organization and content of schooling pose for 'problem' pupils, and the importance of alleviating these in order to avoid precipitating truancy among these children. What makes these children 'problematic' and thus 'vulnerable' (*ibid.*, p. 26) is their family background for officially it is maintained that, 'There seems little doubt that family circumstances play the major role in cases of chronic truancy (*ibid.*, p. 27). The situation may be compounded among pupils who are adolescents, that is, in the transition stage to adulthood, a stage characterized in the Pack Report in terms of a disjuncture between physical and emotional maturity. Solutions involve the establishment of correct links, often by means of guidance teachers, who 'provide the ... link between the school and the other components of a child's life ...' (*ibid.*, p. 8). Difficulties in formulating the nature of 'correct' links are illustrated by the failure to clarify the role of attendance officers. For the function of these officials in some regions is instrumental 'truant catching' whereas in others their function, as reflected in the designation educational or school welfare officer, has a social work orientation.

Official failure to recognize the historically specific nature of issues of transitions and links has meant that there has been no conception of solutions to problems beyond issues of their correct management in relation to problematic individuals. This has meant, for example, the paradox of the 'solution' of day units within schools. These are characterized by fewer teachers and flexibility of timetabling and curriculum in order to provide greater continuity within schooling for 'problem' pupils. But, since the aim of such units is ultimately the reintegration of pupils into the tighter structure of the school outside of the unit, this immediately raises a further problem of transition — the same problem which, it is officially argued, is likely to have precipitated the truancy in the first place.

This brief consideration of contemporary solutions underlines the way in which a historical understanding can offer a different perception of contemporary 'knowledge' about truancy. It has been the lack of such an understanding which has made it possible for those who have considered the topic to have become trapped by the preconceptions about social relations which were institutionalized into the system and which produced the 'problem' in its present form. To point this out is not to be dismissive of the motivations and efforts of those who work in schools. Ultimately, schools are for no child in particular. They are for children in general. The problem is that children are particular. What this implies is that there is a need for flexibility rather than rigidity in the development of education. The issue of truancy raises the question, as I have already indicated, of the role of schooling. It is no longer ideologically acceptable for schools to be about keeping children in their place. But what does it mean to say that schools should be about individual achievement?

The ideology of individual achievement emerged with the development of examinations. Yet after over 100 years of examinations in our schools the reality of the examination has been to teach some children about what they can achieve but to teach most about what they cannot. Education which allows for genuine individual achievement for all children would require a social order in which a broad range of capacities are highly valued in themselves rather than at the expense of others. There is no simple formula for what that education would be like but it is in recognizing the ways in which issues like truancy raise questions about what we have that we can begin to open our minds and to consider what we could have.

Appendix:
Extract from Instructions to Inspectors
(*Source: XX*, 1841)

Report to the Committee of Council on Education, respecting the School in the
County of
> *District, No.*

Date of instruction from Committee of Council to inspect school.
Date of visit to school.
Date of report.

1. Name of chairman or secretary of school committee, as correspondent on behalf of the school.
2. Address — Post town.
3. By what name is the school to be known?
4. In what parish is it?
5. What is the name of nearest post town?
> Distance?
> Direction?
6. When was the school established?
7. Who were the original promoters of it?
8. Is it, or has it been, in connexion with, or has it derived, or received a promise of, aid from any society?
> What society?
> What is the amount of such aid?

Tenure and Site of Building.

9. What is the tenure on which the site is held?
10. Is the school-house erected on ground which is the property of the Incumbent as a spiritual corporation sole, or otherwise belonging to or connected with the Church of England?
11. Are the school-rooms applied to any other purpose than those of the school? to what purpose? under what regulations?
12. Is this appropriation recognised in the trust deed?
13. Is the trust deed duly executed?
14. Has it been enrolled?
15. When was it enrolled?
16. By whom were the trustees named and appointed?
17. The names and professions of the trustees?

18. What means are there for the renewal of the trust on the death or avoidance of the trustees?

19. What is the extent of the site?
Describe it generally.
How is it bounded?
How is it enclosed?
How is it drained?

20. State generally your opinion whether it is a healthy situation or otherwise?

21. In all respects well chosen, or otherwise?

22. Of what materials is the school-house built?

23. Is it thatched, or slated, or tiled?

24. In what state is it as to repair?

25. When was it erected?

26. From what funds was it erected?

27. If it was erected with aid from the Parliamentary Grant, furnish, in Appendix, a Special Report, arising from the audit of the building account, and the comparison of the reports or statements, presented to the Lords of the Treasury, or of the answers to the questions, Form A, with the receipt and expenditure; the description of the building in those replies, and in the plans transmitted to the Committee of Council, with the structure erected, and the examination of the deed of trust.

Mechanical Arrangements.

28. Furnish a rough sketch of the plan of the building if possible.

29. What are the dimensions of the chief school-room in length, breadth, and height to the centre of the ceiling?

30. Does the school-room contain a gallery for 80 or more children?

31. When one or more class-rooms are provided for the separate instruction of a part of the children, state also the dimensions in length, breadth, and height, of each class-room.

32. Are the school-rooms sufficiently ventilated and warmed?

33. Is there a lobby, or closet, for bonnets, cloaks, hats, &c.?

34. Is an exercise-ground provided? and if so, at what distance from the school?

35. Of what extent is it?

36. Is the playground furnished with gymnastic aparatus, flying-course or circular swing, parallel-bars, and gymnastic-frame?

37. What is the nature and height of the fence with which the playground is enclosed?

38. Does the building include a residence for the schoolmaster and mistress? If not, how far is their residence from the school?

Religious and Moral Discipline.

39. Are the children assembled and dismissed every day with a psalm or hymn, and with prayer?

40. Is the Holy Bible read every day? In classes, or in the gallery?

41. Are the children taught private prayers to repeat at home?

42. Are they instructed in the Church Catechism?

43. Are they instructed in the Liturgy and Services of the Church?

44. Do all the children belonging to the Daily School attend school on Sunday and go to church?

45. Are they provided with proper church accommodation?

46. Are means taken to ensure their suitable behaviour during the Service?

47. Are inquiries made afterwards by their teacher how far they have profited by the public ordinances of religion?

48. Do the teachers keep up any intercourse with the parents or confine their attention to the children during the hours they are in school?

49. Is the progress of the children in religious knowledge in proportion to the time they have been at school?

50. Are their replies made intelligently, or mechanically and by rote?

51. Is due attention paid to the junior as well as to the senior class, and in each class to the lower as well as the higher pupils?

Means of Instruction.

52. Enumerate the books used in the school opposite the following heads:—

Reading.
Arithmetic.
Geography.
History of England.
Grammar.
Etymology.
Vocal Music.
Linear Drawing.
Land Surveying.

53. What apparatus does the school contain?

54. Are the children systematically trained in gymnastic exercises?

Organization and Discipline.

55. Are the children classed according to their proficiency?

56. Is each child always under the instruction of the same teacher?

57. Are the children taught by a succession of teachers, each conveying instruction in some particular branch?

58. What is the number of teachers?

59. What is the number of monitors?

60. What is the number of pupil teachers?

61. What is the remuneration of each pupil teacher?

As respects Rewards and Punishments.

62. Is any system of rewards and punishments adopted?

63. State whether distinction depends on intellectual proficiency.
On a mixed estimate of intellectual proficiency and moral conduct.
On moral conduct only.

64. Are corporal punishments employed?
If so, what is their nature, and what are the offences to correct which they are used?

65. If they are employed, are they publicly inflicted?

66. What other punishments are used?

67. What rewards, if any?

As respects Method.

68. Is the method of mutual instruction strictly adhered to?
69. Is the simultaneous method more or less mingled with individual teaching?

Simultaneous, or Mixed Method.

70. How far is the interrogative method only used?
71. Is the suggestive method employed?
72. Is Ellipsis resorted to?
73. Are the lessons tested
    By individual oral interrogation?
    By requiring written answers to written questions?
    By requiring an abstract of the lesson to be written from memory?

Mutual Instruction and Mixed Method of Instruction.

74. What is the number of masters?
    Of assistant-masters (if any)?
    Of monitors?
    Of pupil-teachers?

Monitors and Pupil-Teachers.

75. State the name and age of each monitor and pupil-teacher, distinguishing pupil-teachers from monitors.
76. State the period during which he has received instruciton.
77. State the attainments of each pupil-teacher or monitor, separately, in the following table, marking the pupil-teachers P. T., the monitors M.
78. To whom are the pupil-teachers apprenticed?
    For what period?
    What renumeration do they receive?
79. How many classes are there in the school?
80. How many children in each class?
81. State the proficiency of each class in the several subjects of instruction?
82. In what works of industry are the boys employed?
83. In what works of industry are the girls employed?
84. Obtain a written account, signed by the master, of the routine of employment of each class in the school, for every hour in the day and every day in the week.
85. Is any mutual assurance society or clothing-club connected with the school?
86. Is any library connected with the school; if so, of what books and of what number of volumes does it consist?
87. Is the use of the library confined to the school children, or otherwise?
88. Are the children alowed to take the books to their parents' houses?
89. What number of books was taken out in the last six months?

Attendance, Registers, &c.

90. Obtain a copy of the school-registers of admission, attendance, proficiency, and moral conduct, respectively.
91. How many children were present at the time of inspection?
       Boys.
       Girls.
92. How many have been on the books for the last six months?
       Boys.
       Girls.
93. What was the average daily attendance during the last six months?
       Boys.
       Girls.
94. Is the number of children in attendance on the increase or decrease?
95. At what rate?
96. Is punctual and regular attendance enforced?
97. By what means?
98. Do the children pay for admittance to the school?
99. Do they all pay?
       At the same rate?
100. What is the rate of payment?
101. Do the children take any meals in the school-house?
102. In what part of the premises?
103. Do the children appear to be clean?
       Neat?
104. Do they wear any distinguishing dress?
       Or badge?
105. Enumerate the holidays which occur during the year.
106. At what age are the children usually admitted?
107. To what age do they generally remain?
108. Are there any systematic means of keeping up a connexion with the school-children after their leaving school?

Schoolmaster and Schoolmistress.

109. What are the names of the schoolmaster?
       And schoolmistress?
110. Are they respectively married?
       Or single?
111. Are they man and wife?
112. Are they respectively provided with fuel, candles, and other perquisites?
113. Do they live rent-free in the school-house?
114. Do they devote their whole time to the duties of their office?
       If not, state what other occupation they have, the time it occupies, and its emoluments.
115. Have they received instruction in the art of teaching, in any and what training-school?
116. At what age did he (or she) become a schoolmaster (or schoolmistress)?
117. What was his (or her) former occupation?

118. State your opinion of the teachers as respects their attainments;
    character;
    and method of conducting the school.
119. By whom is the master (or mistress) appointed?
120. Upon what conditions, and for what period, is the appointment held?
121. Is there a written agreement?
122. Is there a sufficient facility for dismissing the master (or mistress) in case of need?
123. By whom is the master (or mistress) to be dismissed?

Government of the School.

124. In whom is the general management and control of the school vested?
125. Name of the visitor (if any).
    Patron.
    President.
    Treasurer.
    Secretary.
    The Committee.
    The trustees.
126. Do the trustees [or committee] meet periodically?
127. Are there general meetings of the subscribers and promoters of the school?
128. Is there any, and, if so, what system of constant superintendence by the committee or otherwise?
129. Is the committee active, or merely nominal?
130. Who are the active members of the committee?
131. Transmit a copy of the printed rules of the schools.
132. Is there any periodic public examination of the school?
    What is its effect upon
    The teachers,
    The children;
    especially as respects character and manners?

Annual Income.

133. State the amount of annual subscriptions and donations.
134. Of annual collections.
135. Of annual produce of endowment.
136. Of school fees.
137. Of any other sources of income separately enumerated.

Annual Expenditure.

138. What is the annual stipend of the master?
    . The mistress?
    Each assistant master and mistress?
    Each pupil teaher?
139. What amount was expended last year in repairs?
    For furniture and apparatus?
    For books and stationery?
    For candles and fuel?
140. What other expenses are incurred?

SPECIAL QUESTIONS ON INFANT SCHOOLS
Mechanical Arrangements.

The questions respecting mechanical arrangements in the former paper having been replied to, the following additional questions may be put:—

1. Are the walls lined with a broad belt of black board. or prepared with mastic, painted black, for lessons in chalk-drawing and writing?
2. Is a small gallery prepared with desks and boards for the instruction of forty children in drawing and in the signs of sounds?

Recreation and Physical Exercises.

3. What amusements have the children?
4. What games are encouraged?
5. Have they any and what gymnastic apparatus?
6. Are the children trained in walking, marching, and physical exercises, methodically?
7. With what result?
8. How often do the intervals of recreation occur daily, and what time is spent in recreation at each interval?

Industry.

9. How many children learn to sew?
   To knit?
   To plait straw?
   To keep the garden-border free from weeds?
   To sweep the school-floors, &c.?

Imitative Arts.

10. Do the children learn to draw, on the wall or on a board, right-lined figures from objects or from copies?
11. Do they learn to draw the Roman capital letters and numerals?
12. Are these steps the preliminaries to learning to write?
13. Do they in this way learn to write the letters with chalk on the wall, or on a board?

Learning Signs of Sounds.
I. READING.

14. Does the school-room contain one of Mr. Prinsen's letter-boxes?
15. Has the master or mistress been instructed in the method of making the children familiar with letters—
    1. By showing them the figure of a natural object having a monosyllabic name?
    2. By analysing this word into its constituent sounds?
    3. By showing the children the sign of each sound beginning with the vowel sound, and then combining them into the word by the phonic method?
16. Are the children expert in the various modes of using the letter-boxes, to spell and read words?

II. SINGING.

17. On what method are the children taught to sing?
18. Do they learn the signs of musical sounds to any extent?
19. Can they copy the notes of music with chalk on the wall?
20. Can they sing many marching or other school songs?
21. Can they sing any hymns?

Knowledge of Natural Objects, &c.

22. Are the children exercised in examining and describing, in very simple and familiar terms, the properties of those natural objects by which they are surrounded?
23. Is there a cabinet in the school stored with natural objects which the children are likely soon to meet with in their rambles, or visits to friends?
24. Is there a cabinet of domestic utensils or implements of industry, of a small size, the uses of which may be explained to the children?

Instruction in the Gallery.

25. Are they instructed in any other subjects in the gallery?
26. If so, enumerate the gallery lessons.
27. How long is the usual lesson in the gallery?
28. Are the replies of the children made intelligently, or mechanically and by rote?

Discipline.

29. Are the children clean in their persons and dress?
30. Are they orderly and decorous in their behaviour?
31. Do they appear to have confidence in their master and mistress, and to regard them with affection?
32. Are any, and, if so, what rewards and punishments employed? On what principles, and with what results?
33. Is their attendance at school punctual and regular?
34. Examine register, and state whether it is kept on a good plan, neatly, and with care.

Bibliography

Parliamentary Papers

1839 XLI
1840 XL
1841 XX
1842 XXXIII
1844 XXXVIII
1845 XXXV
1846 XXXII
1847 XLV
1847–48 XLIV
1850 XLII; XLIV
1851 XLIV
1852 XL
1852–53 LXXXIX; LXXX
1854 LI; LII
1854–55 XLI XLII
1856 XLVII
1857 XXXIII
1857–58 XLV
1859 XXI Part 1
1860 LIV
1861 XLIX
1862 XLI; XLII
1863 XLVII
1864 IX; XLV
1864 Committee *Select Committee On Education (Inspectors' Reports)*
1865 VI; XLII
1865 Committee *Select Committee to Inquire into the Constitution of the Committee of Council on Education and the System Under Which the Business of the Office is Conducted ...*
1866 XXVII
1867 XXII
1867–68 LIII; XXV
1868–69 XX

1870 XXII
1871 XXII
1872 XXII

Internal Documents on School Attendance and Responses to Pack Report from:

Borders Region
Central Region
Dumfries and Galloway
Fife Region
Highland Region
Lothian Region
Orkney
Strathclyde Region
Tayside Region
Western Isles

Secondary Sources

ABRAMS, P. (1982) *Historical Sociology*, Somerset, Open Books Publishing Ltd.

AHIER, J. (1977) 'Philosophers, sociologists and knowledge in education' in YOUNG, M. F. D. and WHITTY, G. (Eds) *Society, State and Schooling*, Brighton, Falmer Press.

AHIER, J. and FLUDE, M. (1983) *Contemporary Education Policy*, Beckenham, Croom Helm.

ALTHUSSER, L. (1972) 'Ideology and ideological state apparatuses' in COSIN, B. R. (Ed) *Education: Structure and Society*, Harmondsworth, Penguin.

ANDERSON, M. (1978) *Family and Industrialisation in Western Europe*, St. Louis, MI, Forum Essay Series.

ANDERSON, R. D. (1983) *Education and Opportunity in Victorian Scotland*, Oxford, Oxford University Press.

ANDRIOLA, J. (1946) 'Truancy syndrome', *American Journal of Orthopsychiatry*, 16.

APLEY, J. (1968) 'Paediatrics and child psychiatry in Great Britain' in MILLER, E. (Ed) *Foundations of Child Psychiatry*, Oxford, Pergamon Press.

APPLE, M. W. (1979a) *Ideology and Curriculum*, London, Routledge & Kegan Paul.

APPLE, M. W. (1979b) 'The production of knowledge and the production of deviance in schools' in BARTON, L and MEIGHAN, R. (Eds) *Schools, Pupils and Deviance*, Driffield, Nafferton Books.

APPLE, M. W. (1982a) *Education and Power*, Boston, MA, Routledge & Kegan Paul.

APPLE, M. W. (Ed) (1982b) *Cultural and Economic Reproduction in Education*, London, Routledge & Kegan Paul.

ARIES, P. (1974) *Centuries of Childhood*, Harmondsworth, Penguin.

BAILYN, B. (1982) 'The challenge of modern historiography', *American Historical Review*, 87, 1.

BALL, N. (1963) *Her Majesty's Inspectorate 1839–1849*, Edinburgh, Oliver & Boyd.

BARKER, P. (1968) 'The in-patient treatment of school refusal', *British Journal of Medical Psychology*, 41.

BARTON, L. and MEIGHAN, R. (Eds) (1979) *Schools, Pupils and Deviance*, Driffield, Nafferton Books.

BEAUMONT, G. R. (1976) 'A comparison of the effect of behavioural counselling and teacher support on the attendance of truants', unpublished Diploma in School Counselling dissertation, Swansea, University College.

BELSON, W. A. (1975) *Juvenile Theft: The Causal Factors*, London, Harper & Row.

BERGER, J. and LUCKMANN, T. (1971) *The Social Construction of Reality*, Harmondsworth, Penguin Books.

BERNBAUM, G. (1977) *Knowledge and Ideology in the Sociology of Education*, Basingstoke, Macmillan.

BERNSTEIN, B., *et al.* (1971) 'Ritual in education' in COSIN, B. R. *et al.* (Eds) *School and Society*, London, Routledge & Kegan Paul.

BERNSTEIN, B. (1973) *Class, Codes and Control*, vol 1, St Albans, Paladin.

BEST, G. (1973) *Mid-Victorian Britain 1851–1875*, St Albans, Panther Books Ltd.

BISHOP, A. S. (1971) *The Rise of a Central Authority for English Education*, Cambridge, Cambridge University Press.

BLAGG, N. (1987) *School Phobia and Its Treatment*, Beckenham, Croom Helm.

BONE, T. R. (1968) *School Inspection in Scotland 1840–1966*, London, Scottish Council for Research in Education.

BOURDIEU, P. (1976a) 'The school as a conservative force' in DALE, R., *et al.* (Eds) *Schooling and Capitalism*, London, Routledge & Kegan Paul.

BOURDIEU, P. (1976b) 'Systems of education and systems of thought' in DALE, R., *et al.* (Eds) *Schooling and Capitalism*, London, Routledge & Kegan Paul.

BOURDIEU, P. and PASSERON, J. C. (1977) *Reproduction in Education, Society and Culture*, London, Sage Studies in Social and Educational Change.

BOWLES, S. (1976) 'Unequal education and the reproduction of the social division of labour' in DALE, R., *et al.* (Eds) *Schooling and Capitalism*, London, Routledge & Kegan Paul.

BOWLES, S. and GINTIS, H. (1976) *Schooling in Capitalist America*, London, Routledge & Kegan Paul.

BOWMAN, M. J. (1972) 'The human investment revolution in economic thought' in COSIN, B. R. (Ed) *Education: Structure and Society*, Harmondsworth, Penguin.

BROADFOOT, P. (Ed) (1984) *Selection, Certification and Control*, Lewes, Falmer Press.

BROADWIN, I. T. (1932) 'A contribution to the study of truancy', *American Journal of Orthopsychiatry*, 2.

BURCHELL, C. (1979) 'A note of juvenile justice', *Ideology and Consciousness*, 5, spring.

BURT, C. L. (1944) *The Young Delinquent*, 4th edn, London, University of London Press.

CAIN, J. (1974) 'A study of the effect of counselling on pupils displaying an irregular pattern of school attendance', unpublished Diploma in School Counselling dissertation, Swansea, University College.

CAMERON, D. K. (1979) *The Ballad and the Plough*, London, Futura Publications.

CAMPBELL, J. H. (1972) 'The central administration of education 1839–1900', unpublished PhD dissertation, Manchester, University of Manchester.

CARROLL, H. C. M. (1968) 'Poor attendance at school: A study of first year children in a comprehensive school' unpublished Diploma in Educational Psychology dissertation, Swansea, University College.

CHAZAN, M. (1962) 'School phobia', *British Journal of Educational Psychology*, 32.

CHITNIS, A. C. (1968) 'The Edinburgh professoriate 1790–1826 and the University's contribution to nineteenth century British society', unpublished PhD dissertation, Edinburgh, University of Edinburgh.

CLARK, E. A. G. (1977) 'The superiority of the "Scotch system": Scottish ragged schools and their influence', *Scottish Educational Studies*, 9.

CLARK, K. R. (1972) 'Non-attendance at school — Towards a coefficient of absence', unpublished MEd thesis, Hull, University of Hull.

CLARK, M. (1975) 'Social problem ideologies', *British Journal of Sociology*, 26.

CLYNE, M. B. (1966) *Absent: School Refusal as an Expression of Disturbed Family Relationships*, London, Tavistock.

COLLINS, R. (1979) *The Credential Society*, London, Academic Press.

COOMBES, F. (1974) 'Truancy on trial' in TURNER, B. (Ed.) *Truancy*, London, Ward Lock Educational.

CORRIGAN, P. (1975) 'Dichotomy is contradiction', *Sociological Review*, 23.

CORRIGAN, P. (1977) 'State intervention and moral regulation in nineteenth century Britain: Sociological investigations', unpublished PhD dissertation, Durham, University of Durham.

CORRIGAN, P. (1981) 'On moral regulation', *Sociological Review*, 29.

CORRIGAN, P. (1987) 'In/forming schooling' in LIVINGSTOKE, D. (Ed.) *Critical Pedagogy and Cultural Power*, Basingstoke, Macmillan.

CORRIGAN, P. and SAYER, D. (1985) *The Great Arch*, Oxford, Basil Blackwell.

COSER, L. A. and ROSENBERG, B. (Eds) (1969)*Sociological Theory*, New York, Macmillan.

COSIN, B. R., *et al.* (Eds) (1971) *School and Society*, London, Routledge & Kegan Paul.

COSIN, B. R. (Ed) (1972) *Education: Structure and Society*, Harmondsworth, Penguin.

CULLEN, M. J. (1975) *The Statistical Movement in Early Victorian Britain*, Hassocks, Harvester Press.

CURTIS, B. (1988) *Building the Educational State: Canada West 1836–1871*, Lewes, Falmer Press.

DALE, R., *et al.* (Eds) (1976) *Schooling and Capitalism*, London, Routledge & Kegan Paul.

DALE, R. (1977) 'Implications of the rediscovery of the hidden curriculum for the sociology of teaching, in GLEESON, D. (Ed.) *Identity and Structure: Issues in the Sociology of Education*, Driffield, Nafferton Books.

DALE, R. (1979) 'The politicisation of school deviance: Reactions to William

Tyndale' in BARTON, L. and MEIGHAN, R. (Eds) *Schools, Pupils and Deviance*, Driffield, Nafferton Books.

DALE, R. (1981) 'From expectations to outcomes in education systems', *Interchange*, 12, 2–3.

DALE, R. (1982) 'Education and the capitalist state' in APPLE, M. W. (Ed) *Cultural and Economic Reproduction in Education*, London, Routledge & Kegan Paul.

DAVID, M. E. (1980) *The State, the Family and Education*, London, Routledge & Kegan Paul.

DAVIDSON, S. (1960–61) 'School phobia as a manifestation of family disturbance: Its structure and treatment', *Journal of Child Psychology and Psychiatry*, 1, 4.

DAVIE, G. E. (1961) *The Democratic Intellect: Scotland and her Universities in the Nineteenth Century*, Edinburgh, Edinburgh University Press.

DEMAINE, J. (1981) *Contemporary Theories in the Sociology of Education*, London, Macmillan.

DENISON, E. F. and PULLIER, J. (1972) Education of the labour force' in COSIN, B. R. (Ed) *Education: Structure and Society*, Harmondsworth, Penguin.

DINGWALL, R. and LEWIS, P. (Eds) (1983) *The Sociology of the Professions*, Basingstoke, Macmillan.

DOCKING, J. W. (1980) *Control and Discipline in Schools*, London, Harper & Row.

DONAJGRODZKI, A. P. (Ed.) (1977) *Social Control in Nineteenth Century Britain*, Beckenham, Croom Helm.

DONZELOT, J. (1980) *The Policing of Families*, London, Hutchinson & Co Ltd.

DREYFUS, H. L. and RABINOW, P. (Eds) (1982) *Michel Foucault*, Hassocks, Harvester Press.

DURKHEIM, E. (1956) *Education and Sociology*, IL, Free Press.

DURKHEIM, E. (1961) *Moral Education*, New York, Free Press.

DURKHEIM, E. (1964) *Rules of Sociological Method*, New York, Free Press.

DURKHEIM, E. (1976) *The Elementary Forms of the Religious Life*, London, George Allen & Unwin.

EGGLESTON, J. and GLEESON, D. (1977) 'Curriculum innovation and the context of the school' in GLEESON, D. (Ed) *Identity and Structure: Issues in the Sociology of Education*, Driffield, Nafferton Books.

EISENSTEIN, Z. R. (Ed.) (1979) *Capitalist Patriarchy and the Case for Socialist Feminism*, New York, Monthly Review Press.

ENCYCLOPAEDIA BRITANNICA , 13th edn, volumes 19–20.

ERBEN, M. and GLEESON, D. (1977) 'Education and reproduction' in YOUNG, M. F. D. and WHITTY, G. (Eds) *Society, State and Schooling*, Brighton, Falmer Press.

EVANS, E. G. S. (1975) 'Truancy and school avoidance: A review of the literature', *Educational Review*, 4, 1.

FARRINGTON, D. (1980) 'Truancy, delinquency, the home and the school' in HERSOV, L. and BERG, I. (Eds) *Out of School: Modern Perspectives in Truancy and School Refusal*, Chichester, John Wiley & Sons Ltd.

FENWICK, K. and MCBRIDE, P. (1981) *The Government of Education*, Oxford, Martin Robertson.

FLEET, L. (1978) Some margins of compulsory education', unpublished PhD thesis, Bristol.

FLINN, M. W. (Ed) (1964) *Readings in Economic and Social History*, London, Macmillan.

FLINN, M. W. (1977) *Scottish Population History*, Cambridge, Cambridge University Press.

FLINN, M. W. and SMOUT, T. C. (Eds) (1974) *Essays in Social History*, Oxford, Oxford University Press.

FLUDE, M. and AHIER, J. (Eds) (1974) *Educability, Schools and Ideology*, Beckenham, Croom Helm.

FOGELMAN, K. and RICHARDSON, K. (1974) 'School attendance: Some results from the National Child Development Study' in TURNER, B. (Ed) *Truancy*, London, Ward Lock Educational.

FOUCAULT, M. (1972) *The Archaeology of Knowledge*, London, Tavistock Publications.

FOUCAULT, M. (1978) 'Politics and the study of discourse', *Ideology and Consciousness*, 3, spring.

FOUCAULT, M. (1979a) *Disciplinary and Punish*, London, Peregrine.

FOUCAULT, M. (1979b) 'On governmentality', *Ideology and Consciousness*, 6, autumn.

FOUCAULT, M. (1980) 'Questions on geography' in GORDON, C. (Ed) *Michel Foucault: Power/Knowledge*, Hassocks, Harvester Press.

FOUCAULT, M. (1981a) *History of Sexuality*, vol 1, Harmondsworth, Penguin.

FOUCAULT, M. (1981b) 'Question of method', *Ideology and Consciousness*, 8, spring.

FOUCAULT, M. (1982) 'The subject of power' in DREYFUS, H. L. and RABINOW, P. (Eds) *Michel Foucault*, Hassocks, Harvester Press.

FRIEDSON, E. (1975) *Profession of Medicine*, New York, Dodd, Mead & Co.

GALLOWAY, D. (1980) 'Problems of assessment and management of persistent absenteeism' in HERSOV, L. and BERG, I. (Eds) *Out of School: Modern Perspectives in Truancy and School Refusal*, Chichester, John Wiley & Sons Ltd.

GALLOWAY, D. (1982) *Schools and Disruptive Pupils*, London, Longman.

GALLOWAY, D. (1985) *Schools and Persistent Absentees*, Oxford, Pergamon Press.

GAULDIE, E. (1976) 'The middle class and housing in the nineteenth century' in MACCLAREN, A. (Ed) *Social Class in Scotland*, Edinburgh, John Donald.

GIBSON, W. J. (1912) *Education in Scotland: A Sketch of the Past and the Present*, London, Longmans Green & Co.

GILLIE, O. (1978) 'Sir Cyril Burt and the great IQ', *New Statesman*, 96.

GLEESON, D. (Ed) (1977) *Identity and Structure: Issues in the Sociology of Education*, Driffield, Nafferton Books.

GOFFMAN, E. (1968) *Asylums*, Harmondsworth, Pelican.

GORDON, C. (1979) 'Other inquisitions', *Ideology and Consciousness*, 6, autumn.

GORDON, C. (Ed.) (1980) *Michel Foucault: Power/Knowledge*, Hassocks, Harvester Press.

GRANT, J. (1876) *History of the Burgh Schools of Scotland*, vol 1, Glasgow, Collins.

GRAY, J. *et al.* (1983) *Reconstructions of Secondary Education*, London, Routledge & Kegan Paul.

GRAY, J. and HANNON, V. (1986) 'HMI's interpretations of schools examination results', *Journal of Education Policy*, 1, 1.

GRIMSHAW, R. and PRATT, J. (1987) 'Truancy: A case to answer?' in REID, K. (Ed) *Combating School Absenteeism*, Kent, Hodder & Stoughton.

GRUNSELL, R. (1980a) *Beyond Control?*, London, Chameleon Books.

GRUNSELL, R. (1980b) *Absent from School* , London, Chameleon Books.

GURVITCH, G. (1964) *The Spectrum of Social Time*, Dordrecht, Kluwer Academic.

HACKING, I. (1981) 'How should we do a history of statistics?', *Ideology and Consciousness*, 8, spring.

HALSEY, A. H., HEATH, A. and RIDGE, J. (1980) *Origins and Destinations*, Oxford, Clarendon Press.

HARGREAVES, D., *et al.* (1975) *Deviance in Classrooms*, London, Routledge & Kegan Paul.

HARGREAVES, D., *et al.* (1979) 'Durkheim, deviance and education' in BARTON, L. and MEIGHAN, R. (Eds) *Schools, Pupils and Deviance*, Driffield, Nafferton Books.

HARRISON, J. F. C. (1973) *The Early Victorians 1832–51*, St. Albans, Panther.

HARTMANN, H. (1979) 'Capitalism, patriarchy and job segregation by sex' in EISENSTEIN, Z. R. (Ed) *Capitalist Patriarchy and the Case for Socialist Feminism*, New York, Monthly Review Press.

HERBERT, M. (1974) *Emotional Problems of Development in Children*, London, Academic Press.

HERSOV, L. (1960–61) 'Persistent non-attendance at school', *Journal of Child Psychology and Psychiatry* , 1, 2.

HERSOV, L. and BERG, I. (Eds) (1980) *Out of School: Modern Perspectives in Truancy and School Refusal*, Chichester, John Wiley & Sons Ltd.

History of Education Society (Ed) (1970) *Studies in the Government and Control of Education Since 1860*, London, Methuen.

HODGES, J. and HUSSAIN, A. (1979) 'La police des familles', *Ideology and Consciousness*, 5, spring.

HOSKIN, K. (1979) 'The examination, disciplinary power and rational schooling' *History of Education*, 8.

HOSKIN, K. (1982) 'Examinations and the schooling of science' in MACLEOD, R. (Ed) *Days of Judgement*, Driffield, Nafferton Books.

HULLIN, R. (1988) 'The juvenile court and non-attendance at school', *Justice of the Peace*, 152, 16.

HUMES, W. M. and PATERSON, H. M. (1983) *Scottish Culture and Scottish Education 1800–1980* , Edinburgh, John Donald.

HUMES, W. M. and PATERSON, H. M. (1986) *The Leadership Class in Scottish Education*, Edinburgh, John Donald.

HURT, J. (1971) *Education in Evolution*, London, Granada Publishing Ltd.

HURT, J. (1979) *Elementary Education and the Working Classes 1860–1918*, London, Routledge & Kegan Paul.

HUTCHINSON, H. (1971) 'Church, state and school in Clackmannanshire: 1803–72', *Scottish Educational Studies* , 3.

INSTITUTE FOR THE STUDY AND TREATMENT OF DELINQUENCY (1974) 'Truancy in Glasgow' *British Journal of Criminology*, 14.

JENCKS, C. (Ed) (1982) *The Sociology of Childhood*, London, Batsford Academic and Educational Ltd.

JOHNSON, A. M., *et al.* (1941) 'School Phobia', *American Journal of Orthopsychiatry*, 11.

JOHNSON, R. (1970) 'Educational policy and social control in early Victorian England', *Past and Present*, 78.

JOHNSON, R. (1976) 'Notes on the schooling of the English working class, 1780–1850' in DALE, R., *et al.* (1976) *Schooling and Capitalism*, London, Routledge & Kegan Paul.

JOHNSON, R. (1977) 'Educating the educators: "Experts" and the state 1833–39' in DONAJGRODZKI, A. P. (Ed) *Social Control in Nineteenth Century Britain*, Beckenham, Croom Helm.

JOHNSON, T. (1972) *Professions and Power*, London, Macmillan.

JONES, D. K. (1977) *The Making of the Education System 1851–81*, London, Routledge & Kegan Paul.

JONES, K. and WILLIAMSON, K. (1979) 'Birth of the schoolroom', *Ideology and Consciousness*, 6, autumn.

KAHAN, B. (Ed) (1977) *Working Together for Children and Their Families*, London, HMSO.

KAHN, J. H. and NURSTEN, J. P. (1962) 'School refusal: A comprehensive view of school phobia and other failures of school attendance', *American Journal of Orthopsychiatry*, 32.

KAHN, J. H. and NURSTEN, J. P. (1968) *Unwillingly to School*, 2nd edn, Oxford, Pergamon Press.

KAHN, J. H. and NURSTEN, J. P. (1978) 'Tribute to Emmanuel Miller', *Journal of Child Psychology and Psychiatry*, 19, 4.

KAHN, J. H., NURSTEN, J. P. and CARROLL, H. C. M. (1981) *Unwillingly to School*, 3rd edn, Oxford, Pergamon Press.

KARABEL, J. and HALSEY, A. H. (1977) *Power and Ideology in Education*, Oxford, Oxford University Press.

KAY-SHUTTLEWORTH, J. (1969) *Memorandum on Popular Education*, London, Woburn Books Ltd (1st edn 1868).

KEDDIE, N. (1971) 'Classroom knowledge' in YOUNG, M. F. D. (Ed) (1971) *Knowledge and Control*, London, Collier-Macmillan.

KERR, J. (1910) *Scottish Education School and University from Early Times to 1908*, Cambridge, Cambridge University Press.

KERR, J. (1913) *Leaves from an Inspector's Log Book*, London, Thomas Nelson and Sons.

KITSUSE, J. I. (1962) 'Societal Reaction to Deviant Behaviour: Problems of Theory and Method' *Social Problems* 9.

KNOX, H. M. (1953) *250 Years of Scottish Education 1696–1946*, Edinburgh, Oliver & Boyd.

LARSON, M. S. (1979) *The Rise of Professionalism*, London, University of California Press Ltd.

LEMERT, E. M. (1971) 'The problem of social problems theory' in RUBINGTON, E. and WEINBERG, M. S. (Eds) (1971) *The Study of Social problems*, New York, Oxford University Press.

LEVINE, D. M. and BANE, M. J. (1975) *The 'Inequality' Controversy*, New York, Basic Books Inc.

LONGMATE, N. (1974) *The Workhouse*, London, Temple Smith.

LUKES, S. (1974) *Power*, Basingstoke, Macmillan.

McCANN, P. (Ed) (1977) *Popular Education and Socialisation in the Nineteenth Century*, London, Methuen & Co.

MCCRONE, D., *et al.* (1981) 'Egalitarianism and society inequality in Scotland', paper presented at the British Sociological Association Conference.

MacDONAGH, O. (1977) *Early Victorian Government 1830–1870*, London, Weidenfeld & Nicolson.

MACDONALD, A. M. (Ed) (1973) *Chambers Twentieth Century Dictionary*, Edinburgh, Chambers.

MACINTOSH, M. (1962) *Education in Scotland: Yesterday and Today*, Glasgow, Robert Gibson & Sons Ltd.

MACLAREN, A. (Ed) (1976) *Social Class in Scotland*, Edinburgh, John Donald.

MACLEOD, R. (Ed) *Days of Judgement*, Driffield, Nafferton Books.

MCMICHAEL, P. (1973–76) 'Delinquency, failure and the schools', *Scottish Educational Studies*, 5–8.

MADOC-JONES, B. (1977) 'Patterns of attendance and their social significance' in McCANN, P. (Ed) *Popular Education and Socialisation in the Nineteenth Century*, London, Methuen & Co.

MARKUS, T. A. (Ed) (1982) *Order in Space and Society*, Edinburgh, Mainstream.

MARSHALL, G. (1979) 'The Weber thesis and the development of capitalism in Scotland', *Scottish Journal of Sociology*, 3.

MARSHALL, G. (1980) 'The dark side of the Weber thesis: The case of Scotland', *British Journal of Sociology*, 3.

MARSHALL, G. (1982) *In Search of the Spirit of Capitalism*, London, Hutchinson & Co Ltd.

MARX, K. (1976) *Capital*, vol 1 (edited by ERNEST MANDEL), Harmondsworth, Penguin.

MASON, J. (1935) *A History of Scottish Experiments in Rural Education from the Eighteenth Century to the Present Day*, London, University of London Press.

MAY, D. (1973–76) 'Truancy, school absenteeism and delinquency', *Scottish Educational Studies*, 5–8.

MERTON, R. K. (1969) 'A paradigm for functional analysis in sociology' in COSER, L. A. and ROSENBERG, B. (Eds) (1969) *Sociological Theory* , New York, Macmillan.

MILLER, E. (Ed) (1968a) *Foundations of Child Psychiatry*, Oxford, Pergamon Press.

MILLER, E. (Ed.) (1968b) *The Problem of Classification in Child Psychiatry*, Oxford, Pergamon Press.

MODEL, A. and SHEPHEARD, E. (1958) 'The child who refuses to go to school', *Medical Officer*, p. 99–100.

MONTGOMERY, R. J. (1965) *Examinations*, London, Longmans, Green & Co. Ltd.

MORGAN, A. (1927) *Rise and Progress of Scottish Education*, Edinburgh, Oliver & Boyd.

MORRIS, N. (1970) 'State paternalism and laissez-faire in the 1860s' in History of Education Society (Ed) *Studies in the Government and Control of Education Since 1860*, London, Methuen.

MUSGRAVE, P. W. (Ed) (1970) *Sociology, History and Education*, London, Methuen & Co Ltd.

MYERS, J. D. (1970) 'Scottish teachers and educational policy 1803–1872: Attitudes and influence', unpublished PhD, Edinburgh.

MYERS, J. D. (1983) 'Scottish schoolmasters in the nineteenth century professionalism and politics' in HUMES, W. M. and PATERSON, H. M. (Eds) (1983) *Scottish Culture and Scottish Education 1800–1980*, Edinburgh, John Donald.

NURSTEN, J. P. (1958) 'The background of children with school phobia', *Medical Officer*, p. 100.

PACK, D. C. (1977) *Truancy and Indiscipline in Schools in Scotland*, London, HMSO.

PARRIS, H. (1969) *Constitutional Bureaucracy*, London, George Allen & Unwin Ltd.

PARSONS, T. (1964a) *Essays in Sociological Theory*, New York, Free Press.

PARSONS, T. (1964b) *The Professions and Social Structure*, New York, Free Press.

PAZ, D. G. (1980) *The Politics of Working-Class Education in Britain, 1830–50*, Manchester, University of Manchester Press.

PICKERING W. S. F. (Ed) (1979) *Durkheim: Essays on Morals and Education*, London, Routledge & Kegan Paul.

POWER, M. J., *et al.* (1967) 'Delinquent schools?', *New Society*, 10, 264.

POWER, M. J., *et al.* (1972) 'Neighbourhood schools and juveniles before the courts', *British Journal of Criminology*, 12, 2.

PRINCE, G. S. (1968) 'School phobia' in MILLER, E. (Ed) *Foundations of Child Psychiatry*, Oxford, Pergamon Press.

RAFFE, D. (1986) 'Unemployment and school motivation: The case of truancy', *Educational Review*, 38, 1.

READER, W. J. (1966) *Professional Men*, London, Weidenfeld & Nicolson.

REEDER, D. A. (Ed) (1977) *Urban Education in the Nineteenth Century*, Basingstoke, Taylor & Francis.

REID, K. (1985) *Truancy and School Absenteeism*, Kent, Hodder & Stoughton.

REID, K. (Ed.) (1987) *Combating School Absenteeism*, Kent, Hodder & Stoughton.

RENTON, G. (1978) 'The East London child guidance clinic', *Journal of Child Psychology and Psychiatry*, 19, 4.

REYNOLDS, D. (1977) 'Towards a socio-psychological view of truancy' in KAHAN, B. (Ed) *Working Together for Children and Their Families*, London, HMSO.

REYNOLDS, D. (1987) 'School effectiveness and truancy' in REID, K. (Ed) *Combating School Absenteeism*, Kent, Hodder & Stoughton.

ROACH, J. (1971) *Public Examinations in England 1850–1900*, Cambridge, Cambridge University Press.

ROBINS, L. N. and RATCLIFFE, K. S. (1980) 'The long-term outcome of truancy' in HERSOV, L and BERG, I. (Eds) *Out of School: Modern Perspectives in Truancy and School Refusal*, Chichester, John Wiley & Sons Ltd.

RUBINGTON, E. and WEINBERG, M. S. (Eds) *The Study of Social Problems*, New York, Oxford University Press.

RUBINSTEIN, D. (1969) *School Attendance in London 1870–1904*, Hull, University of Hull occasional papers in economic and social history 1.

RUTTER, M., *et al.* (1976) 'A guide to multi-axial classification scheme for psychiatric disorders in childhood and adolescence', submission to the World Health Assembly.

RUTTER, M., *et al.* (Eds) (1979) *Fifteen Thousand Hours*, London, Open Books.

RUTTER, M. and HERSOV, L. (Eds) (1979) *Child Psychiatry: Modern Approaches*, Oxford, Blackwell Scientific Publications.

SAYER, J. (1987) 'Why have you come to school today? A pathology of presence' in REID, K. (Ed) *Combating School Absenteeism*, Kent, Hodder & Stoughton.

SCHNEIDER, L. (Ed.) (1967) *The Scottish Moralist*, Chicago, University of Chicago Press.

SCHUTZ, A. (1976) *The Phenomenology of the Social World*, London, Heinemann.

SCOTLAND, J. (1969) *The History of Scottish Education*, vol 1, London, University of London Press.

SCOTTISH COUNCIL ON CRIME (1975) *Crime and the Prevention of Crime: A Memo*, London, HMSO.

SEABORNE, M. V. J. (1971) *The English School, its Architecture and Organisation*, vol 1, London, Routledge & Kegan Paul.

SENN, M. J. E. (1968) 'Relation of paediatrics to child psychiatry' in MILLER, E. (Ed) *Foundations of Child Psychiatry*, Oxford, Pergamon Press.

SHERIDAN, A. (1980) *Michel Foucault: The Will to Truth*, London, Tavistock Publications Ltd.

SIME, J. T. (1957) 'Some aspects of truancy', unpublished BEd dissertation, University of Glasgow.

SIMON, B. (1970) *Studies in the History of Education 1780–1870*, London, Lawrence & Wishart.

SMART, B. (1983) *Foucault, Marxism and Critique*, London, Routledge & Kegan Paul.

SMITH, F. (1923) *The Life and Work of Sir James Kay-Shuttleworth*, London, John Murray.

SMELSER, N. J. (1974) 'Sociological history: The industrial revolution and the British working class family' in FLINN, M. W. and SMOUT, T. C. (Eds) *Essays in Social History*, Oxford, Oxford University Press.

SOJA, E. W. (1981) 'A materialist interpretation of spatiality', unpublished paper presented at the Australian National University, Canberra.

ST JOHN-BROOKS, C. (1982) 'Loose in the city: The underworld of roaming children', *New Society*, 61, 1036.

STRONG, J. A. (1909) *A History of Secondary Education in Scotland*, Oxford, Clarendon Press.

SUTHERLAND, G, (1973) *Policy-making in Elementary Education 1870–1895*, London, Oxford University Press.

SUTHERLAND, G. (1984) *Ability, Merit and Measurement*, Oxford, Clarendon Press.

SYLVESTER, D. W. (1974) *Robert Lowe and Education*, London, Cambridge University Press.

TAYLOR, A. J. (1972) *Laissez-Faire and State Intervention in Nineteenth Century Britain*, Basingstoke, Macmillan.

THOMPSON, E. P. (1974) 'Time and work-discipline in industrial capitalism' in

FLINN, M. W. and SMOUT, T. C. (Eds) *Essays in Social History*, Oxford, Oxford University Press.

TROYNA, B. and WILLIAMS, J. (1986) *Racism, Education and the State*, Beckenham, Croom Helm.

TURNER, B. (Ed) (1974) *Truancy*, London, Ward Lock Educational.

TYACK, D. B. (1976) 'Ways of seeing: An essay on the history of compulsory schooling', *Harvard Educational Review*, 46.

TYERMAN, M. J. (1968) *Truancy*, London, University of London Press.

TYERMAN, M. (1974) *Who are the Truants?* in TURNER, B. (Ed) *op. cit.*

WALDFOGEL, L. *et al.* (1959) 'A program for early intervention in school phobia', *American Journal of Orthopsychiatry*, 29.

WEBER, M. (1971) *The Protestant Ethic and the Spirit of Capitalism*, London, Unwin University Books.

WEDGE, P. and PROSSER, H. (1973) *Born to Fail?*, London, Arrow Books.

WEST, D. J. (1982) *Delinquency: Its Roots, Careers and Prospects*, London, Heinemann.

WHITTY, G. (1977) 'Sociology and the problem of radical educational change' in YOUNG, M. F. D. and WHITTY, G. (Eds) *Society, State and Schooling*, Brighton, Falmer Press.

WILDMAN, R. (1974) 'Workhouse architecture' in LONGMATE, N. (Ed) *The Workhouse*, London, Temple Smith.

WILKINSON, W. L. (1954) 'The development of a state system of education in Scotland (1872–1908)', unpublished BEd dissertation, University of St Andrews.

WILLIAMS, P. (1974) 'Collecting the figures' in TURNER, B. (Ed) *Truancy*, London, Ward Lock Educational.

WILLIS, P. (1981) 'Cultural production is different from cultural reproduction, is different from social reproduction is different from reproduction', *Interchange*, 12, 2–3.

WILSON, T. (1983) 'A reinterpretation of "Payment by results" in Scotland 1861–72' in HUMES, W. M. and PATERSON, H. M. (Eds) *Scottish Culture and Scottish Education 1800–1980*, Edinburgh, John Donald.

WITHRINGTON, D. (1970) 'What is and what might be: Some reflections on the writing of Scottish educational history', *Scottish Educational Studies*, 2.

WITHRINGTON, D. (1975) 'Anxieties over withdrawal from school: A historical comment', unpublished paper.

WOODWARD, L. (1962) *The Age of Reform*, Oxford, Oxford University Press.

YOUNG, M. F. D. (Ed) (1971a) *Knowledge and Control*, London, Collier-Macmillan.

YOUNG, M. F. D. (1971b) 'An approach to the study of curricula as socially organised knowledge' in YOUNG, M F. D. (Ed) *Knowledge and Control*, London, Collier-Macmillan.

YOUNG, M. F. D. (1972) 'On the politics of educational knowledge', *Economy and Society*, 1.

YOUNG, M. F. D. (1977) 'Curriculum change: Limits and possibilities' in YOUNG, M. F. D. and WHITTY, G. (Eds) *Society, State and Schooling*, Brighton, Falmer Press.

Index

Figures in italics refer to tables